# Notions of Grace

Notions of Grace: A Memoir of Climbing, Cancer, and Family
is published under Catharsis, a sectionalized division under
Di Angelo Publications, Inc.

Catharsis is an imprint of Di Angelo Publications.

Printed in the United States of America.

Di Angelo Publications
Los Angeles, California

Library of Congress
Notions of Grace: A Memoir of Climbing, Cancer, and Family
ISBN: 978-1-962603-45-4
Paperback

Words: Jason Kolaczkowski
Cover Design: Savina Deianova
Interior Design: Kimberly James
Editors: Matt Samet, Willy Rowberry

Downloadable via www.dapbooks.shop and other e-book retailers.



For educational, business, and bulk orders, contact
distribution@diangelopublications.com.

1. Biography & Autobiography --- Memoirs
2. Sports & Recreation --- Mountaineering
3. Family & Relationships --- Parenting --- Fatherhood

# Notions of Grace

A MEMOIR OF CLIMBING, CANCER, AND FAMILY

JASON P KOLACZKOWSKI

To my family, both inherited and chosen:

No adventure would ever launch but for
the sanctuary of base camp.

# CONTENTS

CHAPTER ONE

# Presence

It had been over five months.

My son, Connor, stopped under the straining, reaching limb of a lone bristlecone pine. The trunk bent awkwardly away from the prevailing wind, its lowest branch groping in the opposite direction, feeling for something to catch hold of.

"Can you put my mask in my pack, please, Dad?"

"Sure, kiddo."

We were at the last tree we could find between us and the summit of Pennsylvania Mountain, a peak whose grassy slopes would suggest it as a hill if it weren't for its elevation above 13,000 feet. As we paused somewhere near 12,000 feet, we were finally above the smoke from summer forest fires, which had gathered like stretched cotton in the valley below. We turned back toward our trailhead, admiring our first mile of progress and looking toward the rising sun. The sun was well above the foothills now, but it still loomed red and swollen in the smoke-filled sky.

Connor pinched his small, kid-sized mask from his face and casually lifted it above his head. I grabbed it and then took a knee behind him, unzipping the small, lime-green pack he had on. His little legs and lungs were unaccustomed to the uphill or the altitude, and I caught a glimpse of his half-smile of self-satisfaction as I removed his mask. I carefully folded the ear straps into the mask before dropping it into the pack and zipping the pack shut.

"Can you take mine, too?" Connor's twin brother, Kade, asked, having come up to us waving his mask.

It seemed like our masks had been ever-present for these five months. That's when the news reports started showing graphics of big white spheres with little, red, T-shaped spikes protruding from them. That's when they shared "live images" of very dead people in body bags being loaded into freezer trucks. That's when Connor, Kade, their mom, Kristina, and I—along with most everyone else—stopped heading out into the world.

When COVID-19 first emerged, half-a-world away, there was hopeful prognostication that it was going to be like the flu—which is bad enough for someone with my then newly won health problems—but it soon was obvious that this virus was far worse. It was clear that if you had immune deficiencies, as I did, it could get really bad. It was only years later, when the retrospective studies started to be published, that we learned people with my particular condition had, in fact, succumbed to COVID at higher rates than the elderly, transplant recipients, and even other cancer patients.

"You guys having fun?"

"It's hard," Kade replied.

I, again, looked back down into the smoky valley, dotted with the occasional homes that spread from the ranching hubs, with their tractor-supply stores and John Deere dealerships, and eventually out into the windswept high plains of South Park Valley. The people in those homes and ranches, as well as those from the larger towns like the one from which we came, by our governor's decree were "Safer at Home," but I just couldn't be at home anymore.

Today wasn't about cancer or COVID. I tucked Kade's mask into his pack, along with my racing mind.

The twins began to plod up the tundra again on their little five-year-olds' legs, heading toward our ultimate destination just above 13,000 feet. Already, neither had ever been this high before. The mid-August grass, green at its roots, rose in dry, wispy yellows, scratching at the boys' ankles and crunching under their feet. It wasn't yet as dry, here in Colorado, as it was in California, Oregon, and Washington, whose early-August thunderstorms had ignited the conflagrations that were now blowing lung-choking smoke across much of the American West. But Colorado's own fires, it turns out, would be coming soon.

The red dot of a sun and the sharp, early-morning breeze kept our heads in our hoods and our hands in our gloves. The fleece on my fingers felt familiar, like hearing an old friend's voice. Pressing the fleece between my hands and the cork on my trekking-pole handles, I could feel the fibers gently rubbing over my knuckles as I moved. I tucked my chin into my chest, hiding from the breeze.

My breath echoed off the synthetic shell of my jacket, drowning out the wind as I ate up the ground with long strides. Tufts of grass and the occasional rock pushed against the bottoms of my trail runners. My toes splayed inside their shoes in response.

Eventually, the sun crested above the smoke, and I felt the warmth against my back. I called out to the boys, up ahead, "You getting warm?"

"Yeah, Dad," Kade called back. A red jacket punctuated by a lime-green pack spun around, along with another green dot surrounded by blue.

"Let's stop for some water and drop a layer?"

"Huh?"

"Let's take our pullovers off."

I swung my pack off my shoulders and folded myself over, peeling off my jacket and then clawing the fabric into a rough ball that I jammed into my bag. The sensation brought back a memory of the previous fall, a moment of stuffing my outer layer into a white pack set against the white snow somewhere on the shoulder of Gangapurna West, an un-summited Himalayan peak. There, the pristine valley of the rarely travelled east fork of the South Annapurna Glacier stretched back and below me with clouds, rather than smoke, caught and framed by the giants of Annapurna I, Annapurna III, and Machhapuchhare. That climb was a rationalized self-test, a point I had to prove to myself that I contrived to be in service to my boys. Here, with gently rising slopes of grass—rather than precipitously rising spires of rock, snow, and ice—under my feet, I looked up at my boys, whose hands rammed their own outer layers down into their own packs. I smiled broadly in a way that I somehow never quite could amidst the truly high, more dangerous peaks.

I pulled off my gloves and thrust them on top of the jacket, and then dug into the bottom of my pack for my sun hat. I plopped the electric-blue crown onto my head and tried to smooth out its always-crumpled black brim.

The cool air now felt energizing as the breeze swam across my back and through my fingers. Holding firmly to the cushioned shoulder-strap, I threaded an arm through the opening before twisting my elbow through the other strap. I looked up and saw the boys doing the same.

As we marched the final few steps to the summit high on the Continental Divide, we came to a semi-circle of stacked slate and shale, the kind of wind block the miners made atop the high peaks of Colorado back during its gold and silver days.

Kade's red shirt came up on my flank. He was a bit pallid from the altitude.

"Feels good, doesn't it?"

"I'm proud of myself."

"Well, good. It's hard work."

Connor's blue shirt came up on my other flank. "What mountain's that, Dad?" he asked, pointing beyond our rocky shelter. He gazed beyond the next ridge and out past the divide. He excitedly waved his finger, reaching out for the speck of a mountain in the distance. A deep, vertical cleft was cut in two by a horizontal cross, identifying the namesake peak of the Holy Cross Wilderness, over twenty miles away.

"Yeah, that one looks tall. Is it taller than this one?" Kade chimed in.

I gazed out into the expanse of high peaks. Even in the mid-August heat, shadows and pockets contained corners of perpetual snow.

"Yeah, there are plenty of taller and steeper mountains," I said.

Kristina was climbing into bed in our oversized Aurora, Colorado, home, one made affordable by its significant distance south and east of Denver. She was seven months pregnant, but looking further along due to carrying twins. She stopped. In a sardonic voice that only my wife can manage, she said, "Either I've peed myself, or my water just broke." I stopped mid-tooth-brush.

I was calm, and said something like, "Okay, I'll get the bags."

I had yet to register the seriousness of having our boys be born seven-and-a-half weeks early. I was simply fixated on the next thing to do, and that thing was to get to the hospital.

But my wife was keenly aware of the implications. She called our chosen hospital to ask if we should still come in, given the early birth, and was told to go to a different hospital that had a level-three neonatal intensive-care unit (NICU)—which provides specialized care for premature babies and/or those who have critical illnesses.

Mid-pregnancy, we had spent a few hours, spread out over a few weeks, visiting hospital maternity wards. Kristina was hoping for a natural childbirth, no drugs, and so the surroundings were important to her—they needed to be comforting. But we also knew the pregnancy was "high risk," as she was over thirty and bearing twins. So, we also wanted the security of a full medical facility. There are risks and then there are *risks*, after all.

Eventually, we had gone to breathing classes at our chosen hospital, getting exposure to those surroundings so that they would be familiar once the birth process began. I learned time-tested ways to massage and breathe with and comfort my wife, along with ways that were specific to her.

Well, we were five minutes into the delivery, and our birth plan was out the window.

Driving through the dark, the lights got brighter as we moved from the sleeping suburbs into the heart of downtown Denver. I squeezed my eyes into slits, bringing the road into some focus against the glare of streetlights and oncoming headlights.

I parked the car near the roundabout under a broad, red, neon banner with the bold, square-lettered word EMERGENCY protruding in illuminated white. We walked ourselves to the reception desk to describe the situation.

They wheeled my wife to the maternity ward, and we ended up with a private room. My wife was hooked up to an IV, where she was given a cocktail of drugs to delay contractions and speed up the boys' lung development. Even gaining a few hours could make a difference, the doctor told us.

Labor itself was a blur, marked by the milestone callouts of the various metrics that signal the stage of delivery: centimeters dilated, the boys' heart rates, and the like. My usually stoic wife was groaning in pain every fifteen minutes or so, mostly lying on her back but also rocking slightly from one hip to the other. Gently raising a palm to the small of Kristina's back, I made circles and tried to convince myself that I was being helpful.

Attempting to honor the tattered remains of our birth plan, the medical team wheeled Kristina into the delivery room, where she began pushing. And in that room we stayed . . . for hours. A determined look remained on my wife's stony face, but after four hours of pushing, and over twelve hours since our arrival at the hospital, her limbs now flopped to her sides and her head swung back in exhaustion after each contraction.

The first baby in the birth canal—Connor, it would turn out—was starting to exhibit signs of trauma. With each new cycle of pushing, his heart rate would drop.

"I don't think it's urgent—yet," the doctor told us, "But the issues are starting to mount. We may want to consider a C-section."

My wife agreed.

Two nurses set a partition between my wife's face and her pelvis, blocking the view for both of us. I stayed at the head of the operating table, near Kristina's strained face.

The doctor, a petite but powerful woman, climbed onto the table and stood astride my wife. The table wobbled under her shifting weight as she moved her arms about in surprisingly forceful tugs.

At exactly noon, the doctor pulled Connor from my wife; a nurse quickly swaddled him and then held him for just an instant near Kristina's head. She turned with a longing gaze.

The nurse then whisked Connor to the back corner of the room where a team conducted their APGAR (Appearance, Pulse, Grimace, Activity, and Respiration) tests; a wall of crinkled powder-blue surgical isolation gowns blocked my view. Connor was placed into an incubator and wheeled off, briskly, to the NICU.

One minute after Connor, Kade was similarly yanked into the world: a similar "drive-by" appearance for Mom, a wall of powder blue, and then another ride to the NICU.

Someone asked me to follow the boys as others began to close up my wife's midsection.

I followed the boys down the hall, where we passed my parents, Marianne and Alan, and my in-laws, Kathy and Bill, all of whom were seated and waiting. They had come to join us over the course of the morning. My mom smiled at me as I walked by. My dad nodded. Bill sat quietly, with my wife's inherited, stoic countenance. Kathy and I locked eyes. They were all so calm, in contrast to the frenetic energy I was feeling. I said something reassuring—I can't quite remember what—and it was the truth, because the boys and my wife were doing well; but my focus was on whatever awaited me and my sons at the end of the hall.

Later, Kathy would tell me, "You could tell that you were all-in."

The clouds were sporadic but hanging low one Saturday afternoon as I sat in the grass of my front yard, reveling in the lushness of it.

In Albuquerque, all the grass I'd ever played upon was sod, laid down for yards and parks. Soccer had been my game, and I spent my time on windswept fields with hardpan ground and steel-bar-and-mesh-net goals erected at each end, with the grass ending at a concrete sidewalk or giving way to the goathead-and-tumbleweed desert. In Knoxville, in and around the sod, the rich soil welcomes all varieties of flowers, ground cover, and clover.

Knoxville is a football town. Just the day before, my friend Aaron and I had spent the afternoon taking turns pretending to be the quarterback for the University's "Volunteers," leading our team to a series of dramatic, last-second victories.

But today, Aaron was at the game with his dad, who was a drag racer. Aaron's father had some souped-up Chevy Barracuda from the early 1970s that was splashed with sponsor stickers. My dad and Aaron's dad bonded a bit over the time that my father had purchased a brand-new Barracuda, more than a decade earlier, and his lament over letting that car go.

Knoxville shuts down on Saturdays when the University of Tennessee plays. Nothing is open; everyone is at the game; and everything is draped in orange. Our family was too new to the area to easily access tickets to the games. There were waitlists for the waitlists.

So, I sat myself in the clover, squinting down at the leaves, focusing in and counting: *Three clover leaves. Three more clover leaves. Three leaves, again.* I spent hours counting leaves.

Eventually, my mind wandered.

I lay back, looking up to the sky, making shapes of the clouds: a rabbit, a coyote's head, things I remembered from New Mexico.

A few months after I'd turned six, my family had moved from the arid New Mexican desert to the greenery of Tennessee. My dad had taken a job with an engineering firm that was "about to land a big contract" and needed to staff up with people with my father's skills. As it turned out, we would only live there a year before heading back to Albuquerque, the contract having fallen through.

My older brother, Bryan, was somewhere behind our neighbor, Kent's, house. Kent was my brother's age, two years older than me, and a rarity in Tennessee in the 1980s: a hockey player. But when he wasn't on ice or in-line skating up and down the street, he was in the woods behind his family's property that, at our young age, seemed to go on forever. My brother and Kent would spend hours behind that house, building forts, playing soldiers, and generally acting out their own modern-day Mark Twain novel.

I thought about the game and when Aaron would come back from it. Maybe we could act out a few of the key plays.

Sitting back up, I felt the cushion of grass under my seat and legs. This wasn't like the ground that used to push back at me so violently out west.

The sweet smell of fresh cut grass filled the air. Many of the neighborhood dads had spent the morning cutting their lawns before heading to the stadium with their families and trucks and portable grills.

Sighing, I shifted onto my knees and elbows, head bent low,

scanning the grass again with precision.

*Three leaves. Three leaves. Three leaves.*

*Four.*

Still in my crouch, my back jerked straight. *Four clover leaves!* I plucked the treasure from the patch and raced into the house.

"Mom! Look what I found!"

Mom met me in the entryway, and I thrust my treasured prize forward, its cool stem pinched between my fingers. She looked down and exclaimed, "Oh, look, a four-leaf clover! My, you must be lucky!"

"Yeah, I'm pretty lucky, huh?"

"We should take care of this."

My mother was an elementary school teacher, the type who would put in the extra hours at home preparing workbooks and visual aids for her students out of materials she'd paid for out of her own pocket. She knew that school-district budgets never quite stretched as far as they were needed. So, she had access to a small laminating machine.

Mom marched me over to the bookshelves in the living room and crouched down. I joined her. It was dark down below the windowsill.

She tugged out a reddish-brown spine with gold-leaf lettering to produce an encyclopedia volume.

"Wait here."

She got up while I sat—bouncing slightly—with the book at my knees.

Mom reappeared with a strip of parchment paper, which she held out to me, unfolded.

"Put it here."

I placed the clover in her hand, and she carefully creased the parchment paper atop it.

"Can you open the encyclopedia? We'll put it in there to press it."

I opened the book to something near the middle. Mom handed me the makeshift envelope and I placed it on the page. She then slid the envelope until it tucked into the spine. I closed the book over my find.

Spurred on by my success, I continued to spend idle days in the clover patch. Before we left Tennessee at the end of the following summer, I had a second laminated lucky charm, slightly larger than the first one.

The dental hygienist had just finished with X-rays, and I was told to wait for the dentist to come by to interpret them. It was a standard clean-and-check appointment, akin to the physical I'd had with my doctor the day before: no issues, just routine, corporeal maintenance straight out of the owner's manual.

I was getting these appointments taken care of because I had just changed jobs. I had spent the last seven years working in healthcare analytics for a rather large company, and the bureaucracy had gotten to me. I remember telling Kristina, "I could do my job really well, and the company will—more or less—take care of twelve million people next year. But I could do my job really poorly, and the company will—more or less—take care of twelve million people next year."

With the boys nearly four years old, I was becoming mindful of walking back into the house after a workday while feeling deflated by the absurdity of it all. It wasn't the type of life lesson I wanted to pass along. So, Kristina was encouraging when I joined a tech startup as their director of analytics, helping measure when and for whom and how well those prompts to get mammograms or blood-sugar checks or colonoscopies were getting people to take care of themselves. Our goal was to learn what was working and double down, so that patients could enjoy a more targeted outreach.

With the job change came a change in insurance carriers and, along with it, the medical practitioners my insurance covered. I was simply establishing a new primary-care physician and dentist. I was feeling healthy and had no complaints.

My new dentist's office was a converted restaurant with large, garage-style doors that once opened to patio dining. The doors had a lot of glass, which was now frosted to afford some standard of privacy for the patients. But the light from the doors, in combination with the bright examination lamps overhead, filled the room with a harsh glare.

I had risen out of the dental chair and was casually examining the various screens and gadgets that surrounded me when my cell phone rang.

I slid my phone from my pocket to screen the call, just making out the name of my primary-care physician's clinic against the room's bright lighting.

"May I speak with Jason, please?"

"This is him."

"Jason, I'm calling to let you know that we got some blood work back, and we need you to go and get some follow-up blood work. Today." Her speech was hurried.

"Uh . . . okay." My speech was not hurried. I didn't understand the conversation we were having, yet.

"I've put in an order with the lab. They are expecting you. You can head in right away. Your white-blood-cell count is *very* high. It's just the lymphocytes. And I've talked to an oncologist. She said it's pretty rare to have just one of the white-blood-cell types be high, so there's a chance it might not be cancer."

The tumult of words poured over me. I wasn't familiar with all the types of white blood cells, yet. I knew what my lymph nodes were and what my lymphatic system did, but I didn't know what a lymphocyte was.

The word *cancer* had gotten my attention, though. My brain was trying to catch up with my slamming heart, and I edged in a few questions: "So, I might have cancer?"

"It's too early to tell, and we need the additional blood tests. But it would be unusual for it not to be."

"But there's a chance that it isn't?"

"Yes, a chance. But you should go ahead and schedule an appointment with the oncologist. They'll be calling you to get it arranged so that she can interpret the results of the new tests with you. You should expect them to call, today."

"Uh . . . okay."

"Okay. So, thanks, Jason. Please go ahead and get into the lab, today, and get that blood work. We'll be in touch."

"Um . . . thanks."

I hung up and stared through the refracted light of the frosted garage door at nothing in particular. My heart continued to race, and my mind struggled to catch up. It felt like stepping out over a mountain ledge, with the menace of backbreaking boulders, or even just thousands of feet of air, below. *Do the next thing, make the next move.* In this case, get through this dental appointment and then get to the lab.

I sat back in the dentist's chair and closed my eyes to protect my mind from the vortex of light and words ripping through my head.

I folded my hands over my chest and waited for the dentist.

*The clover patch where the two four-leaf clovers were found is in the shade of the trees behind Jason as he plays on the driveway of his family's Tennessee home.*

CHAPTER TWO

# Vulnerability

I was about twenty feet off the ground, maybe halfway up this last tower of vertical rock, which led to a flat, horizontal, coffee-table-sized block marking the summit of Teakettle Mountain, standing 13,819 feet in the alpine kingdom of Yankee Boy Basin in the San Juan Range of southwestern Colorado. From up there, my wife and I could take in the red and white stripes of rock on the surrounding peaks and the light bouncing from the runoff creeks.

But first, I had to not fall.

My left knee was jammed into a wide crack, up to my thigh. The stone in that crack, perpetually in the shade, was cold, and my leg ached from the touch of it. The grainy, volcanic rock scraped away at me, under my pant leg. With my right hand, I groped at the face outside the crack, searching for a handhold.

It was my first "traditional" lead climb: had I fallen, any connection to the rock would have been through removable climbing protection that I would need to place myself, so I was looking for secure placements inside the crack. The climbing was easy—only 5.3 on the Yosemite Decimal System used to rate climbs, and that runs from 5.0 to 5.15—a purposefully picked climb well within my decidedly-beginner abilities.

I came to technical climbing late in life, particularly by Colorado standards. I was already an adult with a mortgage and was only months away from beginning to date Kristina, when repeated knee injuries had ended my soccer-playing days. I came to climbing as a way to continue enjoying movement. Throughout our time dating, and then early in our marriage, Kristina and I would venture out onto Colorado's peaks in these times before children. We'd had a few close calls already, too, including a bad fall Kristina took the week before we got married.

As it was, I hadn't researched the climb carefully, because I didn't yet know how to research routes properly. Thus, I hadn't brought gear wide enough for this gaping "offwidth" crack, a crack too tight to fit your body into but too large for your hands to come into contact with both sides So, nothing connected me to the mountain except my left knee and what handholds I could intermittently find on the face.

I paused and looked down at the "deck," where Kristina belayed me from her stance among some menacing, oblong boulders. My rope made a lazy curve in the air, connecting my climbing harness to her belay device, with nothing in between.

I probably wasn't going to die from a twenty-foot fall, but neither would I escape a plummet onto the uneven and rounding surface below unscathed. Plus, we were deep in the alpine backcountry at almost 14,000 feet; if I got hurt, we'd have to figure out how to descend the 3,000 vertical feet and 3.5 miles over loose shale fragments back to the car. Was that even possible with a broken ankle . . . or back . . . or a head injury?

I wasn't panicked. In fact, I was pretty calm. I was just thinking through choices and risks. The climbing felt secure and well within my limits. The probability of a fall was quite low, but suddenly, the consequences seemed quite high.

Here I was, on my first traditional lead climb ever, and in effect, I was free soloing: relying solely on a cool head and my climbing skill, with no way to catch a fall. Not only that, but I was doing it on my first-ever offwidth, trying to figure out how to jam the small hands that went with my 5'6" frame into a crack that didn't want to securely receive them.

I studied the rock features above me. The wide crack began to narrow until it finally petered out into a few ledges just below the summit block.

I continued wriggling: *Press the hands against the sides of the crack, drag the knee up to a new position, lodge that knee in deeply enough to hold, move one hand, then the other*... As the crack tapered, pushing me out onto those ledges and the face of the summit pyramid, I was surprised to find that I felt worse than I had in the offwidth. This very easy face climbing was the kind of thing I had done plenty of times before, if just not on lead. But I was emotionally tired and raw from holding it all together during the day's novel experiences. Turns out, staying calm takes energy.

I had thought the narrowing crack would finally offer the opportunity for protection; however, because it flared out into the wider crack below, this wasn't the case. Instead, I found a smaller crack around the corner in which to slot in a small nut that compressed into a constriction: a very good placement. I called for tension, so I could gather myself. "Take!" I hollered down to Kristina.

She hauled in the rope on her belay device, until I felt a small tug at the tie-in point on my harness.

My climbing rope no longer continued its unfettered descent to my wife's belay device.

I paused for a moment, hands still on ledges and toes still in the crack so as to not relinquish all of my safety to this single nut placement.

Exhaling with relief, I called out, "Climbing!" The rope tension dissolved from my waist as Kristina pushed slack out from her stance.

I reached a hand onto the flat surface of Teakettle's high point, searching for a ripple to curl my fingers into. A decent left hand. A push from the toes of my right foot, and I swung my left leg onto the summit.

My first alpine rock climb, my first "trad" lead, my first offwidth, and my first free solo (to a point)—all in one.

There was a bolus of weathered nylon webbing attached to a jammed boulder near the summit. I studied its tattered edges and decided to drape my own fresh loop over the rock. With a satisfying click, I clipped a carabiner to the bundle of webbing and traced the carabiner's tether back to my harness, adjusting myself tight to the anchor. Then I set up my belay device on my harness, feeding the rope through and letting Kristina know she was "On belay!"

Similarly jamming, sliding, and pressing against the wide crack and then out onto the face, my wife clambered onto our perch where she clipped into the anchor as well.

There we sat for maybe ten minutes, on a tabletop just big enough for two, looking out onto the red-and-white strata of volcanic rock in Yankee Boy Basin.

The day's climb wasn't a close call, really—more of a calculated risk. Yes, the calculation had changed as the climb evolved, but it always does.

We didn't say too much. My wife commented on how helpless

she'd felt at the end of that lazy curve of rope, but that was about it. I could remember feeling just as helpless when she'd fallen just before our wedding.

The midday sun of early autumn washed the rocks, the creek down below, our helmets, and our faces in a harsh light. The flaring reflections made me squint beneath my sunglasses.

Amy, who was our most regular nurse, and a colleague had rolled another reclining, faux-leather chair up to the boys' stations in the NICU. The brownish-orange plastic "fabric" was a bit too shiny and squeaky, but I attempted to settle in, nonetheless. I pulled down the hem of my full-zip sweater, ensuring it tucked nicely behind my back, and then unzipped my sweater, which I'd worn just for this purpose. Amy handed me Kade, and I placed him against my bare chest. Amy smiled down at me, asked if I was "good," made a quick about-face, and moved with purpose to her next task.

Weighing about four pounds now—a few weeks after the twins' birth—Kade felt reassuring on my chest, like a heavy blanket. But he and his brother would need to be steadily over five pounds, among other criteria, before they could be discharged. I zipped my sweater back up over the both of us. I felt his rapid heartbeat against mine.

I tilted myself back and set my feet up, exhaling deeply. The rushed commute from work to the hospital never seemed to feel routine. The couple across from me were talking, surrounded by three incubators—triplets. The father wore a baseball cap and pulled it low over his eyes. She was moving from incubator to incubator, putting a hand in the open top of each box.

"What time do you want to go?" she asked.

"Pretty soon, I think. Mom has been watching the twins for a while. I think she could use a break," the man said.

An alarm went off from one of their triplet's telemetry monitors: a sudden heart-rate dip, or a bradycardia event—a "Brady" for short. The big white numbers on the monitor plummeted from one hundred twenty-something to sixty-something.

A nurse walked briskly over and pressed a button on the bottom corner of the monitor, silencing the alarm. She then reached into the incubator and started stroking the child's foot from top to bottom.

We were very familiar with this. Another condition needing to be met before being sent home was to avoid having a Brady for six consecutive days. As the children got weeks older and weeks stronger, the foot stroking stopped, and the nurses would just wait as the patient brought his or her own numbers back up autonomously.

So, it was that the ward was like some strange combination of a library and Times Square. Things were usually hushed around you, but there was always a background of sound, buzzing from somewhere just out of sight. White shoes bustling by. A nurse gently rubbing a child's foot, watching as a parent did so, or calmly switching off the alarm and willing the numbers to rise while reassuringly cooing—at the parents.

I spent a few hours in the chair, eventually dozing off, with Kade on my chest.

My wife was next to me, Connor sharing the sweater wrapped around them both. Kristina had already been there for a few hours and had been through a feeding cycle. She was sleeping, now, too. I smiled as I woke up and looked at her, leaned back in her recliner, eyes closed, head tilted to one side. She had not been sleeping well of late.

I needed to use the restroom, so I carefully rose, folding my arms below the bundle on my belly, and moved slowly to the incubator. Keeping Kade seated in the crook of one elbow, I tugged my zipper down with my free hand and slid Kade out of his cocoon, dropping my elbows into the box and placing him gently on his blanket, which I used to swaddle him in movements that came automatically.

The "burrito wrap" was maybe the first thing these, some of the most highly trained nurses on the planet, had taught me. Then there were diaper changes and feedings and baths. Repeatedly, Kristina and I had received professional instruction in the mechanical basics of parenting in a way most parents will never experience.

Grabbing a small, blue stylized baby footprint on the otherwise white blanket, I tucked a pinch of fabric under Kade's chin, assuring his head was free but still semi-cushioned.

The boys received all their necessary fluids and medications intravenously. Connor was born at three pounds, fourteen ounces, and Kade was born at three pounds, eleven ounces. Their tiny arms and legs were too small for the needles, and so their IVs were placed on that vein of their foreheads which now only protrudes when they get really mad.

I looked down at Kade's closed eyes and bandaged head. A long, translucent tube meandered from my baby through a length of winding coils attached to a sack hanging from an IV stand.

I shuttered, recalling that feeling of invasiveness, the line inserted into one's body. Each time that I moved my arm or my wrist, pain would shoot up my limb. How uncomfortable it must be, then, to have to hold your head and neck still or inevitably feel the tugging of the needle resisting your movement and stretching the skin and vein surrounding it.

I carefully stroked Kade's head and then turned away.

The restrooms were in the corner of the ward, and I made my way down the hall over the low-pile carpet, feet shuffling softly. In front of me was a kitchen with a pharmacy-style window that sat attached to the nursing station, with its changing room and lockers and cork boards with photographs of the infants and families in the unit.

There was a bottle on the window counter with a strip of tape on it, a name scrawled on it in black Sharpie. It was here that the NICU would store pre-pumped breast milk to be dispensed to the kids for their rigorously scheduled feedings. Having to feed the babies at certain times meant that you either needed to be there or you needed to have a supply—an inventory—of milk.

For the first weeks, my wife breastfed when she was there with the boys, but she also pumped to build up the inventory. There were two mouths that needed feeding, and two mouths needing progressively more milk as the days and weeks passed. So, over the course of a few days, she resided in the NICU, in a reserved room, and pumped. It took her a couple of hours to get enough milk for the feedings, which happened every three hours. This left her working with one hour when she wasn't pumping—not a large buffer.

Forsaking sleep, she pumped around the clock, building up that precious inventory.

Just recently, however, the milk-storage policy had changed, and there was a limit placed on the volume that could be warehoused. Kristina now had to produce milk pretty much on demand, every three hours, for two hours of feeding. Again, she didn't sleep.

We met with the doctors, pleading behind watering eyes whenever we caught any of them making their rounds. We were met with compassionate half-smiles and empathetic head tilts. But inevitably their shoulders would shrug.

"I can't do it! I've been trying so hard, but I can't do it!" my wife had confided in me one day. She was frayed and crying and collapsed onto my shoulder as we stood guardian over the precious incubator boxes surrounding our more precious boys.

I tried to assure her that "having a cow's milk allergy, I drank plenty of soy milk as a kid. Formula will be okay."

I was mad but without any reasonable avenue for expressing my anger. This wasn't the nurses or doctors. It was the "they," some faceless administrative decision-makers who were never seen nor heard except through the proxy of the medical staff's downturned eyes and shaking heads.

My brow furrowed as I turned left from in front of the window shelf and the bottle, which sat waiting to be transported. Out of the corner of my eye, I noticed that the station at the end of the aisle was vacant—again. There were comings-and-goings of kids and families all the time. Some were our station neighbors for a few days, or a week, and then they'd depart, hopefully to take home a healthy baby.

Eventually, as I left the restroom, I caught a clear view of the corkboard that marked the doorway to the nurses' station: two photos sharing the same thumbtack, one photo pinned at an angle of a tiny infant with a pink bow, and another photo with a young girl running in soccer cleats and a jersey, bent forward, pushing off to race down the field; another set of photos with a newborn sleeping with head tilted, sharing a thumbtack with a family portrait, smiling faces somewhere in the woods; and headshot after headshot of round infant heads and closed eyes protruding from a wrap of blue or pink stylized baby feet on white blankets. Above each headshot was a number made from scrapbooking cardboard, usually in some glittery and shimmering color. Above Connor's and Kade's photos was "thirty-two-and-half," almost eight weeks short of the ideal forty, as it were.

I traced my finger along the curves of the "three."

Below this record of our boys was another number, seeming to be waiting for a photo. It hadn't been here yesterday.

It said, "twenty-seven."

I sat back down in the recliner, pulled the lever, and raised my feet. I closed my eyes, head tilted back, chin up to the sky. A tear welled up. I let it sit there for a long moment, hanging on my eyelashes, until I squeezed my eyes tight.

Breathing out heavily, I rose from the chair, which gave a plastic squeak. I unzipped my sweater. I loosened some coils of IV tubbing, giving us some slack. Then I picked Kade back up, tucking him into my elbow with one arm, unswaddling him with the other. Easing back into the seat, I turned his head to the side and placed him on my chest. I folded one side of my sweater over Kade's back, then the other, and then zipped us back up.

Connor and Kade would be in the NICU for thirty-four and thirty-five days, respectively. We took them home over the course of two days, just before Christmas in 2014. For both trips home, my dad accompanied me. He helped with the car-seat checks and bundling the kids against the cold Colorado winter. He kept a watchful eye in the backseat, next to Connor or next to Kade, while I drove home, where Kristina tended to the snuggling and feeding.

For six years, a shelf of our home library housed the first bottle that either boy finished. It happened to be Connor's. Inside the bottle we'd stashed a coiled twelve inches of the IV tube that had connected his head to the life-saving medications of his very first days.

I had just gotten back from a long run in the heat of August, under an unrelenting New Mexican sun. I was one day away from soccer tryouts and training camp at Sandia High School and one week away from beginning my sophomore year. I was out training in the heat because our high school soccer coach, a former Olympic alternate in Greco-Roman wrestling, was a believer in outworking your opponents. While the local soccer, and even football, teams would take to their fields for twice-daily workouts, we were about to begin thrice-daily practices: a morning, afternoon, and evening session every day for a week.

My parents were up in Colorado for a long weekend, celebrating a wedding anniversary in their beloved Rocky Mountains. They had taken a full day's drive into a far-off corner of the state, away from the summer crowds. My brother and a friend were busy squeezing out the last drops of freedom before their senior year began.

After speeding my jog up to a limb-flailing canter, I then slowed to walk the final hundred yards to my house. It was a single-story, white-stucco home, designed by color and material to reflect away the incessant heat. The nearly circular patch of lawn in front surrounded a single Gambel oak, persistently growing thicker and hardier over its first eight years. Ours and my neighbors' landscapes offered an intermittent set of ground-cover juniper and sage, spaced with too much precision to be natural. Between those bushes, the rounded river rock that would not be found anywhere in our native deserts confirmed that we were clearly in the suburbs.

I entered our house and closed the varnished, heavy wooden front door behind me. I didn't lock it.

I headed to the back room, which we used as a kind of guest bedroom and second den where my brother and I could entertain ourselves or host our angsty teenage friends, playing the latest Nintendo and Sega video games or brooding over whatever ailed us at the moment.

I stood looking out the window at nothing in particular—just the gray cinderblock walls that lined every yard in our neighborhood, as with so much of Albuquerque. As I let my heart and breathing slow after the run, I suddenly felt a strong poke in my back, like someone forcefully digging an index finger into you during a heated argument.

Then I felt it again. I spun around.

As I was spinning, I saw the light flash across the blade of a nine-inch chef's knife, one I recognized from the block in our kitchen.

Another poke, and another. It was only after the fact that I realized that none of the blows ever felt sharp, just these index-finger-like pokes. My eyes were fixed on the knife and the flashes of light from the window upon its blade. It was with disembodied astonishment, not horror, that I saw blood fling off the edge when the knife was pulled back, again, to strike.

A shock of shoulder-length long hair was all I saw of my attacker, and he became distracted as our golden retriever came in. He jammed the knife down on Sunset's front shoulder, and she yelped.

I took the opportunity to slip past the man and into the main living area. Passing the breakfast bar that separated the kitchen from the living room, I noted a three-inch-deep gash on the kitchen counter. He'd swung an angled slash into the counter before coming for me.

Making my way to the opposite end of the house, I sprinted into my parents' bedroom and took the phone's handset off the wall. I dialed 9-1-1 and let dispatch know that I had been stabbed "at least twice, maybe more." At that point, the intruder came in, half-jogging, half-falling toward me. I spun my head low and to the side to dodge a blow, and in so doing was confronted with the tangled hair of his genitalia. He was naked. Continuing in his inelegant lunge, he bounced off my ducking body and seized the phone. With a yank, he and the phone were flung onto the bed, and he disconnected me from dispatch. In doing so, he'd also put down the knife.

I grabbed the knife and dashed from the room. As I came past the kitchen again, this time I made a hard left turn and sprinted out the front door and two doors up the street. The neighbors' solid-wood front door was open, and I could hear laughing and conversation through the screen.

*Good. They're home. Wait—I'm a bloody mess and am carrying a blood-soaked knife*! I placed the knife down and rang the doorbell.

My neighbor came to the door, smiling, then his face fell as he looked me over from top to bottom. He spun around and yelled something like, "Get me some towels and call nine-one-one!"

Someone else—it was hard to register who amidst all the adrenaline—came to the door with a handful of towels and pressed them against my chest. As we all stood on their front stoop, my neighbors moved to my side and pressed more towels into my back. Another on my arm. Another on my opposite shoulder. Each towel placement began to signal to me the extent of my injuries.

It seemed like only moments later that sirens blared as emergency services arrived. The police moved into my home while the emergency medical technicians arrived with the firemen at the neighbors', one of whom had flagged them down from the curb. I was finally sat on the front stoop by the EMTs; after a few minutes of assessment and questions, I was placed on a gurney and rushed into the ambulance.

As my gurney approached the open ambulance doors, I saw the intruder also being wheeled—covered in a white blanket and strapped to another gurney—toward a second ambulance parked in front of my home alongside two squad cars.

Right about then, unknown to me, my parents had coincidently called to check in. In an otherwise empty house, the police answered the phone.

I have often thought about their terror at that moment and what the drive back from Colorado to New Mexico must have been like, racing home, likely testing the speed limit to get back to their youngest son. It feels obscure, vague, surreal, like wandering through a dense fog. Now myself a parent, I can only imagine.

In the ambulance, I had a sense of speed, and I could hear the sirens wailing as we weaved in and out of traffic. The EMTs remained calm. They told me that things looked good, but also that they were going to treat this "very aggressively." They said they wanted to administer an IV and that I would need antibiotics along with other medications to avoid blood poisoning from the metal or from Sunset's blood on the knife. (At the time, I couldn't remember if I had been stabbed before or after Sunset.)

Given that all my wounds were in my upper body—the final tally was two in my back on the left side, one of which had nicked my lung; one in my chest, which got blocked by my sternum; one in my right biceps; a deeper one on my left shoulder; and a nick inside my right elbow—they wanted to run my IVs through my lower body. They chose my feet as the point of entry.

Each attempt to insert a line felt miserable, much sharper than the stabbing had. This would eventually leave my feet so bruised and painful that I could not properly walk, only shuffle, for the next few days.

One attempt; I gritted my teeth. A second attempt; I looked away. A third and a fourth. I lost count and squeezed my eyes tightly shut.

In resignation, they ran an IV in the back of each wrist.

I was rolled into the emergency room at University Hospital, which has one of the best trauma units in all of the country, given Albuquerque's reputation for violent crime. A team of physicians, nurses, and technicians intercepted me at the ambulance doors and began administering treatment while we made our way inside. The view, as I stared upward, was a rush of bright-blue sky; then more gray concrete, this time from the portico; then a convulsing sequence of fluorescent lights.

They needed to check the wound depths and so inserted a sterile Q-Tip into each gash. It was a weird sensation to feel nerves activated by touch in a way they'd never really been before. It didn't hurt, but it made me want to squirm, feeling something foreign circling at some invisible depth inside my body.

They cut my shirt off with medical shears.

The doctors, like the EMTs, assured me that things were "looking good." I remember a few crinkled lines around the eyes, belying a few grins, that I found calming, more than I remember any laughter, despite the jokes I tried telling as a distraction, or more probably as deflection.

Eventually, they were satisfied that most of my wounds were superficial enough to stitch them up. They irrigated each wound, another strange sensation, and began sewing. All but one.

A doctor leaned over me. His mouth and chin were covered by a blue surgical mask, and his hair was obscured by a white cloth. His eyes were penetrating. He spoke quickly and impassively.

"We're going to keep that one in your back, open. It got to your left lung. We don't think your lung will collapse, but there's a chance. If it does, we want to be able to run a tube and reinflate it."

I nodded, pretending to be reassured.

Now in comparatively stable condition, I was left in an observation room, apparently to see if my lung would collapse.

I was pumped full of pain medications, feeling stiff rather than hurting. The open wound was oozing onto an absorbent pad placed behind and under me, and it bothered me. I felt exposed and vulnerable. I wasn't supposed to have these insides of mine open to the outside. I tugged at the hospital blanket, trying to pull it up despite my arms still being locked into IV tubes. I couldn't quite pull the blanket high enough to feel covered.

My first visitor—as my family was still en route—was Jim, the father of my first neighborhood friend, Josh. I lived on a school-boundary line, so Josh went to a different high school than me despite us only being around the block from each other. However, we'd stayed pretty close. Jim was an ex-Secret Service agent who was on Presidential protection details and now worked for the

United Way. A kind, no-nonsense man, Jim squeezed the ends of my fingers, careful with my IV tubes, and I finally felt comforted.

My family arrived that evening and remained bedside with me as the observation period ended and the doctors stitched shut my final wound, my lung having not collapsed after all.

My mom cried the first time I got up and shuffled across the floor to the bathroom, toting my IV tree; the open back of my hospital gown exposed some of the severe bruising that covered my torso. Cold tiles pressed hard against my bruised feet.

The IVs made movement painful as my nerves, already overstimulated, sounded the alarm each time a needle wiggled within a vein. When I wasn't making my periodic shuffle to the bathroom, I laid in bed and tried to keep my hands folded over my chest, unmoving, waiting.

As the days moved forward, I went home and, of course, my family and I began to have conversations about what had happened. I naively marveled at how the violence and uncertainty that was part of late 1980s—and now early '90s—Albuquerque had somehow infiltrated our home, a home that had always felt, to me, far enough away from the chaos. Mostly, though, my parents would ask if I was doing okay, trying to get me to open up about the attack. Mostly, I deflected.

"I'm okay—really."

"Really?"

"Well, it hurts. I'm really sore. But I want to get moving again. Can we go to the soccer practices? I want to see the team."

There were court filings, and interviews. I learned it was acid laced with PCP that had precipitated the attack. I never got back the shirt they had shorn off my body, as it sat in an evidence locker somewhere. I participated as little as possible, and a state-administered buffer was placed between my juvenile self and the incident, designed to protect me from the trauma—and maybe the randomness—of it all. Along with my family, I told lawyers and judges and police, "I'm okay—really." Secretly, though, I didn't feel okay. I slept with my bedroom door locked for the next six months, about the same amount of time that Sunset, her fur filling in over the stitches in her shoulder, refused to go into the back room.

Hiding behind my locked bedroom door, I didn't allow anyone inside. In that room, I ran a loop in my head. *I'm not dead . . . I probably should be dead . . . Why am I not dead . . . ? Well, I guess I'll figure it out . . . There must be a reason.*

I didn't voice this internal conversation. Not with anyone. There was an experience chasm that the people around me couldn't, or I wouldn't let, cross. There was no reason offered as to why I would go into each slide-tackle on the soccer field with fearless determination, dismissing thoughts of potential injury. I didn't talk about why the bullies didn't pick on me and the popular crowd didn't question when I wouldn't want a puff or a hit or a chug. No substances in my body.

But I also didn't explain why I wouldn't go to the theater with my friends and watch the blade-driven battles of the movie *Braveheart*, towards the end of my senior year, even though we had rented and watched *Silence of the Lambs* when I was a freshman. And I didn't say anything about the scars on my chest, back, and arms when, on an almost nightly basis for three years, I would sit on the side of the soccer field, pull off my practice jersey, and replace it with a T-shirt before grabbing my equipment bag, throwing it in my car, and heading home.

I acted out of both determination and fear, not unlike when I'd folded my hands over my chest to avoid stirring the IV tubes tethering me to the hospital bed.

The dentist had come in to provide the usual dentist's chastising for inadequate brushing and flossing, let me know that my X-rays had come back fine, and then left to let the hygienist know that I was ready for my cleaning.

I was a practitioner of merely serviceable, but not exemplary, oral care, it being a habit for which I let lapse my usual diligence. I only have so much room to care about so many things. Today, though, the issue felt even smaller, and I resented the dentist's zealousness, although I didn't say anything.

The hygienist applied the gritty fluoride, I rinsed and spit, and she handed me a little bag of dental party favors: floss, travel-sized toothpaste, toothbrush, a tiny bottle of mouthwash.

I climbed into the car and thought about what, if anything, I should tell my wife. A very clear set of words ran across my mind, as if I was reading them on a billboard: "I should definitely tell her."

This wasn't the thing to hold on my own, even if I didn't really know what was going on, yet. "This is exactly the kind of thing you wouldn't talk about, before," I told myself. "This isn't really about sparing her worry."

My openness, or lack thereof, was a constant struggle in our marriage. It wasn't something I fought against, in principle. I *wanted* to be more open. But I struggled to overcome the baked-in habit of withholding my inmost thoughts, fears, and hopes, a habit I'd honed so sharply ever since that fateful afternoon when I was fifteen years old.

I called Kristina as I steered the car to the laboratory to have my blood drawn. The steering wheel felt hard, unforgiving, under my tight grip.

"Hi, sweetheart. So, uh, I got a call from my doctor, and they need me to go in and get some additional blood work. They said my white-blood-cell count was really high. So, I'm heading over to have my blood drawn, and I'll be home after that."

"Wait, *what!?"*

"Yeah. They are concerned that I might have . . . cancer." The word stuck in my throat.

"You might have *cancer!?"*

"Well, we don't know for sure, but they need me to do more blood tests."

"Did they say what kind of cancer?"

"Nope, just that my white-blood-cell count was really high."

"Okay."

We paused. I worked to focus on the road's gentle curves, which ran me past a schoolyard lined with towering, mature oak trees, newly bare this late-fall day and vaguely menacing, like the giant antlers of some mythological beast.

"Well, I guess we'll do this, huh?" she said.

"Yeah. I guess so."

When I got home after the blood draw, we talked more about the findings, and I tried really hard to rationalize why my white-blood-cell count might be high, coming up with pseudo-medical excuses for the anomaly. *It probably wasn't cancer.*

Over the course of the few days between the follow-up blood test and my pending oncology appointment, I told my wife that it was "the cold I was getting over," even though I hadn't really been sick at the time of the original blood draw, just a lingering cough that my asthmatic lungs always hang onto for weeks after any illness. Or: "It was my immune system attacking that small crumb of food I accidentally inhaled over Thanksgiving." A week or so before my doctor's appointment, a crumb had caused a coughing fit. Maybe it was a combination of the two, putting my immune system into overdrive.

Kristina and I tried to keep to some sort of normalcy during the days we waited for the appointment. There were still our twins, who had just turned four and who still needed raising. And there was work to be done. Which was another thing: *when and what should I tell my employer?*

I looked for hopeful signs in everything.

Kristina and I were standing in the bright glow of our new kitchen. We had moved into our new house in a quiet corner of Littleton, a southern suburb close to the Denver Metro Area's major commuting arteries and mass transit, three months earlier in coordination with my job change. The kitchen had white cabinets and a glossed, light-gray subway-tile backsplash. It opened up into the dining area, which—in turn—opened up through sliding-glass doors onto the back patio. The kitchen got a lot of light.

I lifted my phone and pressed the patient portal app. A happy chime had alerted me that I had some test results waiting. I knew the results didn't come with the doctor's interpretation, but how could anyone resist? Was I supposed to just absently acknowledge the fact that my results were in the palm of my hand but then go about ignoring them until my oncology appointment?

I swiped through the menu options.

My blood work showed “a negative expression of CLL.” That was good news, right? “Negative” always means “no evidence” in healthcare lingo, right?

I looked up what “CLL” meant on the internet: Chronic Lymphocytic Leukemia.

I felt bolstered, but still uncertain.

I showed my wife, vindicated that my pseudoscientific rationalizations had proven correct. But, with a mental nod to my true ignorance, I confessed that I still wasn’t sure.

“I guess the appointment will clear everything up.”

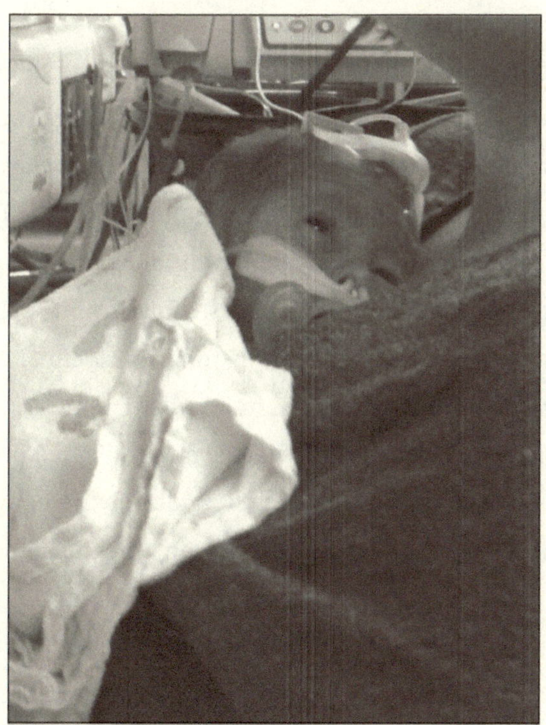

*Kade – IV running to his forehead – on Jason’s chest in the NICU.*

CHAPTER THREE

# Promises

It was mid-March, the height of the late Colorado winter, which really shows up as we approach spring. I pulled my knit beanie down tight over my ears and braced to leave the car, parked at the trailhead for Fletcher Mountain, a 13,958-foot peak in the lofty Tenmile Range near Breckenridge.

As I stepped out, a blast of cold air hit me from the side, blowing through me. I spun out of the way, let the wind slam the driver's-side door shut, and hurried around to the back of my wagon. I pulled the hatch open, but the hydraulics were too cold to hold it up. As I leaned in to fish around for my high-altitude boots and outer layers, the hatch slowly drifted down and rested on my back. After several rounds of this, and giving up on any form of dignity, I crawled into the wagon's hatch and let the door close behind me.

Playing the contortionist, I wiggled and squirmed into my eight-thousand-meter down pants (pants made for the cold conditions on the Himalayan giants); the loft from the insulation doubled the circumference of my legs while also making them stand out with an unignorably bright yellow-and-sky-blue outer shell. I was pretty sure that, as we—me and my fellow members of the Colorado Mountain Club (CMC)—got out onto the trails and began our training, I could be seen from outer space. Perhaps I'd end up somewhere in the next round of satellite-map releases, an Easter egg for intrepid cyber-sleuths to find.

Unsnapping the button at the bottom cuff of each pant leg, I unzipped the legs from bottom to top, opening the pants from foot to knee. I slid my feet from my comfortable tennis shoes and began the next round of contortions: pulling on my high-altitude boots while inside the cramped car.

With an elbow thump against the side of the car, I got the liner boots pulled from the outer boots and secured the first one on my foot with a Velcro flap. Then, hooking an index finger in a pull loop on the back of the outer boot, I rammed my liner-booted toes into the outer and yanked hard up on the loop, driving my heel downward until it slid into place with a *thunk*. From the pressure of my pulling, the loop had left an imprint on the inside knuckle of my finger, but I still had to repeat this inelegant dance on the other side.

Boots on and pants zipped back up, now came the process of getting on the boots' waterproof, knee-high gaiters. It was comparatively simply: I pulled apart the Velcro that ran down the front of each gaiter, mashed and folded the billowing down until it appeared the gaiter fabric would be able to encircle my lower leg, and then tugged the Velcro fronts back together, sealing them shut.

I shimmied and turned and bridged my back and managed to get my parka on and zipped up to my chest.

I placed over my mouth and nose a heat-exchanging mask: a foam mask with a vent that warms air by holding it close to your face before you breathe it in. This helps me stave off my cold-induced asthma as well as protects my nose, cheeks, mouth, and chin from the elements. I put on my climbing helmet, pulled my goggles down over my eyes, pulled my hood over my head, and zipped the parka all the way up, snug around the mask.

Now in my spacesuit, I opened the hatchback, again, and stepped into the gale. I could feel the wind ripple my parka and try to spin me, though less viciously than when I'd first stepped out of the driver's-side door.

Groups of the CMC's High Altitude Mountaineering School (HAMS) consisted of one senior instructor—me, in this case—with, usually, two assistants who all were there to ensure the education and safety of eight to nine students. We'd usually have three or four groups a season, so about twenty-five to thirty-five students in total.

The point of HAMS is to help prepare students for glaciated peaks around the world, and as such, it usually culminates in a spring/summer climb of Mount Rainier, the most heavily glaciated peak in the Lower 48. It is then a subset of these students who go on to climb the bigger peaks in Alaska, South America, and Asia as they develop more experience.

That's how I had started in high-altitude climbing, and that diligence—which fell into inanition at least with oral hygiene—was on full display in the mountains. Besides daily fitness routines, I had added daily routines of practicing technical skills. I had daily routines of equipment modification and maintenance. I had regularly scheduled instructional weekends with accomplished high-altitude guides. And I had organized expeditions to high summits in South America and Alaska. With two three-year-olds at home, I took it as de rigueur that I have the knowledge and abilities to return home safely.

Glaciated peaks at high altitude mean weather, wind, and crevasses. Colorado has no true glaciers with crevasses, but you can simulate the vertical walls of these deep, icy features with one-sided cornices. Colorado does, however, have weather and wind, especially in the late winter and early spring when the jet stream dips south and cuts across the higher peaks.

In these conditions, then, from late January through March of every year, I'd head out into the high country most weekends, with a group of ten or so, and go through the mechanics of how to efficiently and safely move over snow and ice.

This day, I marched over to the other carpooled vehicles to make sure the assistant instructors were having our students gear up properly.

When I'd parked my car at the trailhead, the temperature read -9° Farenheit. It was hard to know what the wind speed was, but with gusts that started to make balance an issue, that was usually around 40 mph (for me). That would make the windchill somewhere around -35 or -40.

I paused to examine myself in the side mirror of a student's car, ensuring I had zero skin exposed.

The students were beginning to partner up into three groups of three, and I came to each group and did the same examination, making sure their skin was covered up. I mentally checked off names with corresponding helmet and pack colors, which is how I would recognize the students today.

We weren't going to get far in these conditions, but the students would get a sanity check on what big-mountain weather can be like, helping them decide if this kind of thing was for them.

In all, this was my fifth year teaching with HAMS, three of them as a senior instructor, for which my responsibilities include planning the logistics of the field days and delivering lectures on topics of particular expertise. I usually delivered two lectures a season, one on physical fitness and the other—usually the opening lecture of the school—about my Rainier climb as a student, during which my team and I organized and executed a rescue of two imperiled climbers.

This was going to be my last year teaching for at least a little bit. Next year was going to be taken up by planning my own big Himalayan climb. I was going to attempt that unclimbed peak in the Annapurna Massif, an audacious goal for someone who had not climbed in the Himalaya before. But my previous experiences making ascents up progressively taller and progressively more committing peaks had emboldened me.

I was also going to be moving homes, as I had very recently left my big, bureaucratic job for a small startup that was honestly trying to do some good in health care. I only had so much time.

Mountaineering instruction is a delicate balance between pushing students beyond their comfort zones—the whole point of learning, after all—and ensuring that they stay safe in these very harsh environments, all while we cover mentally and physically demanding skills such as route-finding, moving as a unit when tied into the same rope, and self-arrest (using your ice axe to stop a slide down a snow slope or glacier).

Today's field day was originally designed to summit the nearly 14,000-foot Fletcher Mountain, bringing these skills we had been practicing on other field days onto a real peak with real consequences. As the students—now organized into their three-person rope teams—all gathered round, I made sure to set expectations, shouting through my mask to make myself heard above the wind.

"Can everybody hear me!?" Nods in the affirmative.

"It is going to be hard moving today! With the wind the way it is, to be honest, you'd likely stay in your tent if you were on a big mountain! But we'll see if we can't get above Blue Lake and then reassess! Maybe we'll even get as far as the bench at 12,500 feet!"

Nods in the affirmative.

"If, at any point, you feel hands or toes starting to go, you pull on me or one of the other instructors, and we are all turning around!"

Nods in the affirmative.

"Alright, who wants to lead us out?"

We marched up a packed-snow track that was a mountain road in the summertime, the semi-compacted, wind-hardened snow crunching underfoot. A wide corridor of pine trees lined the road, and at the occasional clearings, we could see the corners of homes I can only imagine were owned by hearty mountain folk.

It wasn't long until the trees began to become sparser, until they eventually disappeared altogether. To our right was Quandary Peak, one of the taller peaks in the state, standing slightly above most of the other 14,000-foot mountains. Its south face jutted skyward at an angle that wasn't sheer but that wasn't "hike-able," either. To our left was the shorter, steeper-yet north face of North Star Mountain, a long, ridgelike peak. North Star's north face is a series of rubble gullies that shed rock in the summer and cascade avalanches in the winter.

It wasn't unusual for these types of harsh field days to weed out a few aspiring high-altitude climbers. They wouldn't quit the school very often, but you wouldn't see them climb anything beyond the graduation climb on Rainier, if even that.

Typically, no one was ever really in danger, but every year a few students would pass a rather uncomfortable day during one field session or another by mismanaging their layers: getting too hot, breaking a sweat, and then cooling to a chill.

That wasn't going to happen today. No one was going to be breaking a sweat. I was geared up in more insulation than I'd worn two years earlier on Denali. No one could afford to learn lessons the hard way today. No, today needed to be about doing it right. Skin can flash-freeze at these temperatures.

Above Blue Lake, we began to make our way up a ridgeline to the expansive bench at 12,500 feet. The students fell into file, the lead climber kicking in steps for the others. Occasionally, the leader would fall to the rear to allow a fresh climber to take on the chore of breaking trail.

We paused at the point where the slope steepened and headed up toward the bench to discuss the avalanche potential. The ridge would keep us safe. Anything that we let loose would fall away to the sides. No one was below in any direction; no one else was crazy enough to be out here. Topping out on the bench, we huddled together.

"How's everyone doing!" Nods in the affirmative. "Anyone want to keep going!?" No nods.

On the way back home, we stopped at Tommyknocker, a local brewery in Idaho Springs, the last mountain town before the freeway funnels travelers down into the western suburbs of Denver. One of our more gregarious instructors had long ago negotiated a deal with the ownership, helping defray the costs of the post-climb beers CMC's students would effortlessly down. The school's various groups, who had gone off independently to various mountains, now converged here.

We sat in baseball caps and comfortable sneakers on the hard, wooden chairs that encircled the hard, wooden tables. Goggle lines wrapped around our eyes. Disheveled beards and long hair draped over fleece tops in bright reds, blues, and greens. I finally felt warm, and my toes and fingers still tingled a little from the increased blood flow.

Coming in a bit after some of the other groups, I'd chosen an empty seat at the table with the school's joint directors: John and his wife, Debbie (whom we all called Deb).

John was a decade older than me, a bit taller, and wirier. He had the chiseled and weathered face of a person who spends time in the mountains. His baseball cap was greased with sweat stains where the brim met the crown from long days toiling with a pack in the sun.

Deb, also my senior, was of average height, but carried a mountaineer's pack with ease. She had crow's feet from decades of squinting under the high-alpine sun and against glacial reflections. She was John's willing adventure partner, tempering John's vocal enthusiasm with a quiet and empathetic manner, though she was no less determined.

They met at work, as my wife and I had, and they fell in love after each had lost a spouse to cancer. They had kids roughly the same age, and one could mistake them for the Brady Bunch if it were not for their sojourns into the oxygen-deprived heights.

I mostly climbed with John, as he had a more expansive set of climbing partners. But it was Deb who really took me under her wing when I was a rising instructor, not only imparting the necessary climbing skills, but more importantly spending time discussing the art of teaching and coaching.

Deb took Kristina under her wing, too. Sure, there were the finer points of peeing as a woman when tied into a rope on a glacier. But there was also the role climbing could play when balanced against motherhood and the joys and challenges of sharing a life with another diehard climber.

Deb often talked openly to Kristina and me about the conversations she and John would have with their own kids, who were now young adults. "We tell them, now that they are adults, John and I are consciously taking more risks. Controlled risks, but more risks, nonetheless," Deb would say.

"How was your day?" John asked.

Our server came by, and I asked for the brewhouse's oatmeal stout and a bowl of tomato-artichoke soup. "Cold!" I said with a grin.

"Did your group make it up?" Deb asked, giving a knowing smile from beneath her wind-disheveled dusty-brown hair.

"No, we stopped at the bench at twelve-five. It was pretty brutal, honestly. But the gang did great! They worked together. We communicated well. We made good decisions. Yeah, it was a good day."

"It's a good class, this year," she replied.

"It is. You two put together a good roster. How'd the other groups do?"

"Seems like they all did really well. Kind of the same as yours. Got out and experienced these conditions."

"That can be such a good thing," John chimed in. "Sometimes really experiencing how the mountains can be is so beneficial for growing as a climber. When Deb and I were on Cho Oyu, so much of what we were doing was just being in a harsh environment."

Our server returned, and I took a sip of the frothy ink-black ale.

"So, Ecuador, Denali, Cho Oyu. What's next?" I asked.

"We've been talking, and I don't think we'll go back and do another 8,000-meter peak. You just don't do that much actual climbing," John replied.

"It was really hard work, and a lot of feeling uncomfortable. I don't mind feeling uncomfortable, but I'd rather feel uncomfortable while climbing, while actually moving," Deb confirmed. "There's lots of great stuff to climb just in and around Colorado. We'll probably just climb here for a bit."

"Of course, there's the Rainier trips with the school or maybe Baker or other climbs we can take them to, but we are just so lucky to live in Colorado."

That was John's usual refrain. We heard about how lucky we are to live where we do half-a-dozen times each school season. But he wasn't wrong.

I flashed a smile and said, "Well, I was a year behind you to Ecuador. I was a little further behind to Denali, because of my knee. The two of you keep plotting the course! Maybe the Himalaya are coming, but I don't think the 8,000-meter peaks interest me, either. I'm finding I like things that are more under the radar."

Deb looked out at the students, sitting at broad, community tables around us. I followed her lead and turned my gaze outward.

For a while we sat quietly. We sipped from our pint glasses and rolled them around the wet coasters. Over the echoing hum of exuberant chatter and clanking silverware, the students shouted stories of the day's internalized struggles. Another soft grin spread across my lips.

We called it the slowest jailbreak in history.

Kristina and I had a series of one-foot by one-foot foam pads that snapped together like a puzzle. They came in preschool-approved bright greens, reds, blues, and yellows. Careful to make sure that no two adjacent squares were the same color, we fashioned a twelve-foot-square bit of makeshift flooring on the hardwood between our breakfast bar and the seating of our great room, surrounding it with plastic, inter-connecting baby gates. The kids thus had a play area right where we spent most of our home time.

"Play area" might be a bit overstated. At eight months old, the boys couldn't yet stand up.

I had just gotten back from my summit of Denali and was now in the routine of work, commuting, grocery-store runs on the way home, diaper changes, late-night feedings, and groggy mornings. I refused to be a "coffee drinker," still sensitive to the random attack I'd weathered by someone under the influence of drugs and not wanting to become dependent on any substance for normal human function.

I was at work when the jailbreak happened, so I only saw it from stitched-together video clips later that evening.

My wife was typing away at work emails and data queries on the couch, glancing back over her shoulder every few minutes to monitor the boys. Over the course of forty minutes or so, the two determined, slightly chubby lumps of human-cuteness wiggled and rolled to one corner of the play area then lay on their backs, gathering strength.

The navy-blue and red striped onesie produced a small, pale leg, and the leg kicked out at the gate. Then the powder-blue onesie produced an identically sized and identically pale leg, which—likewise—kicked out at the gate.

*Rest.*

Needing to get closer to the gate, which had been pushed farther away due to the kicking (as per the plan), the kids rolled and wiggled some more.

*Rest.*

*Kick. Kick.*

The baby gates slowly parted. The rolling and wiggling moved from the padded flooring to the hardwood.

*Kick. Kick.*

The opening became wider, until the escapees rolled through the breach.

Between the emails and data queries, Kristina recorded the great escape a few seconds at a time. The video remains a prized entry in our family's digital archive.

Kade and Connor always have preferred open spaces. When the boys would fuss—around this same age—they were most readily calmed by a walk, not a walk around the house—it had to be outside. My wife and I had various wraps and shawls that doubled as baby carriers. As the boys got bigger, we upgraded to what seemed like industrial, rope-access harnesses, but with padded kangaroo pouches.

In the carriers, the boys faced out. We tried to face them in, which we were told would help them fall asleep, but they would have none of it. The world was too full of colors . . . then colors and shapes . . . and then details: red-breasted robins, green grass, and—in the right season—the deep purples of the maple trees that ornamented our very planned, suburban neighborhood. Eyes remained wide; fingers stretched out and reached.

The long walk around the houses or through the open grass of our manicured neighborhood park or down to Aurora reservoir, where dirt (not sand) met docks, became part of the routine. It put the boys at ease to be outside, and they preferred the mesmerizing wobble that came from their rides in the industrial harnesses. At times, they would tolerate their double stroller or even the big-wheeled child carrier latched behind a bike and which could go over packed dirt, but when they'd had enough, they'd let us know of their displeasure.

The kids' baby shoes didn't stay dainty and ornamental for long; in fact, we quickly traded them in for treaded and robust shoes instead.

Eventually, the baby gates just stayed open. The boys napped in a nest of blankets placed on the padded floor, and they played with the similarly stashed stuffed animals and blocks and jingly, textured toys meant to awaken their senses. But they also rolled, and eventually crawled, out onto the hardwood, knees padded with baby fat and the gaps in their joints making them oblivious to the hard surface.

Within the confines of the main floor of the house, the little boys were free-range and happy about it. They moved constantly, even when moving was hard and time-consuming, with an unmistakable intensity of purpose: sometimes, as on this first day and others thereafter, to get out of gated "baby-jail," sometimes to grab a cord and discover how it wrapped around a finger. Well, oftentimes it was a cord. Thankfully, they never really cared about the ends of cords and the plugs into which they terminated, preferring instead to haul themselves up on the cords like climbing ropes.

Of course, that intensity of purpose isn't very different from Mom and Dad. Before the boys, we had our own trips outdoors, with ropes, and deep planning sessions regarding important details like which crampons and boots made the most sense or which ice axes to bring.

We encourage the boys' exploration, but we also pledge to shepherd it. Our brains know full well—even if our hearts, to this day, can't fully conceive—that someday those explorations will expand beyond the reach of our parental grasp.

When I was growing up in Albuquerque, our dining room table's primary function was as a filing cabinet. Not all the time. We'd have holiday meals and guests, but the number of days with food on the table paled in comparison to the number of days with paper on the table.

It was a deep, walnut-stained thing, eating up the space. To my small self, the table seemed huge, like I could have had all of my friends over for a birthday party, brought everyone to gather around it, and still have had seats left open.

I raced my Hot Wheels cars around the table's base when I was home from school sick. A large pillar branched down from its center into a sleek curve, from which stretched two "wings." The wings, in turn, grabbed the floor. The route around the table base made a perfectly sized oval track for my casted-steel miniatures.

My dad, Alan, was a nuclear safety engineer. His job was to find the probabilities of mechanical, human, or—late in his career—terrorist safety incidents at all types of nuclear facilities. Those risks would then be targeted for mitigation work, be that power-plant redesign, technician training, or security enhancements. He was good at it and was sought for his expertise.

I noticed elegance and creativity in what could easily be assumed to be tedious work. For one power-plant, he and his colleagues were charged with finding the likelihood of human error when running through the safety procedures in the event of a fire in the control room. Well, there weren't fires in control rooms, fortunately, in the numbers that you would need to draw firm conclusions. And you certainly weren't going to set up an experiment. So, they got black-box recordings from airplane flights that had had fires in the cockpits. Using this proxy data, they then modified their findings based on the complexity of safety protocols across the two different operator environments.

The rich-brown tabletop was frequently covered in my father's stacks of white- or yellow- or green-striped papers. "Horizontal filing," as my mom called it.

My dad was always writing proposals for work or finalizing reports to clients. And he taught classes to federal regulators, so there were lesson plans and handouts, too.

As each deadline approached, my dad would sit at the table, maybe in his favored yellow polo shirt with horizontal blue pin stripes, contrasting with the dark wood as the sunlight from the dining-room window turned from white to yellow to red before disappearing entirely. Then the lights came on. As the light changed, the paper stacks grew, nearly to a foot tall.

My dad did not miss deadlines. His version of integrity hinged on the motto, "Deliver on what you say you will deliver." But the firms he worked for signed clients who always needed more and needed it faster (just like every other business); so, the cycle of ever-more-pressing deadlines was always accelerating.

The papers piled higher and higher.

At a time when home computers were just becoming a thing, he was bent over the dining-room table, scribbling notes into a legal pad, or on a draft copy of a report, for his assistant to type up the next day. He would pause to think, his curly brown hair bobbed up and to the side, before he lowered his head and scribbled with his pen some more.

As the deadlines tended to show up at the end of each week, the evening hours bent over the legal pad would stretch into the wee hours of the morning in the work week's latter days.

After dinner, I would gather up my remaining Hot Wheels, making a basket of my shirt's belly, clearing the floor for Dad's return to work. At night, I would shuffle off to bed, passing the open entrance to the dining room.

I panned my head as I walked by, eyeing my dad's back, clad in his standard striped shirt; the scribbling and the head bent in concentration; the stacks of paper. Must be a Thursday.

The next morning, shuffling back through the open entrance and into the kitchen, I found the chair now vacant. The stacks of paper were slightly higher.

"What are you working on?" I might ask that evening.

"I promised Mary [or Gordon or whomever] that . . ." my dad would respond.

Around the house, implied promises fueled my father's activities as well. I don't recall whimsical statements like "Perhaps I'll build a clubhouse in the backyard." I became aware when I saw the schematics. Nor do I recall him saying, "Perhaps I'll set up the new basketball hoop." Instead, concrete bags were soon lined up next to the posthole digger. I sat on the driveway, on a scorching summer day, and "helped" as my dad planted the hoop's metal support into the ground and filled in the concrete.

Despite my busy father's minor resentment at losing a whole weekend day to yardwork, the lawn was kept mowed and he dispatched whatever else had made it onto the upkeep list, such as hedge trimming or picking the ripe fruit from the cherry tree before the birds devoured them all. The cars got washed, by hand, when a warm day presented itself. There were also the hours behind the wheel, caravanning from New Mexico to some adjacent state for a soccer tournament, myself and a couple of teammates talking nonsense in the back of the car while he and my mom tried to converse up front.

When I woke up on Monday, shuffling groggily to the kitchen to get ready for school, the light showered through the dining-room window in a soft yellow, on its way to white. The table was clear then, and I could see the nearly black streaks of grain and knotted wood winding through the chocolate-colored surface.

By Wednesday, the first few stacks of white and yellow had reappeared.

While I was waiting for my oncology appointment and definitive diagnosis, I had a few workdays that still demanded my attendance. I was in a new job, part of the leadership team at a startup looking to sell a software-as-a-service package to help healthcare companies figure out if they were helping nudge patients towards both lower cost and more satisfying preventative care rather than waiting for sickness to set in.

Say an insurance carrier was trying to get more diabetics to get their feet checked as part of their routine health maintenance; to do so, the carrier launched a text-message campaign. Maybe more diabetics actually scheduled and attended their appointments with their doctors. So, had this text-messaging campaign worked, or was it the fact that the American Diabetes Association had just done a series of radio ads reminding patients to get their feet checked, too?

Or maybe a group of doctors was trying a new accountability app that allows patients to self-report taking their prescribed medications. So had the real—not just the self-reported—adherence improved?

These are difficult questions, and it takes a series of statistical steps to isolate the effect of the intervention as distinct from any other potential cause. Our company boxed those statistical steps into a software package, with the goal of helping healthcare companies understand what was working rather than endlessly throwing money at things that weren't truly working—a cost eventually passed on to the patient.

I was pretty experienced at this stuff, having spent three years evaluating program effectiveness for the State of Colorado's Medicaid agency then eight years working for the nation's largest nonprofit healthcare company, Kaiser Permanente, eventually leaving as head of analytics for the Colorado region.

Here at my new job, first thing on Friday mornings, we had a leadership team meeting. All of the senior personnel would walk past the café area, stocked with snacks and beer; through the conference room doors; and into the glass-lined conference room, which was supposed to demonstrate our transparency to the team. We were definitely a "tech startup."

On this particular Friday morning, I sat through the meeting trying to dig in and pay attention. From up on the twenty-sixth floor of our downtown Denver skyscraper, the sun from the wall of glass facing the skyline crashed into the room, blending oddly with the electric light washing in from the café through the opposite wall of glass.

As we wrapped up the meeting, and the group stood, I remained in my seat. "Gang, can I have two minutes with all of you?" I asked.

My coworkers were hurrying to get to their next meeting or to-do list item, and I could sense their restlessness. Still, one of them—I can't remember who—said, "Sure."

I just blurted it out: "I need you all to know that I got some bloodwork back from my doctor. It could be nothing, but it could be cancer. My white-blood-cell count is really high, and they need to do some additional tests to make sure they know what is going on."

A few people sat back down.

"I just need you all to know, because you've made an investment in me, and just as I'm coming up to speed here, there is a reasonable chance that I'm going to be out for a while . . . and you all have a business to plan. That's it. I just need you to know so that we're not all surprised one way or the other."

I stood up, relieving them of the pressure of staying in a room filled with awkward silence, and we all filed out.

Melissa, our chief marketing officer, was quick to find me and let me know that she was available to talk. Megan, our head of human resources, asked if I, with her, wanted to review our employee crisis-counseling benefits and extended-leave policies. Anne Marie, who was not my boss but who had hired me, assured me that people would be covering for me and that I could take some time to focus on myself.

Later that day, I stopped by the office of our CEO, Eric, to talk about something or other. At the end, as I turned to leave, he stopped me.

"How are you doing?"

"Well, you know."

"I did some searching. At worst, it'll be a few months of you beating up on cancer, and then you'll be back and helping us out."

"Yeah, we'll see," I said over my shoulder as I moved toward the door.

On the train ride from downtown to our new home on the south end of town, I kept my sunglasses on and my headphones in my ears, pretending to scroll through my music files.

It was nice to know that I would be welcomed back. It was nice to have permission to focus on treatment, if treatment was where I needed to focus.

I looked up from my phone as the light flickered from the windows. The train squealed around a bend, carving a route down the side of I-25. The cars on the highway inched forward and then stopped, inched forward and then stopped. A sea of paired red lights flashed on and off, as if choreographed.

I glanced back down at my phone but then turned my gaze to the blue vein running from the inside of my wrist into the crook of my elbow. I imagined gently lifting the vein out of my arm, as if it was a stray piece of tinsel on the Christmas tree in our living room, wishing away the poison in it.

I furrowed my brow and squinted down at my arms, turning

them to see the veins on the backs of my hands. I rolled my free hand into a fist, squeezing tightly. The veins protruded toward me, like a challenge.

Then I slowly let my fingers loosen, trying to move the tension out through my fingertips. I unfurrowed my brow.

"I will not make this a battle," I audibly whispered. "I will not war with myself." Cutting myself off from the world or cordoning off cancer from the rest of myself sounded exhausting.

I looked back up at the brake lights, stuck in traffic, now unmoving, and mouthed, "If this is cancer, it is not 'Other.' It is 'Me.'"

*The checkerboard floor of the living room playpen, site of the "slowest jail break in history."*

CHAPTER FOUR

# Tests

We had just turned from the "two-thousand-aughts" into the "twenty-tens," and it had been several years since I had graduated Hight Altitude Mountaineering School, had become an instructor, and had climbed glaciated Mount Rainier via multiple routes. It was time to try high-altitude mountaineering, and so I started the lengthy planning process.

Climbing at altitude—for Coloradans like me, who regularly go above 14,000 feet, we are talking about 17,000, 18,000, 20,000 feet, and above—makes altitude-related ailments (like acute mountain sickness, pulmonary edema, cerebral edema, etc.) part of the risk calculation. This, in turn, requires climbers to mitigate those risks through acclimatization.

Ecuador quickly became my first high-altitude-mountaineering destination for two reasons: the government required that mountaineers from outside the country hire a local guide; and each climb had a refugio—or a climber's cabin—on the mountain. Having a guide meant that I would be less responsible for route planning and in-country logistics, which would let me focus solely on understanding the terrain and climate demands in order to help us pack the right equipment for our climbs. Having refugios meant that each climb was—in essence—a single, overnight endeavor:

drive near to the refugio, make the thirty-minute hike in, have a meal, get some sleep, and wake up well before the sun (an "alpine start") for a summit bid. We'd then return to the refugio, pack up, and drive out: a day-and-a-half per climb, each.

So, in essence, all my partners and I would be testing was our abilities to deal with the climbing and the altitude; we would limit the other variables we'd be encountering. Kristina would come along, and she and I recruited another climbing couple, Andine and Richard, to join us.

I knew Andine from the Colorado Mountain Club, and she had recruited her husband to become a HAMS student. Andine was born in (what was then) East Germany, but didn't have stories of oppression or yearning for freedom. She was just too young in the time before the Wall came down. She was passionate, well read, multicultural, and a nurse. Richard was an engineer and came at climbing with an engineer's analytical mindset.

While no one climb would be extreme unto itself, the combination of five peaks in about ten days would take its toll. We planned a progression of summits, getting higher and higher as part of an acclimatization schedule. We would start with snow-free Corazon; progress through the glaciated peaks of Illiniza Sur, Cayambe, and Cotopaxi; and finish with Chimborazo.

The first climb was really a hike, like a walk-up Colorado Fourteener. Vulcan Corazon is about 15,700 feet high and made for a lovely day, complete with an actual trail. In the warm climates near the equator, it lies well below the snow line.

From the summit, it was a refreshing saunter back down to about 10,000 feet, after which we had a day of rest inclusive of the drive to our next objective.

On the next climb, a steep glacial ascent up the 17,000-plus-foot Illiniza Sur, we learned that my body acclimates well and that my wife's does not. When we woke up in our refugio at 2:00 a.m. for our alpine start, fishing for our gear and getting ready to step out into the cold, Kristina felt slow, nauseous, and mentally fuzzy. She let us know that she was evaluating her ability to join us on our summit bid. The night's "sleep" above 15,000 feet had taken its toll, and after forty-five minutes of trying to put on her climbing boots, she decided that she was in no condition to attempt the summit . . . which the rest of us did make.

Our third summit bid, Vulcan Cayambe, resulted in the whole team turning around after two of our party became altitude sick. We were at around 18,000 feet, about 1,000 feet shy of the summit, when we made the choice to return to the refugio and drive out to lower elevations. My wife was, again, one of those feeling the effects of the altitude.

On Christmas Eve of 2012, in keeping with our progression of increasing altitude, we attempted Vulcan Cotopaxi, standing about 19,350 feet. Kristina's rather miserable experiences with altitude had made her dread the climbs, especially compared to the ease and enjoyment of in-town rest days.

As we bounced and lurched and jerked in the back seat of the Isuzu Trooper that Jorge, our guide, steered up the "road" to the refugio at Cotopaxi, Kristina and I discussed her trepidation. Jorge's assistant and fellow-guide, Rafael, looked back at us with a smile from the passenger seat. I was compressed against the glass of the rear door, as the four of us filled the back bench seat. Being that it was a volcano, Cotopaxi's terrain steepened as we drove higher. Deep canyons of glacial runoff cut down the volcano's flanks, and

Jorge would have to drive diagonally across the loose boulders and washed-out clay, so that only one tire dipped over the void at a time. At each bounce of the car, a duffel of gear, in turn, spilled onto our heads from the rear storage area. Outside the window there was seemingly no life. No vegetation. No animals. The reddish-brown lower mountain gave way to bright white, the glacier reflecting the equatorial sun directly overhead.

A few hundred vertical feet from the refugio, Jorge parked the Trooper in a scraped-out semi-circle of leveled dirt. Then Jorge and Rafael pulled our duffels out of the car. Kristina and I unzipped the blue-and-black bags on the dusty red ground and began to pull out the gear we'd need: a clang of a snow picket, a hollow clop of a helmet, and a gentle rustle of an insulated jacket. Finally, a flurry of arms as we stuffed our summit packs and lashed the metal pickets to the sides.

The six of us marched up toward the refugio, at 15,700 feet. My heavy mountaineering boots hit the hard dirt with a *thunk* at each heel strike as I then rolled the rigid sole up onto the toe, in an awkward, stiff-footed stride. Those of us in the lead on the thirty-degree slope sent a continuous cascade of dirt down onto those behind, and each step seemed to slide halfway back to its starting position. We struggled upward. After ten minutes, I looked up and there, dug into and built above a sloping basin, was a gray stone structure. We approached the basement garage, which reeked of gasoline and wherein was parked a motorcycle in some state of disassembly.

Grabbing the handrails, I made my way up the stairs and into the common room. The inside was cavernous, and the wood floors echoed at each step.

After we claimed our bunks and organized our gear, I took a walk around the grounds. For the first time in my climbing career, I passed not one but multiple memorials to the adventurers who had lost their lives on the peaks near where I stood: names and dates carved into wood, tin, and rock. The boys were still a few years away, so my thoughts turned to my wife, and her struggles thus far on these taller mountains.

Cotopaxi is a popular destination, and I counted seventy-nine people in the refugio that evening, all tucked into bunk beds that were, in turn, tucked into every corner beyond the kitchen and dining area.

Back at my bunk, anxious from the grim reality brought to light by the memorials, I had another first as a climber: my first experience with Cheyne-Stokes breathing. Cheyne-Stokes is a type of sleep apnea. You simply stop breathing for a bit because the rapid respiration of high altitude has kept you from accumulating carbon dioxide, which is your body's normal signal to breathe. You then take a quick inhale to get oxygen into your system. Those forced inhales were enough to wake me up, which meant I passed a terrible night's sleep.

Luckily (I guess?), we woke up exceptionally early: at 11:30 p.m. We wanted to be out in front of the throngs of climbers to avoid the dangers of debris—ice chunks and loose rocks—dislodged from above. In an hour, we were out the door. Kristina was with us, determined to make the attempt.

The first thousand feet was a slog up the loose, red, volcanic rock, dusted by sediment as if glazed by Martian snow. Each step had its requisite back-slide as Cotopaxi reclaimed our hard-earned progress. I could hear the clacking of rocks below as the army of climbers from the refugio began their ascent, loosing pebbles and small stones into the darkness.

Higher, we came to the snow and ice, navigating a maze of seracs—stacked ice blocks, some as large as buses. Being the first ones up, and in the dark, we strained our eyes to navigate by headlamp as we weaved beneath, around, and onto the tops of these ominous monoliths. We lost time finding a way around a vertical face that we were not equipped to climb with only one mountaineering axe, each. (Normally, vertical ice is climbed by using two smaller, specialty axes called "ice tools.")

As we exited the seracs, we came to a large crevasse cutting in front of us. Its lower lip was at our feet, but its upper lip lay across a four-foot-wide chasm at head level.

We stretched out our party to bring the climbing rope more tightly against all of us, each climber anchoring in place by jamming his or her ice-axe spike and shaft deep into the glacier. That is, all of us, except Jorge, who was in the lead on the first of our three-person rope teams. He swung his axe above his head and jammed the pick into the upper lip of the crevasse. Placing his feet up onto the ice face in front of him, he leaned back over the gaping hole and worked his hands up the shaft of his axe, holding his cramponed feet in place on the ice. And so he levered into an upright position swung a foot over the lip, rolled onto his chest, and then swung the second leg up and over.

Each of us repeated this sequence, in turn. I tried to focus on only two things: making good kicks into the ice, securing my feet to allow them to act as the fulcrum of my lever, and focusing my eyes on my hands as I walked them, hand-over-hand, up my axe, doing my best to ignore how the white snow turned to blue glacial ice, then to midnight blue, and finally to black, as the hole fell away below me.

It was a marvelous little piece of gymnastic climbing, at somewhere approaching 18,000 feet. With the rope and so much counterweight from the other climbers to catch any fall, we were in little danger, but you still had to be able to surmount the crevasse lip.

We all completed the move.

As the sun rose, the wind kicked up, the warming of the earth creating an updraft. Our team was far up on the shoulder of Cotopaxi now, and the headlamps below us seemed to be thinning out as a few teams retreated. At our first sun hit, I felt a rush of warmth and zipped my collar down from over my mouth, sucking in more air.

As we continued our march upward, each of our rope teams was stretched out on a fifty-meter rope, making communication difficult. Between that and the wind, I retreated into my own thoughts.

I was feeling strong. My energy was good. My focus was high. I exalted in the views of the High Andes all around and their wild, snowy and rocky terrain. My mind was open and drinking in the experience. As we paused for a quick bite of food, which we carried in our pockets to keep from freezing, I took a photo of the conical shadow that originated from the peak still above us and which pointed out to the western horizon, past llliniza Sur.

Kristina later told me that, at this same point, she was counting steps, a mental game from her backpacking days: set a step goal; count the steps until you reach it; set another goal.

Hitting "the wall" can be a personal kind of hell on a big peak, because stopping is not an option. Taken to its absurd extreme, if you stop and never get back up, you will eventually die; it just becomes a matter of time. So, you can keep going up or retreat, but you must move.

Feeling hypoxic and queasy, Kristina put one foot in front, and now the next . . . thousands of times. Isolated on the rope like the rest of us, she had no one to share her suffering with. There was just the seemingly unchanging view of the snow, her feet, and the yellow rope attached to me somewhere in front of her, snaking away and guiding her to take the next step.

We snapped a succession of summit photos, with arms raised, big smiles, and cartoonish sunglasses shaped as oversized, blue stars. Buoyed by the sense of accomplishment, we congratulated and thanked each other, just as one other team made the summit. In all, of the seventy-nine souls in the refugio, nine made the summit that day; the rest were turned around by the wind or the "layback" move to cross the crevasse.

Kristina didn't attempt our final climb of the trip, Chimborazo, standing 20,700 feet. Only Andine and I made the attempt, and we turned around at 20,0000 feet when my right crampon failed, slowing our progress to a point where fierce winds began to coat us in a thin layer of ice.

Scrolling through those summit photos of Cotopaxi, you come to one of my strong and willful wife. She isn't standing with arms upraised. You see her sitting with one leg crossed under the other, hands in her lap, a tired smile across her face. Cotopaxi's dark, volcanic crater sits behind and below her, a cloud trapped in its maw.

Connor and Kade climbed before they could walk. When they were in the "cruiser" stage, wobbling around on new legs while keeping hands on the furniture for support, they began to plot their first vertical efforts.

Of the two boys, Connor completed the first "climb."

In our home's main living room, we had a broad, cherrywood TV stand, about three feet high, two feet deep, and six feet long. On the floor next to it was a small speaker, facing out into the room. On top of the TV stand was—well—the TV, and coming out of the TV were cords. Ah, magical cords.

Against the wall near the TV stand, stacked messily, were some faux-brix cardboard boxes, the same ones my brother and I had as kids and with which we endlessly made forts.

Climbing mostly on his knees, Connor made steady progress about halfway up the teetering talus-pile of cardboard bricks, intuitively and carefully maintaining three points of contact by not moving one limb to a new position until the other three limbs were secure.

Kristina took out her phone and began filming him. Kade stood hopefully nearby.

At the halfway point, a few of the cardboard blocks gave way; Connor maintained his crouched and crawling position as the strange floor sunk away beneath him. He had lost half his vertical gain.

Undeterred, he resumed his ascent.

A chubby little knee dug into a yellow block. A hand groped for a hold near the wall. Another knee moved up onto a blue block . . . then a broad red block.

Kade, unable to contain his enthusiasm, leaned against the face of the TV stand and shuffled his way over to the corner, where Connor had now reached the speaker. Connor edged his knees out onto the speaker, placed his hands on the TV stand, and, emboldened by the comparatively sturdy top of the speaker, hoisted himself to his feet. Keeping one hand on the TV stand and both feet firmly planted on the speaker, he reached his other hand out and examined the coaxial cable running from the back of the TV.

*Success.*

This would be far from the last ascent of our furniture, and the boys' dreams only got bigger. The next major objective was the kitchen counter.

The boys, a year old, had a green plastic table with four matching, toddler-sized chairs purchased for when they would be in their finger-food stage and regularly having snacks. However, they'd kept trying to use the chairs to surmount the table, and eventually we had to store the chairs in the basement to mitigate the hazard.

The twins also had small, seated scooters with which they wheeled themselves around on the hardwood floor of the kitchen while we cooked. On their scooters, they had made several reconnaissance runs. I believe they eyed a fine line of ascent at the end of the kitchen counter where it opened up into the living area, offering the most freedom of movement and an easy approach.

It was also where we kept a little CD player, which we used to play the kiddie march "We Are the Dinosaurs." As with the previous generation's Barney, the purple dinosaur, and his insufferable music, this song was our home's version of parental torture; the kids demanded to hear it again and again. But more than the song, what played the song was more fascinating yet—a device with cords.

I'm not sure if it was a fortuitous "weather window" or the memory of, and confidence gained by, the summit of Mount TV Speaker. Maybe it was simply the realization that all their planning had to be put to use some time. But whatever it was, they chose a day, threw caution to the wind, and launched their next climbing expedition.

The climb began, we would later discover, as all good expeditions do: by lining up logistics. We did not see this one, or we would have stopped it. Because of that, the details of their perilous ascent will remain only with them. We found the boys on the counter. Pushed up against the counter was the plastic table, the scooters parked next to it as stepping-stones. The Southwest Buttress of Countertop Peak had seen its first ascent (FA). Although, with Mom's and Dad's hands under their chubby armpits, the boys were airlifted from the summit; so, the legitimacy of the FA remains controversial, the climbers having not descended by their own power.

As the boys aged, the raised mattress on Mom and Dad's bed became a goal. Superior grip strength was required, as the comforter made the only good handholds. The boys would "cut feet" (swinging their feet off the footholds, to dangle by their hands) and hoist themselves into a belly flop onto our bed.

The boys would later "stem" the space between our bed and the wall, pushing their feet wide in the splits and pressing against the opposing facets to create friction. Closet rods became jungle gyms until we discovered this fact and reminded the boys that they were getting heavier. Kade mastered traversing the monkey bars, demanding that we stop just about any time we encountered any at a park, and Connor developed a strange fascination with being upside down, finding any way possible to grab something, hoist his feet up to his waist level, and then pivot upward, thrusting his feet overhead.

I took up golf at the age of fifteen. Neither of my parents played, but something drew me to the game. Watching golf on TV—watching the professionals hone their craft—I could sense the inner quest that golf required, although I couldn't have articulated it, then.

Winston Churchill described golf as ". . . a game whose aim is to hit a very small ball into an even smaller hole, with weapons singularly ill-designed for the purpose." And while I didn't know of the quote then, I can now appreciate the truth in it: the "weapons" truly are "ill-designed" for the outcome you are after.

Also, the sport is not reactive. There is no one hitting a ball back at you or trying to stop your progress. So, it becomes you against the course. This is the heart of the inner journey that golf requires: you pursue perfection, come up short, have no one to blame but yourself, find self-forgiveness (ideally), and then begin yet again with the pursuit of perfection.

Over the course of my first year playing, which happened to be the winter of my sophomore year and following the stabbing attack of the previous summer, I went from shooting in the mid-nineties to the low-eighties. I joined the high school team, which was easy enough given that the nearby country-club development fed into a different high school. So, I played many a round at the unspectacular but perfectly serviceable Arroyo del Oso public golf course near school, and I also commuted to the west side of town for weekly lessons with a local pro out at Ladera Golf Course. Through this dedication and volume of practice, during my junior and senior years, I became a scratch golfer, with scores ranging from the mid-seventies to the high sixties.

Consistency was a struggle, however, and as a new golfer I could still balloon up a score back into the upper-seventies or even low-eighties.

I certainly wasn't going to be recruited to play college golf, but my trajectory of improvement was phenomenal. I started to imagine a life tied to golf, although I wasn't sure in what way, yet.

My senior year, in the Albuquerque City Championship, I placed third. Every high school within the incorporated city competed, and given that the city is the population center of New Mexico, most of the major high schools were there.

Coming up the eighteenth fairway of Los Altos Golf Course, and on my final hole for the tournament, I was aware that I was somewhere near the lead. The eighteenth hole was a straight par five. A large fairway bunker sat on the left side of the landing area for the tee shot, forcing most drives into the right side of the fairway. From there, a greenside lake protected the green, coming in from the right and cutting in front of the green's right half. With my ball likely middle-right of the fairway, I would have to fly the lake to make it on the green "in two."

I had struggled that day, though I still managed to score well. My ball-striking had been off, and I was hitting only slightly more than half of the greens for the round; I was hanging in with the leaders by chipping and putting exceptionally well.

Standing over my ball that was, indeed, middle-right in the fairway, I could "lay up"—that is, take an iron and hit a shot to somewhere short of the lake and try to continue my excellent "wedge play" and putting; the likely outcomes would be split between scoring four or five. Or I could take out a fairway wood and attempt to fly the lake and land the ball on the green; this would make it possible to score a three, and potentially win the tournament. With a quality shot to the green, four would be likely, and five would be unusual. However, trying to fly the lake to the green could also put big numbers—like sixes and sevens—into play. In essence, the dilemma I faced was whether to consolidate my position somewhere around third place or risk it all, bringing first place—or maybe tenth—into the realm of possibility.

It was early afternoon in late spring, and the sun hung high in the desert sky. The wind was mild, but coming in off the left, pushing any shot toward the lake. With a muffled rip, I plucked and tossed some grass to measure the breeze and adjust the desired line of my ball flight. The grass felt spongy underfoot as I paced back and forth between my golf bag and the ball.

The shot called for a "fade," hitting the ball starting out left of the target and then moving it back right, cutting a curve around the lake that would never put the ball over the water. But I was too far out to get there with a fade. I could, instead, hit a right-to-left "draw" about twenty yards farther; that was my natural shot shape and also the distance I needed to reach the green. I tugged at the supple, pearl-white golf glove on my left hand, loosening, pulling, and then retightening the Velcro, cinching the glove around my palm. Reaching into my bag, I pulled the head cover off of a wood and then unsheathed this longer club from my bag.

I strode behind my ball, facing the green. I imagined the flight of the ball, a white speck against an achingly blue New Mexican sky, arching over the lake's dingy waters and landing on the front third of the green.

"You've hit this shot a thousand times," I said to myself.

Holding the club by the shaft with my right hand, I raised it in front of me and wrapped my left hand around the grip. My left thumb pointed straight down the shaft toward the club head. The thin leather of my glove bit into the rubber glued around the shaft's terminus. Then I placed my right palm loosely over my left thumb and curled my right fingers.

I took three practice swings, feeling my muscles manipulate the club head. I mentally stretched my nerve endings down the shaft into the face of the club, feeling its arch and position, trying to synchronize my movements to the ball's imagined flight. I made long arcs with the club, feeling the head brush the ground in order to sweep the ball upward. My arms felt loose as I breathed purposefully with each swing, trying to control my heart rate. The pungent smell of reclaimed water wafted from the lake.

I strode around to the left of my ball and placed the club head behind, lining up the face toward the green, slightly squatting and bending into my stance. My thighs tensed up, readying to release my body's potential energy. The breeze patted my back as I took one final look out at the target and back down at the ball. On an inhale, I pulled the club back and cocked it above my shoulders.

I did fly the lake and land on the green, the ball arching up and right, dangling out over the water, before spinning back left toward the pin. I thought I had "knocked it stiff," landing right next to the hole. Peering at the green, I could see the ball and the pin with only a fraction of space between them.

It turned out that the ball had landed on the front third of the green about four feet right of the hole, but then scooted to the back third of the green. I walked over, saw the fresh ball mark, stuck a tee into the green, and pinched the pockmark closed, smoothing the surface. My ball lay in line with the pin, but maybe fifty feet behind the hole. I took two putts to hole out, hitting a ticklish, down-sloping, left-to-right putt to within about eighteen inches of the hole. I tapped in to make a birdie four.

The leaders behind me made four as well, though, so I'd gained no ground on them.

The night before my appointment with the oncologist, I wrote down the questions I wanted to ask. I had never done this before. My potential health issues had always been small enough to easily keep my questions in my head. This felt wildly different; I was just beginning to learn about five different types of white blood cells, blood markers of my liver and kidney functions, platelet counts, and immunoglobulin levels.

I sat in my living room and scrolled, once again, through the test results on my phone, navigating a record of my body chemistry, seeing a lot of numbers surrounded by green highlights. A few markers sat just below or above the normal range, in the "yellow" zone. Most of that was still mundane. Apparently, I'd been a little dehydrated when my blood was drawn.

But some of the yellow signals stretched beyond my understanding, and I stared for a long time, as if some meaning would reveal itself. Then, of course, there were the two numbers that were way out of whack: my total white-blood-cell count, and the lymphocytes.

While I had been working with healthcare data professionally for a decade, I didn't know enough to really interpret all of this information. Turns out, that's one reason doctors train for a very long time in specialties like hematology, the study of blood.

I did know just enough, however, to scare myself. So, I was trying to gather my thoughts. I was going to need to write some things down in order to ask properly informed questions.

I went down to the basement. Most of my trips to the basement involve a stop at one of three sets of industrial garage racks, the types you find holding up hardware and supplies at your local Lowe's or Home Depot. It's there that I spread out my climbing ropes, hang my helmets and clothes, and organize my nuts, cams, and other climbing protection into bins. This time, though, I moved past my climbing gear to an open office carton filled with books, the kinds you don't really want to read and so store in the basement: for me, mainstream business-strategy and professional-development books. I just could never get past the authors' claims of having done research, when really what they had done is observe and then categorize their observations. And those categorizations usually came from some biased perspective: "Seventy-five percent of healthy organizations have a clearly articulated purpose." *Well, how did you define "healthy?" And after defining it, how did you measure it? And what about "clearly articulated," for that matter?* I have no doubt that having and articulating your purpose is a good thing, but I chafe at the false precision of these cooked-up numbers.

Today, however, was not a day for eyerolls.

I pushed a stack of these bold-font titles aside and came to a black, leather day planner. I got it at a conference after delivering a talk on how decision-makers are biased *against* using data to make decisions and how we can work within those constraints. I stuck it in this box because, with smartphones in everyone's pocket, no one needs a day planner anymore. Inside the day planner was a calendar and a notebook. I removed the calendar and placed it in the box. I carried the notepad, encased in its leather housing, upstairs to the living room.

The planner had been untouched, and stored in one cold basement or another, for years. I sat on our couch and felt the cool of the leather against my hands, running my fingers over the embossed "PMI" lettering on the cover—Project Management Institute. From my seat on our living-room couch, I gazed out my picture window. The sun was setting behind the homes across the street, and the outside was brilliantly lit with rolling and tumbling red clouds stretching a wave across a purpling, twilight sky. I flipped the planner back and forth in my hands.

The cream-colored fabri of the couch caught some of the red and purple light from outside, reminding me of alpenglow, when the alpine snowfields and cliffs turn purple or pink in the soft light of a sunrise or sunset. The twill upholstery scratched just a little on my elbows, but the worn-out cushion was now well shaped to my contours, this end of the couch being my favored location over the years.

My four-year-old boys ran through the space between the couch and the kitchen, yelling something to each other as they circled in front of the kitchen a few times. Then they halted, said something more quietly to one another, and then burst out laughing. After completing a final circle, they ran back out of the room.

Returning my gaze to the black leather and swallowing hard, I flipped the planner open and scribbled "December 3, 2018" in the top corner of the first page, leaving room for more text.

My first questions for the doctor were about my pseudoscientific rationalizations and the possibility of them being true: "How much do white-blood-cell counts usually go up when you are sick? What about when fighting infection?"

The next set of questions were about the numbers. I wanted to understand the numbers: "Which numbers are important? How much 'in the yellow' becomes too much? Can I influence these numbers? How?"

Gradually, my questions got around to the more haunting issues. I pressed my pen into the paper with a little more vigor and my thumb began to tire with the strain.

When I had looked up what "CLL"—chronic lymphocytic leukemia—meant after seeing it referenced on my lab results, I had also, uncomfortably, noticed that the various presentations on the disease that dotted the internet looked at survivability as being over or under five years. *Is that the median life expectancy!?* I jotted down a note. Also, having learned that the genetic markers of the disease seem to be the major indicators of life expectancy, I made a note to ask about the genetics of my particular brand of malady.

I put my pen down and rolled my thumb, loosening the tense muscles in my palm.

I stared over the arm of the couch and back into the kitchen, where the glow of the yellow overhead lights bounced off the nickel-plated appliances. The light reflected back at me off of the window glass too, as it was now dark outside. I was bathed in manmade light that looked like the glow of the sun but provided no warmth.

Less out of hope, and more out of resignation, I jotted down, "Referral for second opinion." And before closing the notepad gently, I spelled out, "Mental health resources."

Kristina and Jason on the summit of Vulcan Cotopaxi (19,347').

CHAPTER FIVE

# Beginnings

My dad tells a story of an attempt he made to climb Longs Peak, the 14,255-foot monarch of Rocky Mountain National Park and the northernmost 14,000-foot peak in the Rocky Mountains. It also juts up from the eastern boundary of the Front Range; it is barely removed from civilization, and on a clear day you can see the pronounced, squared summit from up and down the Denver/Boulder/Fort Collins urban corridor. It is not much over 25 miles from the Longs Peak summit to the city center of the roughly 100,000-person city of Longmont, and along those miles, one would lose a bit more than 9,000 feet of elevation.

That kind of prominence creates weather. Longs Peak is notorious for its wind as well as, in summer, its afternoon thunderstorms. The two highest wind speeds ever recorded in Colorado both came from Longs Peak, and both were more than 200 mph. Wind speeds that extreme usually happen in winter, but winds are consistently strong on the mountain regardless of season and have even blown climbers off the mountain to their deaths. The climber's rule of thumb is to be off the summit and heading back down by noon due to the persistent threat of thunderstorms (except in winter, when—obviously—the dangers of snow travel replace that of lightning).

My dad's story featured weather, prominently.

In the summer of 1972, after two years of marriage but before my brother or I came along, my parents were living in Longmont, and my dad was in his first job out of graduate school. He was in Colorado on a temporary assignment, combining his bachelor's degree in electrical engineering with his master's in nuclear engineering to redesign the electrical busbar—a central hub that distributes electrical power to the various control panel circuits—at the Fort Saint Vrain Generating Station. He and my mom spent almost every weekend hiking in Rocky Mountain National Park. Besides being a series of shared adventures, these forays into the wild also helped my dad get his East Coast body used to life at altitude. On an August day that summer, he and a group of friends left from Sprague Lake and headed up the Boulder Brook Trail. From there, you enter what is known as the Boulder Field, an open slope of rocks on the northern flank of the mountain.

The Boulder Field is about six miles from the trailhead, and gently rises from 12,700-plus feet to above 13,200 feet, where one crosses from the east side to the west side of Longs' north ridge. It is, therefore, well above tree line, which typically is at around 11,800 feet in Colorado.

The Boulder Field is a moonscape, an otherworldly place of car-sized blocks of reddish schist and lightly toned granite completely exposed to the elements. Climbers shuffle and hop over the boulders, making careful foot placements to avoid the twisted ankles and knees that such terrain can bestow.

Here is where my dad's trip turned. In this time before cell phones and emergency beacons—and even before detailed mountain-weather forecasts—they were hit by a severe thunderstorm. The air began to vibrate with static electricity, then the space around them illuminated with the three hundred million volts that accompany each strike of lightning. The booming thunder was accompanied by the higher-pitched staccato of tinkling rock: the lightning wasn't nearby, it was upon them, and the murderous flashes began exploding the boulders, raining rock particles onto the climbers.

Scampering and jumping back down-slope, my dad and his companions scanned the landscape for a modicum of shelter. There would be no escaping the lightning now—random probability would decide that fate—but something could be done to avoid shrapnel. Eyeing a van-sized boulder with an overhanging face, Dad and his group took shelter as best they could, squatting low beneath the overhang.

When the lightning finally abated, the rain did not, and the group made a soaked trudge back to the trailhead. As they drove home, my mom overheard on the radio that a member of a climbing party had lost his life on the shoulder of Longs Peak that morning. When Alan walked through their front door a few hours later, she squeezed him tightly, tears welling.

This all occurred almost five years before my birth, and eventually life and family commitments moved my mom and dad away from Colorado and further attempts at any of its higher peaks. But the story stuck with me.

In the summer of 2009, I was a year out from back-to-back knee reconstructions. A soccer injury tore my right ACL, and the repair failed only six months later. No longer able to enjoy the typical "ball" sports that used to make up my recreation, I was looking for another form of physical endeavor. My mom and dad had moved back to Colorado, now both retired and living in the suburb of

Broomfield, about halfway between Denver and their 1970s home of Longmont. Take the confluence of my need for physical activity and my parents' return to the Rocky Mountains, my father and I decided it was finally time to get him up Longs Peak—some thirty-seven years later.

That was also the summer I broke with norms and began dating my work colleague and now wife, Kristina. Kristina grew up in a Colorado mountain town and had scampered among the state's creeks and rocks for as long as she could remember. She thought the goal and the work leading up to it sounded like fun.

On the drive up to one early-courtship hike, she had told me, "I think my mom likes that I have someone to hike with besides my dog." Later, Kathy, my future mother-in-law, would make the same point to me directly. I assume she could probably thank her daughter's semi-solo excursions for one or two worry lines.

Working at the Medicaid administration office for the State of Colorado, Kristina and I shared a wall in a cubical quadplex in the middle of a sea of cubical quadplexes. With her back to the window, the light would shimmer through the loose stands of her hair in an alluring way. Beyond that, she was also smart and challenging and had opinions.

We both had studied some philosophy in college. Kristina earned a double degree in philosophy and economics before acquiring her master's in economics. I minored in philosophy, while majoring in political science, before getting my master's in public policy.

We both thought René Descartes dug too deep of an intellectual hole to climb out of by imagining away the corporeal world and then finding God's perception to be the proof that the world existed; we agreed that the line between existentialism and nihilism is a chasm, yet somehow still easy to cross; we felt consequentialism has its limits, as Ursula Le Guin had so aptly pointed out when she imagined a citizen of fictional *Omelas* walking away from a utopia that was paid for by the abuse of a child; but on the flipside, forever trying to do the right thing without ever accomplishing anything . . . well, we figured, you may as well be planted under the tree, *Waiting for Godot.*

For two years we were just colleagues, either she or I dating someone else, in various cycles.

Eventually, we were both single for a couple of overlapping months, and I made clear my intentions by inviting her to my house in the suburbs of southern Denver and then getting sloppily drunk while failing at my attempts to play Settlers of Catan by her side.

She didn't run the other way. My prior two years of sober interaction had probably saved me.

For our attempt at Longs Peak, I was happy to have her along. So, my dad took the lead on planning a series of training hikes in the Front Range, collecting objectives that progressively pushed us a little higher and a little farther.

The standard route—the Keyhole—of Longs Peak covers a 15-mile round trip with over 5,000 feet of elevation gain. Throw in that need to be off of the summit by noon, and a 2:00 or 3:00 a.m. alpine start is not unusual. The novices that we were, we needed to build up fitness for the mileage and the pack weight. We needed to get used to the altitude. And we needed to get used to the dreaded alpine start.

We began with a trip up Rosalie Peak, in the Front Range southwest of Denver, but just to the gentle curve of the saddle between Rosalie's east ridge and the peaks of Pegmatite Points. The saddle sits at an altitude of about 12,000 feet on a mountain that rises to over 13,500 feet. The next week, we followed that initial session of self-discovery by going all the way to Rosalie's summit.

Our first Fourteener (a peak standing 14,000 feet or higher) was Mount Blue Sky (back then called Mount Evans), standing a whole 9 feet taller than Longs. But it is a much easier hike, beginning at a trailhead considerably more elevated. The round trip is just above 9 miles, as opposed to 15, and the elevation gain is about 3,100 feet as opposed to 5,000-plus.

We learned a few lessons from this one. We learned that early summer means lots of mud from snowmelt. Kristina had a shoe sucked off her foot in the muck but was able to fish it out. We learned that navigating through head-high willows is as disorienting as being in a corn maze. And I learned that my surgically repaired right knee does worse going downhill than it does going up.

We continued bagging peaks each weekend until late August, when we decided to try for Longs. After lunch on August 22, 2009, we loaded all our day-hiking equipment into the car and headed into Estes Park, at the foot of Rocky Mountain National Park. We found a local Italian restaurant and feasted on garlic bread and pasta, in effect "carb-ing up." After dinner, we checked into our bargain hotel; it was high season in the Park, and reservations were required for most other accommodations.

It was a very short night's sleep. The alarm went off at 12:30 a.m., and we were out the door by 1:30 and driving up the Peak to Peak Highway to the trailhead, attempting to stuff muffins and bananas down our throats.

The perpetually busy Longs Peak Trailhead was already filling up, and I heard hopeful conversations wafting from open hatchbacks and flatbeds of trucks as people donned their packs and extended their trekking poles.

We collectively switched on our headlamps and began a westward, ascending march, filing into an army of fellow headlamps snaking up through the trees at the lower elevations.

Like on previous ascents, our little team of three had become accustomed to stepping through the six-foot-diameter ring of light as we gazed at our feet hoofing up the trail. The wider surroundings remained in the dark, with no sensory input other than trees creaking in the breeze, with their piney smell, and the rush of some mysterious creek down below the trail.

When we popped out at tree line, the breeze kissed my face. I added a fleece layer to combat the chill. Now that we were on open ground, the sheer number of climbers became more apparent, as all of the headlamps both forward and behind were in view. As we paused for a drink, I watched the circles of light inch their way up the switchbacks below, as the climbers navigated around, first, the creek and surrounding thick willows, and then the unstable, ankle-biting talus along the footpath.

We made the Boulder Field as dawn's red glow appeared on the eastern horizon behind us. We began plotting a choose-your-own-adventure path over the rocky tonnage. I skipped lightly, balancing and spanning and bracing myself in starts and stops across the Field. Kristina did much the same, plotting her own path alongside me when we could and then deviating a few meters away when the angle of the boulders demanded different steps. Dad, now sixty-one, stepped more cautiously, placing two trekking poles forcefully down on a new rock opposite some small span of air before lifting one leg over the expanse. We remained silent, each focused on the task at hand.

We were ascending to 13,000 feet, making our way toward the iconic Keyhole, an almost complete ring of vertically stacked boulders. The mass is huge, with the hole as wide as a house, as you thread between the rocks while crossing from the mountain's east to its west side.

We stepped into a stone lightning shelter that now sits as both a haven for today's climbers and as a memorial to the tragic winter-of-1925 summit that led to both death and dismemberment on the descent. The placard outside the Vaille-Sortland Shelter made for sober reading, as we learned about Agnes Vaille, Herbert Sortland, and Walter Kiener. Vaille was the daughter of a wealthy Denver family and was secretary of the Chamber of Commerce. She also became the first woman to summit Longs Peak in winter during her fateful climb. After a storm set in, which contributed to Vaille taking a 150-foot, injurious fall, Vaille's climbing partner Kiener, who was a Swiss-born son of a butcher, raced down mountain to organize a rescue. They had become climbing partners after meeting at the Colorado Mountain Club, founded thirteen years earlier, and had attempted the Longs ascent twice before. Vaille died from exposure while waiting for a rescue. Meanwhile, Sortland was part of a group that had fanned out across the mountain, and he did not report back after the initial search; his body was not found until over a month later. Kiener lost all of his toes and part of a foot to frostbite during the rescue attempt. The tragedy prompted the Park Service to build the shelter in an attempt both to honor the victims and provide an added layer of security for future mountaineers.

I stood in the shelter, peeling off portions of a soft bagel and stuffing it into my mouth. My dad held out a bag of raisins and peanuts, and I readily pinched a few as well.

"How're you feeling?" I asked my dad.

"I feel good."

"Moving okay?"

"Yeah. A little tired, but I'm fine."

"Weird being here?"

"No, not weird . . . but I remember squatting down in the rain and lightning."

"Yeah?"

"I don't remember where in the Boulder Field we were. It was kind of chaotic, and we were just moving down the mountain until we found a big boulder to hide under."

He was stoic. We were still in the middle of something, and that something demanded impassive attention.

"You good?" I asked a final time.

"Yeah. Let's keep moving."

We stepped out of the shelter, crossing through the Keyhole on a peak awash in the reds, pinks, and purples of alpenglow.

We now made a left turn and headed across the Ledges, a single track of rock-hopping that is stable but poised over a 2,000-foot drop, often requiring you to keep your left (uphill) hand on the rock for balance.

The wind kicked up as I dragged my hand along the flanks of the peak, grazing my gloved fingers lightly against the cold rock. The rising heat from the sun kicked up a stiffer breeze, and gusts whipped at us. Twisting, and leaning my back against the rock wall, I pulled my hat tightly down to my ears, cinching up its leash until it grabbed my chin. With a pivot, I returned my left hand to the ramping cliff. The rocks were changing color, the deeper, brick red of the alpenglow giving way to a pale gray-brown as the day brightened.

We crossed the Ledges and uneventfully ascended the Trough, a rocky gully of fairly secure scrambling, as well as navigated across the Narrows, a three- to five-foot-wide ledge similar in size and exposure to the Ledges but which crosses the south side of Longs' summit ramparts.

And then we reached the Home Stretch, a marginally polished, forty-degree sloping ramp up a wide-open, right-facing dihedral—open book—of granite.

Flattened stones nestled side by side to make a consistent floor, running between two-story-high rock walls lining each side of the hundred-foot-wide ramp. For the final two hundred vertical feet, the whole thing wants to pull you down and right, but in an unassuming way; you wouldn't notice gravity's fall line until it was too late.

Ever cautious, we made a point of bear-crawling, keeping our "three points of contact." I was attentive, but calm, like I had been for the entire climb. Each foot placement, smearing with friction against the sloping rock, was a matter of full investment, not out of fear but out of purpose. I peeked my head over the last edge of the Home Stretch, seeing the football-field-sized summit plateau, strewn with boulders and talus. We could go no higher, and soon Kristina and my father joined me. The clouds were just starting to accumulate as we took the obligatory summit shots, high above the towns, cities, and hustle-and-bustle of the Front Range. Willing climbers, joyful in their own successes, took photos for us. My dad, a black baseball cap on his head, smiled broadly and gave a "thumbs up" in front of the summit-scape of variably sized red-brown boulders.

Kristina sat next to me on a couple of cooler-sized blocks. I chewed a little too quickly and washed down each bite with a swig of water: more bagels and trail mix.

"That was fun!" she said through a smile.

"Yeah. Not done, though."

"I know, but your dad seems happy."

"Yep. This was pretty great."

"Hey, 'Is this the mountain we are about to *dominate*!?'" Kristina recounted a shirtless twenty-something's words when we sat, sipping water, next to where he and his party had stood, staring up the mountain from the bottom of the Trough. She chuckled.

"I know!" I laughed in reply.

I imagined all the times Longs Peak felt deep shame, having been *dominated* by such robust displays of masculinity.

We talked as fast as we ate, knowing we had to descend before the ever-threatening afternoon storm rolled in.

As I danced my way over the boulders and back to the ledge that marked the top of the Home Stretch, a few specks of rain blew in from a cloud that was pouring down a few miles away. As I looked back at the cloud and the gray sheets of rain below it, a prism of late-morning light arced between me and the torrent.

Stepping my first foot onto the sloping ramp of the Homestretch, holding a gloved hand on the ledge behind me, I dared allow myself to ask, *Which mountain is next?* Then I placed my second foot, feeling the rock bite into the sole. I turned my attention to the next foot placement, stared intently at the crack where my toe would go, and let go of the summit ledge.

When the boys were born, in the fall of 2014, I was in the midst of training for Denali. Before that, I was training as part of my rehabilitation from knee surgery. And before that, I was a lifelong soccer player, training in order to play in various competitive, amateur leagues from age four to thirty.

Now, training is more or less about freedom: the ability to take off on a climb, maybe not an expedition but a nearby climb, at a moment's notice.

After the boys were born, scheduling became a challenge. Between of the needs of little ones and the rigors of a professional career, my focus would regularly shift midday, placing demands on me that I'd never anticipated when I'd woken up that morning. The report I thought I needed to get out at work was placed on the back burner because of the rush of urgent requests from senior leaders. Or on a weekend, one or the other boy would develop an earache or spill milk all over the carpet or enrich a wall with a crayon mural, suddenly introducing a half hour or more of logistics or cleanup.

I quickly learned that if I wanted any time to myself, I needed to have it in the morning. The more the hours ticked by, the less likely it would be that I would have the luxury of focused time. Given my reliance on my body, and the joy I had developed over the years from pushing my body hard, I made my workout time my "me time," and if I really wanted to guarantee a quality workout, it would have to happen before the boys woke up.

This morning in 2018, the late-summer sun was skimming off the horizon quite early, and I could see it crack through the garden-level windows: illuminated rectangles against the black recesses of the cavernous room. I picked up the forty-five-pound dumbbells at my feet, lifting deeply from my knees, and then waddled them over to the weight rack. I coaxed the first weight into its spot, then the next.

Exhaling deeply, I returned to my spot in the middle of the basement floor and paused, just standing, feeling my breathing relax and my heart rate return to normal.

Then, I began breathing hard, again, pushing out breath purposefully through pursed lips. I jumped in rapid succession, tucking my knees into my chest with each hop. As my toes hit the ground, I was immediately back up into the jumping tuck. *Twenty . . . thirty . . . forty.*

A dribble of sweat moved down my forehead; my glasses began to slide from my nose, so I took them off and set them aside.

My breath broke into a pant. *Fifty . . . sixty . . . seventy.*

I was at the tail end of "leg day," pushing now-tired legs with rapid movements and ramping up my metabolism at the workout's end.

"What are you doing, Dad?" Connor appeared near the weight rack, looking up at me from thigh-height, his hair messed from the night.

But he was dressed. He had on a gray T-shirt, one of the moisture-wicking kind that feel cool to the touch; a pair of electric-blue shorts; and his sneakers, Velcro straps over each forefoot but with the left shoe on the right foot and vice versa.

"Working out," I stuttered, breathless. *Eighty . . . ninety.* I stopped.

"Working . . . out?" he repeated.

"Yeah. Doing exercises to keep my body healthy, like we've talked about."

“I want to work out. What is that exercise?” he asked.

“It’s called ‘tuck jumps.’”

“Tuck jumps?”

“Yeah. You jump up off of both feet and try to bring your knees up to your chest. And when you land, you immediately jump up and do it again. Like this.” *Ninety-one . . . ninety-two.*

Connor sidled up to me and gave it a whirl. He wobbled on the landing, gathered himself, and jumped again.

“Yeah, great! Can you try to jump high?”

Connor jumped and brought his knees up exaggeratedly. He didn’t leave himself time to fully straighten out and so landed in more of a squat. He gathered himself and jumped again.

He then tried to speed up. His knees didn’t really come up any, but he was able to more rapidly get into his next jump.

Legs still on fire, I started jumping alongside him.

The rhythmic, deep thump of my two feet, hitting simultaneously on the hard floor, was now joined by the higher-pitched patter of two smaller feet hitting the floor not quite simultaneously. Connor, hearing my panting, began to force his own breath, sounding like the antagonist from a bad horror movie.

A few days later, Kade eventually became curious and wandered down as well, and we were three straw-colored heads bobbing up and down, making a strange music of stomping and breath, looking over our shoulders at one another.

I kept my glasses on, pushing them back up my nose seemingly with each jump, in order to better see my children.

My parents enrolled me in youth soccer when I was four years old. This was well before international football was widely available on television in the United States, and there was no internet. So, the sport was just beginning to blossom in a few regional centers. New Mexico, with its strong Latinx influence—and particularly Chicano culture—was one of those centers.

Living on the roof of the high desert—Albuquerque sits at 5,000 feet, with the Sandia Mountains rising to 10,000-plus east of town—I sprinted across fields on cloudless days that always carried a breeze. I can still feel the juice in my mouth as I sucked on the half-time orange slices and recall the puckeringly sweet postgame Capri Suns slurped through impossibly thin straws.

A bevy of small boys, from in and around the same suburban neighborhoods in the city's Northeast Heights, were placed on a team by the volunteer-administrator powers that be, and our group called ourselves "the Dragons."

At the sporting-goods store, I tried on tiny cleats and tiny shin guards. I was proud to have equipment. And I was also allotted a reversible jersey, so that we could change colors from orange to white or back on a moment's notice, to contrast with that day's opponent.

This was before the time of national coaching standards that began developing skill and positional awareness with soccer tots on fields the size of a tennis court, complete with smaller teams and tiny goals that did not require a goalkeeper. The youth games I played were a full eleven-versus-eleven on a roughly 80-yard-long field and with a goal that was only slightly miniaturized: a 6-foot high by 16-foot-long target as opposed to the 8x24, adult-sized standard. And our goals were made from permanently affixed steel pipes planted in the turf, such as you found in Albuquerque's many community parks.

With little by way of real instruction, our games turned into hornets' nests of flailing feet. Under each steel frame stood a lone goalkeeper, one for each team, and in the expanse between them was a ball and a horde of twenty children all attempting to somehow kick that ball through the maze of tangled limbs and forty flailing feet.

Sporadically, the ball would squirt free of the throng and roll into the no-man's-land between the mass of kids and the lonely goalies.

It was in these instances that Paul and I shined.

Paul was my best friend on the Dragons, and the two of us happened to be blessed with speed. He and I lived for these moments: the ball suddenly breaking into the open; a burst of effort, feeling our legs tense and drive; resistance from the ground as our cleats grabbed at the hard soil and thin grass; the writhing mass of children left in our wake; seeing the open field in front of us, no mob blocking our view, inviting us to collect the ball and awkwardly drive it, along with ourselves, toward the opponent's goal; a final push forward; then heaving a right leg through the ball while leaning back; and the joy of seeing the ball sail . . . right over the six-foot-high crossbar!

Paul and I were constantly trying to kick the ball over the goal, rather than into it. We were only successful about half the time, meaning that the other half of the time, we ended up scoring quite a few goals given how easy it is to kick a soccer ball past or over a tiny, four-year-old goalie.

And in this way, Paul and I became standouts on the team.

I don't believe the coaches were ever the wiser that we were not attempting to score. I think their view was that we were simply getting too much loft on the ball half the time, though in reality, we were not getting *enough* loft half the time. We had invented our own challenge, if somewhat outside the norms of the game.

As I grew older, I came to embrace the challenges of the purpseful soccer everyone else was playing. I recall a deep sense of satisfaction, orange peel in my mouth, a few years later when I finished the last game of a short, eight-game league season on exactly fifty goals scored. Going into that last game, I'd been four goals shy of fifty, a target I'd decided to pursue once I hit thirty goals at mid-season.

For that fiftieth goal, there were maybe ten minutes left in that final game. I was standing near the halfway line with a defender on my hip. A lazy, lofted ball was put into the right channel and landed between me and my attacking goal. In those days, I was going to win this kind of footrace. I had a full ten yards on my defender once I reached the ball. The goalie came out to cut down my shooting angles. I feigned left and popped the ball right, leaving the keeper—who was now leaning the wrong way—helpless as the ball rolled by him. Not a spectacle of a move, but certainly an effective one that belied my youth.

That fifty-goal season brought me to the attention of other coaches and teams, the kinds with tryouts and invitation-only signups. And thus started a highly competitive youth-soccer career all because I had been playing a game within a game for years and had produced, by happenstance, a string of goals.

I thrived on the travel with the teams and the practices at all hours of the day. And I enjoyed putting in the work. I enjoyed pushing my body and mind, and I enjoyed defining new aspirations for myself.

What followed were years of car caravans to cities all over the Southwest for Thanksgiving and Memorial Day and Labor Day tournaments, in Colorado, Arizona, Texas, and California. I bounced around a few teams in the Duke City Soccer League, and my parents were willing spectators, cheerleaders, and chauffeurs even if the competitive level of play pre-empted their participation in coaching.

I enjoyed living hour-by-hour with my teammates, haunting the hotels and restaurants. The comradery was always thicker when we were on the road, and it showed up on the field. We worked harder for each other the more we came to really know each other.

Over my youth career, I got a lot of trophies; this was right around the advent of the "participation trophy" era, so I was guaranteed one a year. But then there were the earned trophies and medals that came from placing first through third at the various tournaments. And there were also the year-end awards for most goals scored and the like. I collected those, too, because in the early years I maintained my prodigious speed.

I played high school soccer just before the advent of America's first truly thriving professional league, Major League Soccer, and thus before the monumental shift away from school-sponsored youth soccer and toward youth soccer sponsored by professional soccer clubs. Back then, it was still big "schools" rather than big "clubs" that manufactured the talent.

My particular high school, Sandia, was perennially nationally ranked. The highest rank we received in the four years I was at school was seventh, and the highest while I was a varsity player was fourteenth. One season, we graduated eleven of the varsity's eighteen players into Division One college ball. So, it was rare for athletes to play all four years of varsity soccer at our school. I was not one of those rare athletes. Rather, I worked my way up through the ranks, putting my work ethic into practice.

At this point, most of the athletes had grown while I had not. I'd started high school as the proverbial "5-foot, 100-pound weakling." When I graduated, I was only 5'6" and 120 pounds. I wouldn't grow another inch, and it took dedication to a workout regimen, when I went off to college, to bulk up to a *massive* 140 pounds (a size I have ended up keeping my entire adult life).

As my opponents grew, the speed gap closed—although not entirely. I was still slightly faster than most, but not by nearly as much. The other physical gifts possessed by my teammates and the level of competition began to separate out those who would, for example, go on to claim Division One scholarships and myself, who could compete but who no longer stood out.

Both my greatest asset and my greatest weakness was my intensity. It drove me athletically and academically. I remember my parents telling me, as early as elementary school, that it was "okay to get a 'B.'" I ignored them. It might have been okay for some, but not for me.

In soccer, and to borrow a British phrase, I liked "to get stuck in." I liked the physical contact and the tough tackles. I had long since learned that my smaller body got hurt when I went into a challenge half-heartedly rather than full bore. My willingness to put my body on the line tended to make up for my smaller size. But that intensity would also lead to a lot of negative self-talk that would creep in and compound my mistakes. When I made an error, I had a hard time "moving on to the next play." Maybe I would miskick a pass, putting my teammates in a tough spot, but now those difficulties would only compound as I became too immersed in self-flagellation to be of much use.

To adjust, I played to my strengths. I was positionally aware and effective at breaking up my opponents' play; I was a good communicator and endeavored to keep my team organized; and I showed up to practice every day, trying to get better. I didn't mail it in.

My competitive soccer career would pause after high school, when I switched my focus to golf and an eventual (but brief) professional career in that game. I wouldn't resurrect my competitive soccer days until my mid- to late twenties, playing in national amateur leagues, which were filled with the ranks of those Division One athletes who were obviously good but not good enough to take their game to the professional ranks. Again, I more than held my own. But finally, when I was thirty, with a knee injury and three subsequent surgeries, my playing days ended altogether. And while eventually all my trophies would get donated to be reused or thrown away, I did end up keeping one: the Unsung Hero award from my high school days.

I was surprised when they called my name at the year-end banquet. In the dim light of the banquet hall that evening, I moved to the front of the room, around the tables draped in the scarlet red of our school colors. I collected my plaque, posed for a picture, and squinted at the flash. Then I rather sheepishly returned to my chair as the players and parents applauded. Taking my seat, our coach and MC moved on to the Most Valuable Player award.

The year-end awards were voted on by the team, and the Unsung

Hero award went to the player we collectively felt put in "the dirty work," in both the games and in practice.

Over the arc of my playing days, after I could eventually all too easily kick the ball over the goal, I switched my focus to scoring goals. When I got outclassed as an athlete, I focused on helping the athletes on my team be more successful. As a player, no articles were ever written about me. I didn't earn (and didn't deserve) any playing scholarships. I just tried to do what I could do well. In the end, those guys I suited up with and nursed bruises with and pushed my fitness and focus with, well, they thanked me for it.

I sat in the waiting room, looking at the magazine headlines, inspirational signage, and lots of older people wearing hats or scarves or bandanas over their heads. I got a hot chocolate from the coffee-pod machine; it was the least the universe could grant me for putting me through this.

It *probably wasn't cancer* right up until the point when it was, in fact, cancer. As I sat on the cold aluminum examination table, white paper crinkling under me with every weight shift, my oncologist sat on a backless, round stool, her elbows on her knees. She leaned forward, arching her head up to look me in the eye as she earnestly and patiently listened to me while I explained the cold I had caught and the food I had accidentally inhaled. Then she gently called my attention to the diagnosis: CLL, or again, chronic lymphocytic leukemia: a blood cancer. CLL creates defective B-cells, the white blood cells that mark invading bacteria and viruses for destruction, that destruction then being carried out by our T-cells.

"We don't know what causes it," she emphasized. "The median age of diagnosis for CLL is seventy-one, so when we see it in younger people, it's usually people who have been in the military or have dealt with a lot of chemicals. But really, we don't know what causes it." She didn't want me to be looking for some past choice to perseverate over, and I still appreciate that.

She continued, "Because most patients are diagnosed later in life, yes, survivability is not particularly long. But that doesn't mean cancer was the cause of death. Younger patients can live very long lives. We are coming up with new treatments all the time. Now some people treat their CLL with a pill."

Then, Doctor Sarah began to talk me through the life-expectancy statistics. She was around my age or younger, with straight brown hair that fell several inches below her shoulders. She carried an easy smile and had gentle eyes. I very distinctly—like the clearest of bells ringing in my head—remember her saying, "I don't know that this will be the thing that kills you." My reaction was all on the inside, like the words were squirming around in my stomach. I now had a reasonable hypothesis as to how I might die. I might die from cancer. I was only forty-one.

CLL isn't always treated. Because it is a slow-moving disease that shows up in a very elderly population, when treatment becomes an option, the patients aren't necessarily going to be in the physical condition to tolerate it. While chemotherapy is no longer the first-line treatment of choice, the pills targeting the proteins involved in cancer-cell proliferation still come with plenty of side effects, from cardiovascular issues to easy bruising and bleeding to increased risk of infections that your depleted immune system struggles to fight off. And at that age, many of them pass on treatment or never get around to treatment because of some other illness they're dealing with.

There is also no benefit to early treatment. Clinical trials have shown no better results than waiting until treatment was absolutely needed, typically at the point when you either start to have organ impacts, usually in your spleen; your blood markers start getting wonky across your immune system; or you start having symptoms like unhealed bruising, dramatically swollen lymph nodes, or shedding blood platelets into your urine. Those types of things.

"So, our first order of business is to figure out what brand of disease you have. The way this disease impacts people has a lot to do with the genetics of their particular form of the disease. There are certain versions that are better or worse."

"What does that involve?"

"Just some more blood draws. We're going to do some genetic testing to figure out what type you have."

Sarah continued to sit forward, talking slowly and sincerely.

We had moved from the diagnosis stage to the prognosis stage, and it felt like it had happened in the blink of an eye.

Yellow fluorescent light bouncing off the taupe walls made everything look warmer than it was.

"So, I guess this isn't dire?" I questioned, fishing for an affirming reply.

"No, it's not dire. But there are different types of the disease that are faster moving and harder to treat. We need to know which type you have."

"When they called me, my primary care provider made it sound like this was very urgent," I protested, still fishing.

"She was pretty panicked when she called me," Sarah, my—now—oncologist said. "I tried to reassure her that this was manageable."

"So, is this manageable?"

"Of course, but the genetics will dictate the options. We should also get you into the University Health system for a second opinion. It will be good for them to know about you, because if we need to do some really aggressive treatments, that's the place."

That wasn't a particularly affirming statement.

"So, let's get you back to the lab, and get another blood draw for the genetic tests," Sarah said.

Of course they had their own lab. A third needle wiggling in my vein in a week.

"These tests are harder to run, so it'll be about ten days or so."

Ten days. This was going to be a harder conversation to have with Kristina.

Having lost my train of thought, I looked at my notes and asked about community and mental health resources. Sarah referred me to the Leukemia & Lymphoma Society and the social worker they had on staff, Jackie, who was trained in counseling.

"What about for my kids? Are there resources for my kids?"

As hard as the conversation with Kristina was going to be, I had no sense of how to navigate this news with my newly-turned four-year-olds. My stomach, already fluttering, now knotted as I asked. Part of a dad's business was supposed to be protecting his kids from trauma, or at least creating a safe place for them to feel secure when things go wrong. But here I was, bringing trauma home to them.

"Yeah. There are some pretty good groups and camps for kids who have parents who have cancer. Jackie can get you more information," Sarah said. "And I'll be sure to have her reach out to you today or tomorrow to schedule some time."

I noticed as we took more blood from inside my left elbow that I now had a bruise from the repeated punctures.

Still reeling from the news, I was in no hurry to get home, so I lingered in the waiting room, reading the headlines on the magazines more closely this time. The stories seemed to intermingle celebrities and athletes with ordinary people, all touched by cancer in some way. There was a former New York Yankee and a mother of three and a doctor-turned-patient. There was a lot of advice and numbers for helplines. There were calls for research participants and a mountain of pharmaceutical ads.

I picked up a magazine and set it down on a waiting-room chair. I then went over to the side table with the coffee-pod machine and brewed another hot chocolate. I held the warm cup in both hands, feeling the heat run through my fingers, before going back to my seat.

There were no windows in the waiting room, and the fluorescent light from overhead felt as false and contrived as my pseudoscientific self-proclamation of "cancer free" had been.

I picked up the magazine, again, and stared at the woman on the cover. Then I looked up and read a thank-you note that had been turned into a plaque—made by a former patient's family—which hung on the wall next to the reception desk. I took a sip of my hot chocolate. The liquid was sweet and thick, if only a bit artificial tasting. The comforting heat ran down my throat with each swallow. I crossed one leg over the other and took another sip.

*I like this hot chocolate.*

I opened the magazine to the article about the mother of three but couldn't bring myself to read it.

Sarah's office was only a ten-minute drive from our house. When I got home, I told my wife what I knew, which actually wasn't too much beyond that it was cancer and that it had a name.

"What am I going to tell the kids?" I tossed out after a long pause.

"What do you want to tell the kids?"

"I don't think anything, yet. I don't have answers for the obvious questions."

"Okay. We can wait, for now," Kristina replied.

Then, I let the truth seep in: "I just don't think I'm ready."

"This is days old," she said. "Of course not."

*Alan, Kristina, and Jason (left to right) on the summit of Longs Peak (14,255').*

CHAPTER SIX

# Smallness

As my wife's and my alpine-climbing skills improved, we began to pull ourselves away from Colorado's Fourteeners and instead try the Thirteeners, peaks above 13,000 feet. The Thirteeners are far more numerous, with 637 in the state as compared to the 58 Fourteeners. They are also far less popular and frequently remote—it's not unusual to find that you and your group are the only people on a Thirteener on any given day.

Also, with 637 options, you can find everything from easy hikes to scrambles to fully roped, technical climbs.

In climbing parlance, "scrambling" usually refers to class-three or class-four routes. Class-three routes can be loosely defined as being steep or craggy enough that you need to use your hands to assist with balance and climbing. Class-four climbing is steep enough, relying on using hand- and footholds, that many climbers will want a rope, as the consequences of a fall can be dire on this exposed terrain. And class five—fully technical rock climbing on a near-vertical to overhanging cliff—requires ropes and protection to safeguard against a fall.

Of course, these classifications all blend into each other; for example, very skilled climbers will often "scramble" the easier class-five routes, opting to move fast rather than use ropes, which add immediate safety but slow progress and thus increase one's risk of being caught by weather or darkness.

Kristina and I got engaged in the winter of 2009/2010, after our ascent of Longs Peak, and in the months and days leading up to our wedding, we moved slowly toward more technical climbing, enjoying quite a bit of scrambling. We found we enjoyed the isolation on the less crowded and more difficult routes as well as the feeling that comes from flowing through the mountains with your whole body.

The last week of September in 2010, the week before our wedding, we woke up early and headed out to "The Citadel" (officially unnamed), standing at nearly 13,300 feet in the Front Range above the old mining town of Silver Plume. Via the standard route, it goes as a class-three climb, but all the scrambling is at the very end: the final 60-odd feet. As we'd be on a mostly well-maintained trail, but for a little light rock-hopping on the way up, we brought our dogs and planned to leave them with one of us just below the summit pitch, have the other tag the top, then switch.

We started with a relaxing hike to Herman Lake, which sits just below 12,000 feet. We meandered along through an alpine forest, full of evergreens. The smell of spruce and the brisk air were energizing, and we moved quickly. This early part of the trail hadn't yet filled up with those hiking to the lake, a popular destination. We were still in the dark, embracing the "alpine start."

I don't remember everything that we discussed as we hiked along with our two canines: Francesca, a curly-haired Wheaten Terrier that I brought to the relationship, and Ayer, a lovably goofy cattle-dog mutt that Kristina already had. I'm sure the pending wedding was a topic. However, I do recall one topic of conversation, explicitly: we were talking about the afternoon and our plans to go celebrate the birthday of my soon-to-be father-in-law, Bill.

With the early starts we typically have in Colorado, it's not unusual to make a local climb in the morning and then spend the rest of the day relaxing après-climb. We had planned to enjoy this relatively fast scramble and then head to Kristina's parents' home in the nearby foothills.

We wouldn't get there.

From Herman Lake, we ascended another 500 feet to the mountain saddle over a broken trail and bread-loaf-to-microwave-oven-sized talus. Then we scampered up the southeast ridge until we stood at the bottom of two summit towers of almost identical height, one to the southeast, one to the northwest. Each tower is almost a cylinder, with heights up to several stories depending on the line taken. Climbing them calls for finding a weakness in the wall, following a cleft in the rock that brings the otherwise fully technical climbing down to a scramble.

I held the dogs as Kristina went first, scampering up the southeast tower. She moved up a small fissure, about hip wide, which wasn't deep enough to really pull herself into fully; so, the crack left her exposed to a fall down the face.

This certainly looked more like class four than class three. But at this point in our climbing, my bride-to-be was bolder than me, and neither she nor I was particularly worried.

I watched her disappear over the lip of the cylindrical tower and onto the top.

I waited a few moments, expecting to soon see her reemerge and begin the downclimb back to me,Francesca, and Ayer.

I waited longer.

After the hours of approach, the early-fall weather proved to be stable: blue skies so bright that it hurt to look at them. A few wispy, stretched, and unthreatening clouds fragmented the blue. There was a chill in the breeze that bit at my fingers, reminding me that fall was here and that winter would be moving into the mountains soon.

I waited some more.

The dogs' collars jingled as they turned their heads. I heard something faint, like a yell, off in the distance. It wasn't unusual to hear whoops and hollers, called from the summits of surrounding peaks, as they reverberated across the enormous basins below.

I continued to wait, but with ears now perked.

The breeze made a soft, rumbling noise as it moved past me, coming out of the northwest, up where Kristina had been climbing.

Then I got a phone call, which was surprising given the spotty service in the mountains, even up here near the major ski resorts along the Interstate 70 corridor. Kristina's name appeared on the screen.

"Jason, I fell." Kristina's voice was shaken but matter-of-fact.

"Are you okay?"

"I think so, but I'm hurt."

"Where are you?"

"Around the other side at the far tower."

"I'm coming to you."

I led the dogs around the base of the southeast tower, moving clockwise. As I started to move towards the farther, northwest tower, I found Kristina on her hands and knees, crawling toward me. Her face was bloody, and she shook as she crawled.

When I got to her, she stopped crawling.

The blood coming from her nose and forehead let me know that she clearly had a head injury; the question was, *how bad of one?*

I helped her unclip her pack and get it off her shoulders. Her shirt was bloodstained at her lower back.

I threw my pack to the ground and quickly dug through it to find the first-aid kit.

I dribbled some water from my water bottle down her face.

I took one of her hands in mine as I looked deeply into her eyes, searching.

"What happened?"

"My handhold came out. The whole block just pulled right out," she said, her hand and her voice both shaking.

"How far did you fall?"

"I don't know. I landed on my back and bounced down the gully some."

She was clearly coherent. That was a good thing.

But now I was worried about her back . . . although her earlier crawling, pack still on her back, was a good sign, too.

I raised the tail of her shirt and saw a four-inch-long gash in her lower back. I poured water over it to reveal a wound that was deep but, fortunately, not pouring blood.

"What about your wrist?"

Now sitting up, Kristina was holding her other hand palm-up, but in a curled position across her chest.

"I think I broke it."

"We could sling it."

"No."

"Do you want gauze for your nose?"

"No." (Turns out, she would later have gauze uncomfortably

stuffed up her nose for a week after a surgery to repair her broken nose.)

"Well, we can do a Band-Aid for your forehead. I think we should let your back bleed a bit—at least it will keep it clean."

There had been mixed perspectives in the outdoor community on using things like quick-clotting powders, which can lead to infections, and I didn't have any materials or skills to put in stitches in the field.

"Can you get up?"

Kristina wobbled to her feet.

"Do you want me to call for help?"

Kristina took a few steps and said, "We don't need a rescue; we'd be out by the time they got here. But we should call my dad."

I quickly repacked my things and slung my pack on my back. I then took her pack and placed it backward, on my chest. I fully extended its hip belt and, reaching behind me, clipped her pack's two hip straps together around the lower part of my own pack.

We began to hobble out, and using our surprise cell-phone service again, we called Bill and gave him quite the poor birthday surprise.

We made good time on the mellow trail despite the ginger steps Kristina was taking. Every so often, I asked how she was doing but tried not to dwell on it. I wanted to make sure I was aware of any new information or worsening in her condition, but I also didn't want to repeatedly draw her mind back to her pain.

Carrying one throbbing arm tucked against her and curled in front of her chest, my soon-to-be-bride worked her way down 3,000 vertical feet and about five miles of terrain. From time to time, I held her uninjured hand, for additional support on one of the many awkward step-downs.

Kristina kept her head low, hiding beneath the bill of her hat, so as to not scare the occasional group of hikers we passed. Nonetheless, some groups noticed and asked if they could help. Kristina would sheepishly let them know, "I took a fall, but I'm okay . . . and we are almost out, anyway." Their group would then part to let us pass.

Stopping as soon as Interstate 70 spit us out into the Denver Metro, we spent that afternoon at one of the city's many freestanding emergency departments, getting wrist, spinal, pelvic, and skull X-rays. Her wrist was just badly sprained. Her back was lacerated but not broken. She had, however, broken her nose and eye socket.

Kristina had made the southeast summit. When she'd looked across at the northwest summit, however, she couldn't tell which one was higher. So, she downclimbed the first tower to go up the second tower. It was while descending the far tower that, facing in on a downclimb, a large block that she had both hands on detached from the wall. She fell backwards, landing on her pack, and then tumbled. We estimated about twenty feet. We will never really know if it was the loose block or the subsequent tumble that had smashed her face.

I never saw it. I never even really heard it, but maybe that whoop I'd heard wasn't exactly a whoop but a cry of terror. Another thing I will never know for sure.

Kristina spent the next week on a four-hour cycle of sleeping and then waking up to take painkillers and reapply antibiotic ointment to her cuts. She slept on the couch, unable to make herself comfortable in our bed.

Seven days after the accident, Kristina began our wedding day by having one of her bridesmaids, a labor and delivery nurse, remove the stitches from her back. She was zipped into a borrowed wedding dress, as her still-swollen body could no longer fit into the dress she had bought.

On our wedding day, I met her on a flagstone patio at the bank of a community-park lake near my parents' home in Broomfield, an idyllic setting beneath Longs Peak, which towered in the background and served as our wedding altar. Fifty or so family members and close friends stood with us for the short ceremony as we exchanged vows.

I was looking deep into her eyes, which were alight when she grinned mischievously and concluded her vows with, "I über-love you."

I took one of her hands as we moved down the aisle between our guests, who parted to let us pass.

The house of the "slowest jailbreak in history," the home the boys were born into in far southeast Aurora—an already southeasterly suburb of Denver—had a park at the end of the block that was home to a three-story-high hill. When it snowed, the neighborhood teenagers would build a jump at the bottom of the hill and then trudge up its slopes with a snowboard or sled in tow.

In the summer of 2017, when our kids were two-and-a-half, they both grabbed a trekking pole from our gear-storage area. Their little hands could only cover about half the circumference of the grips. They pulled on their Velcro shoes, and Kade pulled a Superman cape around his shoulders.

We headed out to the hill.

The boys grew up around photos and stories about their parents' climbs. The movie-length video I made of my Denali expedition was early viewing for them. My library was full of climbing books that were full of images of iconic peaks and how-to technical illustrations. Climbing was in the air, all around them.

After their ascents of the TV stand, the kitchen counter, and their parents' bed, the twins had noticed the hill. We would pass by it on walks—stretching out their toddler legs now that they were getting too big for the double stroller—to the play area at the far end of the park.

The hill was covered in a native, prairie grass that was a perpetual mix of green and the color of straw no matter the season—except for a strip of trampled dirt that was the up and down ramp for the teenagers' wintertime, aerial adventures.

This day, the boys were chatting about going to "climb a mountain," and I did my best to set the adventure's context in terms of an expedition, despite my shorts and flip-flops. I carried a trekking pole, too, to ensure we were all appropriately "equipped," while Kade's Superman cape bellowed heroically behind him as we prepared to cross the park.

As we moved toward the "mountain," the long grass was sticky underfoot. The boys developed a cadence of carefully placing their trekking poles down, and then shuffling their two feet behind and repeating: *Place, step, step. Place, step, step.* It was not unlike how a mountaineer would use an ice axe.

Kade's tongue peeked out from between his lips. He had developed my dad's habit of sticking his tongue out when he was doing something physical that also required concentration. (I still have memories of my dad cutting lumber at the table saw with his tongue poking out.)

We crossed the field, landing at a dry bed of decorative river rock at the base of the hill. Each stone was rounded and roughly the size of my foot. The rhythm of the trekking poles stopped, and the boys began a kind of waddle, looking down at their feet with ferocious concentration, their blond heads bobbing with each careful step across the uneven rocks.

They paused at the foot of the hill, looking up at it, in turn. "We're going to climb this mountain!" Connor proclaimed.

They started up, back into their cadence: *Place, step, step. Place, step, step.*

The clouds were thickening, graying, and lowering upon us, as was often the case in monsoon season in Colorado. The sun would hide and reappear, and the boys' faces—in turn—went dark and then became illuminated.

Each boy stopped once, about midway up, just to look around. I imagine, for people standing barely three feet high, the world looks a lot different when you are above the trees and rooftops. From that short height, maybe the world looks too big for you, built for beings other than you. From up here, however, above it all, perhaps their world now seemed conceivable—maybe unfathomably large and broad and full of possibilities too numerous to count, but conceivable, nonetheless. We could literally see our place in it.

Reaching the summit, we all turned to my camera, to take the obligatory summit selfies. Connor sat in my lap as Kade stood behind us. Their eyes were alight, and their chins were propped up in infectious grins. Kade unleashed a victory roar.

Spring was turning into summer in 1995, and I had secured my place as valedictorian of my graduating class at Sandia High. The administration asked me, per standard protocol, to deliver a commencement speech.

Each of our 365 graduates were allotted 10 tickets for guests at the ceremony. Give or take, then, I would probably be presenting to a crowd of somewhere between 2,000 and 3,500 people at the Johnson Center, the University of New Mexico's indoor volleyball arena.

I wasn't particularly nervous. I was fortunate to have both an upbringing and a sense of self that allowed me to trust my own voice. However, I felt a sense of responsibility . . . to the audience, yes, but more so to my fellow graduates. My speech would perhaps be some small part of their lasting memory of this day, so I needed to make it a good one—a sincere one, free of clichés like "The world is our oyster."

To be honest, I was haunted by one particular thought: statistically speaking (at the time), about four members of our graduating class wouldn't be alive four years from now. It's the sad reality of life that things like car accidents and drug abuse and freak collapses of amusement park rides happen. I didn't want to stand in front of those four poor souls, whoever they were, and set a bar of success they might never have the opportunity to reach.

It wasn't that I was pessimistic. It was more that I felt compelled to express, having come prematurely to confront the randomness of mortality, that there was one ultimate and universally shared human experience. From this place of terror, I had grown in empathy, and I saw much more commonality across our humanity than I had before. I wanted to talk about this commonality without invoking death—this was a celebration, after all—but while still acknowledging the finite nature of our lives, too.

I opened my speech by quoting the closing lines of "Ulysses" by Alfred, Lord Tennyson. After spending so much time earnestly practicing the delivery, I still have the lines memorized:

> Come, my friends.
> 'Tis not too late to seek a newer world.
> Push off, and sitting well in order smite
> the sounding furrows; for my purpose holds
> To sail beyond the sunset, and the baths
> Of all the western stars, until I die.
> It may be that the gulfs will wash us down;
> It may be that we shall touch the Happy Isles,
> And see the great Achilles, whom we knew.
> Though much is taken, much abides; and though
> We are not now that strength which in old days
> Moved earth and heaven, that which we are, we are—
> One equal temper of heroic hearts,
> Made weak by time and fate, but strong in will
> To strive, to seek, to find, and not to yield.

The imagery is striking, of course; it's Tennyson.

Here is the hero Ulysses, never quite able to settle at home after his years fighting in the Trojan War and experiencing "the passion of life to its top" (as Justice Oliver Wendell Holmes, Jr. described his service during the American Civil War). It's a sense of adventure that was only heightened during the intervening years of his odyssey to return home after the war. Facing his old age, Ulysses passes—literally—the scepter of home rule to his son, and then invites his friends and battle-hardened colleagues to set sail and move their journey forward. He will abandon the home that has been the source of his disquiet and fill the remainder of his life with the sea and its adventures.

Some of us are closer to the end of our lives than we know. Ulysses, by Tennyson's imagination, chose to fill his ending life with a journey. And that was the whole point. The journey, itself, was the whole point. To hang a life's meaning on the outcomes is just unfair, because life can be cut short at any point.

I found a freedom in coming to grips with the lack of control I had in the world. Sure, there were many things I could influence, and plenty of things I could influence greatly, but there was little I could *control.* I found comfort, not horror, in the notion that I could tilt all of life's various odds one way or the other (and further, had a responsibility to do so), but could never run the game.

I caught a cold just before commencement, and laryngitis set in. I had asked my fellow student who introduced me to please ask the audience for quiet, given my inflamed vocal cords. Quiet befell the audience in Johnson Center, and thankfully my voice held up.

I still wasn't nervous, even as I took the podium flanked by flags representing our country and our state. I glanced around the arena, taking in the crowd. I tried to find my best friend, Chad, who went to a different high school and was attending as a guest, but the house lights were dimmed, darkening the surroundings. Small rectangles of dim yellow light crept through the windows at ground level.

Then I focused my attention on the gym floor, where sat

my fellow graduates: a sea of scarlet highlighted by splashes of Columbia blue. The graduates sat on folding metal chairs, glinting around their gowns and legs from the wash of flashbulbs popping in the seats above.

Down on the volleyball floor, I found my girlfriend, Jessica, also graduating this year, and then I let the rest of the scarlet sea flow over me.

Ham-fistedly, but earnestly, I continued. In retrospect, I probably shouldn't have set it up so that I was following Tennyson, but rather let him be the closer.

> The future is exciting, but it is not exciting because we will see our dreams fulfilled. Some of us will try and succeed. Some of us will try and fail and then try again. Those are the realities of life. But the important thing is that we all will try. We will never get everything we want. Achievement isn't everything. The fulfillment of our dreams doesn't make the excitement of the future. The opportunity to try is exciting.

I spoke about finding uniqueness in opportunity. I spoke about the redeeming qualities of failures and missteps. But mostly I spoke about journeys: I spoke about how we never really know where those journeys are headed, let alone each turn they will take. I spoke about our journeys' durations, and how we never really knew those, either. I spoke about the honor of having a journey at all.

The words came easily, and they felt right.

I had come to bury my fears and anxieties after I had been stabbed, and that was a habit I was still a long way from unlearning.

But in this moment, I felt profound authenticity, and that brought me calm and self-assuredness as I spoke.

I closed:

> . . . we realize that the weight of the world is on our shoulders but also realize that we don't have to carry all of it. We grow if we take the responsibility handed to us with grace, poise, and a bit of uncertainty. This day is worth celebrating if we celebrate just the chance to make things happen and remember that it is still up to us to make our lives worth living.

As I left the lectern, I received a hearty congratulations from my teachers, including a beaming smile from Mrs. Harris, my senior-year English teacher. She had round-rimmed glasses and wavy salt-and-pepper hair pulled behind her ears to expose a tanned face that had been weathered by the New Mexican sun. She was, no doubt, thrilled by my use of Tennyson. She would succumb to breast cancer a few years later, her own journey cut short by the seemingly random cell mutations that cause the disease.

About ten days after my diagnosis appointment, I was on a business trip to Chattanooga, Tennessee, when I got the call from my oncologist. She had the results from the test that would let me know if my genetics and the particular manifestation of my disease were a virulent combination likely to progress my cancer aggressively or if maybe it would move more slowly.

I had decided to keep working, as best I could, while I waited to find out if I would be dropping out of the workforce to immediately begin treatment or if I would face a different set of challenges, learning to live with this disease over a longer time horizon.

We had spent the day at a client site: a sprawling business campus sitting high upon a flat-topped green hill, overlooking the Tennessee River and town. It was an idyllic location, but I was in no mood to take in the views. I was doing my best to project a professional face, taking the client meetings, nodding at the earnestness with which one or another pending business exigency needed to be avoided or leveraged.

I was mid-career in healthcare analytics, and our firm's work really could have an impact in people's lives, pointing the American medical system toward populations that could be better served by complex care support, to impart improved "clinical outcomes"—i.e., living better and longer lives. However, what we were doing still felt far removed from the day-to-day realities of the physician-patient relationship that I was now experiencing, even if I knew our efforts would eventually have an impact.

There were times that work was a welcomed distraction, but there were also times that the "distraction" could just not cut through my slow burn of stress.

My co-workers and I were having dinner at the restaurant attached to our hotel when my phone rang, interrupting my polite nodding as I tried to focus on the team debrief regarding our client and our relationship with them.

"Excuse me. I have to take this," I said.

No one questioned my abrupt departure.

I stepped outside onto the restaurant's attached patio, which was empty, with winter only days away.

The breeze off the Tennessee River blew cold. It was dark out. Yellow light seeped onto the patio from the lamps overhanging the indoor-outdoor bar, which had been shuttered for the season, splashing off water pooling in the gray pavers. From above, aside, and below me, my surroundings seemed to twinkle.

My nose and fingertips felt cold. My business-casual attire was not quite enough to keep me warm, and I had left my tweed sports jacket folded over my chair inside.

I paced back and forth across the patio to both keep warm and to provide an outlet for my new spike in adrenalin.

"Hi, Jason, this is Sarah," my oncologist said when I picked up. "I have the results of your blood test."

"Uh huh."

"So, you don't have any of the chromosome mutations or deletions that can mean bad news, but you don't have any of the positive variations either."

As I would learn, CLL patients can have a deletion of the short arm of chromosome 17 within the cancer itself. At the end of chromosome 17 is the TP53 gene that helps suppress tumor expansion. If we cut off—or "delete"—the place where the TP53 gene is supposed to be, then you end up with an aggressive, more treatment-resistant cancer. Without the deletion, TP53 can be there but be mutated, which would have a similar effect.

On the flipside, having mutations in the "V" region of the immunoglobulin-heavy chain gene (IgHV) in the cancer, which would make them different than the linage material passed on to other new cells, is a positive indicator, with shorter times in treatment, longer spans between treatments, and better outcomes.

In the grand scheme, though, the positive variations are only *slightly* positive, while the negative variations are substantially negative.

I pulled my mouth into a pucker and blew out a long and very audible exhale. Then I did it again.

"That's great news," I squeezed out, tearing up. I moved to the back railing of the patio and leaned out over the river and riverwalk, both of which seemed to be flowing below. I blew out a pronounced exhale again.

"You okay?"

"Yeah. I'm good. It's been hard."

"I know."

"What do we do from here?"

"Well, we wait and watch. I'm going to want you to come see me in a few months, and we'll take some blood ahead of time. We'll just watch your symptoms and your blood markers for a while."

"Okay."

"Like we talked about, there is no benefit to early treatment, and treatments are changing all the time. It seems like there is a new trial every day. So, we'll monitor things until it starts to make sense to evaluate treatment options . . . and there are lots of options these days."

"Okay."

Despite the news that my prognosis was not the worst, nor the best, the reality is that deletions, mutations, and other presentations of CLL can change over time. Just because things were okay enough now didn't mean they would stay that way.

"We'll call you tomorrow to get your lab and follow-up

appointment set up. I'm sorry for calling so late, but I knew you'd want to know as soon as possible."

"No problem. I appreciate that you called. Have a good night."

"Have a good night."

I hung up, still leaning over the railing, whose cold metal bar had numbed my fingers. My nose stung, likewise, from the cold. I lingered on the railing for a few more minutes, watching the river.

The Tennessee River seemed big . . . and powerful. The water was black in the dark of night. It wasn't roaring but rather seemed to softly rumble or hum in a way that I sensed in my body rather than with my ears.

I followed the river upstream to the east with my eyes before heading back inside.

"Everything okay?" my boss asked.

"Yeah. That was my oncologist. Everything is okay . . . well, as okay as it can be." I paused. "I need to go to bed."

"Yeah, go get some sleep. We'll see you in the morning."

"Thanks. Have a good night."

"You, too."

I don't know what they talked about after I left—if it was about me or business. Probably both. I went up to my room and called Kristina.

The Tennessee River forms from the confluence of the Holston and French Broad rivers, just outside of Knoxville. It was there, in Knoxville, that I had sat as a six-year-old, scanning, purposefully, the clover in the grass of our front lawn.

Kade "roaring" while Connor sits on Jason's lap, all atop the local hill at the park near their home.

CHAPTER SEVEN

# Awareness

It was the beginning of summer in 2012, nearly two years after our marriage and just over two years before our kids would be born. Kristina and I had selected the longest day of the year, the solstice. We wanted as much daylight as possible for our climb before we had to switch on the headlamps.

We sought to climb Little Bear Peak (14,037 feet), a difficult Fourteener in the Sangre de Cristo Range near the border with New Mexico, when no one was on it. That was hard to do if you weren't doing a winter ascent. On Little Bear's standard class-four route, the big issue is a section called the Hourglass, a funneling rock formation with a wide catchment area at the top that channels any falling rock onto the climbers moving through the constriction below.

Most of Colorado's high peaks are moderately to extremely crumbly. So, the odds of having a climber above you accidently kick down a loose rock aren't exactly small. On a busy day, climbing through the Hourglass becomes a game of roulette.

Kristina and I decided that the easiest and most absolute way to mitigate this danger was to climb Little Bear when no one else was on it, which meant climbing it at night.

Again, the standard logic for a high peak in the summer

monsoon season of Colorado is to start very early, be on the summit by eleven o'clock or noon, and be back down below tree line before the thunderstorms move in, but those same storms tend to move on or dissolve in the early evenings.

So, Kristina and I hiked up the four-wheel-drive track of Lake Como Road under a midday sun beating down on the San Luis Valley, making the notorious trudge up rounded, bowling-ball–sized stones, broken talus, and boulders.

The road is a favorite off-roading location for super-modified jeeps and rock crawlers. Along its switchbacking, 5.5-mile length, it gains almost 4,000 feet, ending at the lake and the last of the trees at around 11,500 feet.

We didn't have a straight ankle for just about any step of the entire approach.

We'd brought with us two bivy sacks, lightweight and minimalist shelters kind of like a sleeping bag made of tent materials. Finding a flat location next to some deeply set boulders, we laid out our sacks. A clump of evergreens stood nearby, casting shade that did little to mellow the blistering June heat.

Being zipped into the nylon was stifling, but it did spare our faces, arms, and legs from the mosquitos that swarmed the lake shore. We napped through the late afternoon, dozing to a serenade of knocks echoing through the basin, sounding like two-by-fours slapping together in quick succession: rocks tumbling down the mountain as descending climbers headed down.

At 6:00 p.m., we stuffed down some food and prepared for our ascent. I didn't eat well because I was nervous. I had done alpine starts before, starting a climb by headlamp, but had never purposefully climbed into progressing darkness. And it was still, typically, more dangerous to head up a mountain that was totally devoid of people, removing the "safety net" of others, though in this case that was the goal.

The ascent began up a steep, miserable, north-facing gully of loose dirt and scree above the lake. For all the talk about the Hourglass in the online forums, no one had really mentioned the sheer frustration that comes on this section from sliding back six inches to a foot for every step upward. The terrain wasn't difficult, but it was demoralizing and not particularly fun. Kristina and I were constantly chatting, using sound to ensure that we were either spread out or bunched together; you either want to be far enough apart that any rocks you kick down don't head toward the other as you zigzag upward, or you want to be close enough together that those rocks can't pick up speed before they reach the second climber.

I focused deeply on each footstep, gently placing my boots down rather than kicking into the mountainside. The goal was to dislodge nothing. We were only mildly successful, but our spacing added safety and made up for any deficiency in our technique.

We stopped at the top of the gully, where I took a GPS waypoint so that we could relocate it on our descent, which would be in the dark. We still had about 1,400 feet of vertical gain to the summit, and the next major component of the climb was a mile-long, ascending traverse that stayed just below the ridgeline.

As the sun sank in the sky, the mountain turned a familiar, muted pink, a hue of alpenglow I was used to seeing in the morning hours. Above us, a series of small rock towers stacked by people—cairns—appeared every hundred feet or so, marking the faint sidehill trail up the ridge.

Then we were at the Hourglass, at the base of the constriction. Above, a solitary climbing rope hung down from some unknown anchor. We each attached a friction hitch to the rope, looping the cord back to our climbing harnesses. We weren't going to trust this mystery fixed rope and certainly wouldn't pull on it, but should we happen to slip, maybe we would get lucky and the rope would hold.

While we were attaching our cords, the last rays of light disappeared, and we were left in the gloaming. The rock transmuted from reds to grays as we switched our headlamps on.

As we reached the constriction in the Hourglass, the rope became saturated. Runoff from the late-melting snow was still dripping down the gully.

Kristina stayed to one side of the rope, and I to the other—just off of her hip—limiting the chances of knocking rock onto each other. We placed our hands and feet carefully, both to avoid sending a projectile down as well as to maximize our grip on the wet rock. The climbing moves, themselves, were easy, and without having to worry about climbers above sending down rocks, we found this crux section of the climb to be comfortable rather than harrowing.

Once above the Hourglass, I took another waypoint. We still had several hundred feet of scrambling to complete in the dark. From here, we relied on Kristina's far superior sense of direction. She led up to the summit, scratching our way up a mazelike tumble of person-high, weathered granite blocks. She guided us rightward from atop this one, leftward from atop that one, with always another block looming above. Full night had set in, and the dark washed the color completely from the stone.

We ran out of blocks to climb just before 10:00 p.m. There, on the summit, I caught a glint of white reflected from the light of our headlamps, and so we fished in the cracks for the PVC-pipe summit register. It was covered in stickers representing climbing culture: various outdoor-equipment brands and local breweries. We unscrewed the lid, pulled out a roll of lined paper and a dulled pencil, and signed our names. Our headlamps also carried our own "light pollution," so we were seeing nothing except each other, smiling. Already focusing on the looming descent, it didn't occur to us to switch the headlamps off and take in the dark forms of the surrounding mountains under the light of a half-moon.

Kristina led the downclimb back to the Hourglass, and I followed her willingly, disoriented from all of the twisting and turning in the dark. Once there, I tied two seventy-meter ropes together and draped them behind a boulder as an anchor. We simul-rappelled—each of us on one side of the rope, counterbalancing each other—down the 50-degree slope of the Hourglass. This technique, while adding danger because each of us needed to be consistently and equally weighting the rope to avoid the rope simply being pulled down by a singularly weighted strand, let us descend side-by-side, again avoiding the potential of loosing rocks onto each other. By the light of our headlamps, each strand of the green and purple ropes jumped out from the colorless ground; the reflecting paint from our helmets and threads from our backpacks kept us in sync, and a tether between us added an additional measure of safety.

On the return traverse, we moved slowly. Coming to each cairn, we stopped, scanned the slope by headlamp until we spotted the next cairn, and then moved on.

Back on the spine of the ridge, I took out the GPS and located the top of our entrance gully.

We slowly picked our way down the scree and shale of this

entrance gully that had been so frustrating on the way up. The constant grinding of colliding rocks must have been confusing to those camped down at Lake Como. Some natural rockfall was part of the mountain environment, yes, but thirty- or forty-five minutes' worth? We stayed close and connected, communicating constantly about any errant, larger rock that might have come down with us.

We skated down the slope. I tried to stay directly in Kristina's wake. I found each skid mark of dirt, stripped clean of the loose rock and pebbles by her shoes, and matched my feet to these paths.

With legs now strong enough to make it to and up the hill at the park, the boys extended their regular walks. Beyond the park and the hill, and beyond the playground at the park's far end, was an underpass beneath a four-lane street, carved into our master-planned community to allow bikes easy access to and from the eastern and western sections of the development.

The underpass, itself, was a rectangular tunnel of drab and dark concrete. However, from the corner posts of the roadway above, framing the tunnel ends, cascaded artfully rusted sheet metal in a nautical green, keeping with the confusing sailing theme of our decidedly-landlocked Colorado sub-development.

Connor and Kade were with my parents the first time they walked far enough to reach the underpass. My wife and I were shown videos, taken by my parents, and regaled with the boys' stories upon their return.

Our walks through the park now had to reach "the tunnel."

Kristina and I each had one boy in hand the first time we entered the tunnel as a family. They announced their entrance by, first, stomping their feet. A *clap-clap-clap* bounced off of the concrete walls, and the boys broke into broad smiles.

The smiles quickly turned to giggles, which now chirped throughout the tunnel, and it wasn't long until hearty laughs were reverberating all around us.

We stayed in the tunnel for fifteen minutes, the boys testing the echo with all sorts of sounds. Kade would stomp, and Connor would stomp. Connor would clap, and Kade would clap. Kade let out one of his lion's roars, and Connor tried one, too. Connor unleashed a screech that could have shattered glass, and Kade, not as practiced at this as his brother, attempted a choppier version. They tried a few songs that they knew. They bellowed indecipherable shouts.

Each new test produced the same riotous laughter.

I had taken a Greek-mythology course in college. In legend, Echo was a wood nymph cursed to only be able to repeat whatever was said to her. When she fell in love with Narcissus, she was rejected by him when she could not answer any of his questions but rather only repeated the questions back. Overcome with grief, Echo retreated to a cave, where she withered away through starvation until only her voice remained. Now, we still hear her repeat back whatever is spoken to her.

But the story doesn't end there. Narcissus was punished by the gods for his rejection of Echo and was made to fall in love with himself. Catching his reflection in a pond, he was unable to leave the sight of himself, and he similarly starved to death.

Their parallel deaths, while highlighting the auditory and visual "reflections" in the myth, bring another layer of metaphor to the story: what we put out into the world is sent back to us.

I have heard unnerving and dangerous rockfall echo across chasms of unfeeling stone. I have heard joyous shouts of climbers reaching the tops of their climbs. I have heard roped up climbers call out safety commands and words of encouragement to their partners. The strange architecture of the alpine behemoths would often carry sounds, both good and bad, from miles away directly to my ears.

The boys had to be pulled away from the tunnel that day. And the walk back was filled with excited chatter about the experience.

"We had an echo!" Connor half-screamed. His grandparents had explained the concept to him.

"That was fun!" Kade called out.

We spent as much time reliving the echo on the walk back home as we'd spent in the tunnel itself.

"Can we go back sometime?" Kade asked on behalf of both twins.

"Of course we can, baby," their mom answered.

We went to the tunnel many times over the following months. Sometimes, the kids would have to be herded out of the tunnel and back home in order to get them lunch or dinner or to a swim lesson or whatever. But unfailingly, with each trip, what the boys put into that tunnel was thrill and laughter. As we took their hands and began the walk back home, that thrill and laughter came echoing back from the darkness.

My mom, Marianne, taught elementary school up until my older brother, Bryan, was born two years before me. Aside from some substitute teaching, she didn't return to her profession until I was in middle school. So, I remember my mom being around for my walks to school as a small child as well as her leaning into lesson planning as I moved into my teenage years. She would be on the sidelines for the afternoon soccer practices and would then spend the evening surrounded by tissue boxes or pencils or notebooks, organizing these items she had purchased out of her own pocket for donation to her classroom. She was there to make me the somewhat unnatural amount of French toast that I could pack away over breakfast and was also upcycling our personal libraries of children's books into her classroom library as we outgrew the material.

My mom also got her master's degree in education after heading back to the workforce. So, I watched her put in a job on top of the job. My mom is a nurturer, and she felt that teaching was her calling, no matter how many demands it put on her time and energy. But that's my mom. She truly cares about people. All kinds of people: people she's met, like the kids in her classroom; and people she hasn't met but knows she is connected to, like the migrant workers who bring food to our tables. So, she tries to balance all of these various depths of relationships.

When she was back teaching, Mom was always experimenting, trying to find ways to reach more kids. Some of the experiments were small, like using a box of sand to have kids tactilely write out their spelling words, bringing kinesthetic learning to children who might benefit from it. Some of the experiments were large, like when she convinced the administration of a school with a hard-to-serve population to allow her to teach a "third-fourth inclusion" class: bringing both third- and fourth-graders into the same classroom. This allowed for lessons with a broad range of possible activities, from more rudimentary to more advanced for the grade levels. Because it was already understood that there were different ages, and therefore different abilities, represented in the room, it removed the stigma of any student needing additional assistance.

But my strongest memories of my mom's teaching career are the few times I helped set up her classroom during the "teacher-service days" before the first day of school.

Back then, we had a gigantic Buick station wagon, so large it should have had its own zip code, an ideal vehicle for hauling me and half of my soccer teammates around town or to those tournaments in neighboring states. One day in August of 1990, when I was thirteen years old, my mom stacked totes and boxes in the back, and we drove to Eubank Elementary School, where she taught.

As I helped her unload, the contents of the containers were unknown to me, but I could guess. I had seen the supplies in neat stacks on the floor of our family room over the weeks and days before.

My mom opened the heavy, metal door to her classroom with a creak. A sliver of light pierced the darkness from the small window on the far wall before Mom flipped the light switch with a satisfying *thunk.* The room exploded in full color—everything was bold. Cardboard, laminated addition, subtraction, multiplication, and division signs, all as big as my head, adorned the math area. A poster was on the wall at each learning station, bordered in the same looping cut of paper but in varying blues and yellows and greens.

As I placed one box down on a small student desk near the door, my mom placed a box and a tote on her own desk at the room's front corner.

Next to the green chalkboard that dominated that front wall was a corkboard. A fringed, rectangular border made of white, laminated construction paper framed off part of the cork. The border surrounded a neatly made grid of boxes, numbering seven across and five down. Outside the frame hung numbers and months, all done in brilliant blue. Centered above the grid, it read "August."

Everywhere, it looked like a giant scrapbook: all the important information had been framed to draw attention, with my mom's carefully prepared words, numbers, pictures, and cartoonish animals all at the ready for little hands to move and order.

Books crammed the shelves of the classroom library. I recognized many of the titles, and the pages I had dog-eared back when I'd read the books. Under the front cover of each one, Mom had glued a small manila envelope and inserted an index card so that "her kids" could check them out and bring them home.

Mom opened a tote and began removing supplies for her desk: scissors, tape, pens.

I opened my box: crayons and assorted construction paper. Mom came over and began to remove the contents to stock the metal supply cabinet behind her desk, placing items on the shelves.

I went back to the station wagon and removed another box, carrying it to my mom's desk this time. Notebooks and pencils. Mom moved them to the bottom shelf.

Another trip, another box. Tissues. These light items went up top, and then heavier folders and three-ring binders we placed near the bottom.

Several middle shelves in the cabinet, right at kid height, were still barren when my mom and I went out to the car together a final time. She handed me a box and took up the final two herself. This one felt a bit heavier than the others.

Mom placed her boxes down, and I placed mine beside them. She unfolded the tops of the boxes and, unspeaking, moved the items from the boxes to the barren middle shelves. The industrial metal cabinet began to fill with individually packaged snacks: raisins, crackers, granola bars, all at kid height, facilitating a quick grab, done before prying eyes could notice hungry students needing the snacks.

I was working in downtown Denver, and my parents and I had arranged for a semi-recurring lunch date. They would drive down from the northern suburbs and meet me on a Friday. We tried to do it weekly, but it was easy for things to interfere.

This day, we were in a little tapas bistro on the ground floor of my office building. The outer-facing wall was almost completely glass, and light bounced off the blue mosaic tiles that adorned the booths and bar. The light's bluish hue matched the cold December temperatures outside, and I kept on a fleece jacket over my dress shirt.

We began with the typical small talk about the drive, the challenge of parking downtown, and what was happening at my work this week. But, having been holding back all of this for too long—weeks now—I stopped pretending I could find the perfect time to tell my parents that their child has cancer. "Okay, I have some news. I'm going to use a couple of words that will sound very scary, but it isn't too bad. I have a very treatable form of cancer, chronic lymphocytic leukemia. CLL," I said.

"I knew something was wrong," my mom said. She was referring to my general aloofness as I was going through the diagnostic and prognostic blood tests that would tell me what I had and how bad the cancer was going to be.

I had been out of touch, pawning off the work trip to Tennessee—as well as the pre- and post-work around the trip—as an excuse. *Busyness.* No one questions it . . . and it was partially true. A sin of omission.

I responded with the whole truth, this time: "I wanted to know what I was dealing with, and I wanted to be able to give you actual information. You didn't need the uncertainty."

"We could have been there for your uncertainty," my dad said, gently. His eyes were kind, holding a soft droop of empathy.

My dad's prostate had been removed many years before due to cancer. The operation went well, and he'd suffered no spread, but he had become intimate with this kind of health uncertainty.

"I'm sorry," I replied.

I meant it, too, but I also didn't feel especially guilty. I had already abandoned the notion that grace would be the presiding virtue of my journey with cancer. Sarah had warned me that CLL can be one of the more difficult cancers, psychologically. You are just getting worse, waiting for things to get bad enough to finally take action.

Well, now I was atrophying on the inside, and I was supposed to just take it and wait. This was likely going to be messy—messy enough that I would have no choice but to embrace and forgive my all-too-human flaws.

"How are you?" my mom asked.

"I'm fine, I guess. I don't have any symptoms."

"And, so, will you have chemo?"

"We don't know, yet."

I proceeded to tell them about the vagaries of CLL, such as the fact that the median diagnostic age is seventy-one, so often people don't get treated at all; but it was also likely that I'd need treatment due to my being thirty years younger. I told them that treatments are always changing due to advancements and that they'd be dependent upon which symptoms I was experiencing . . .

"So, there isn't really any point in guessing what my treatment will be. We don't know when it will be. We don't know what treatments will be available when it's time. And we don't know what shape I will be in, either."

"So, what are you supposed to be doing?" Mom asked.

"I will go in for a blood draw every three months, and we'll see how my blood markers are doing. There have been studies, and there is no benefit to early treatment."

"But you're feeling okay?"

My mom had a look on her face that I hadn't really seen before. Her jaw was locked with what looked more like resolve than an effort to contain her emotions.

"Yes, I really do feel fine. This is a kind of cancer that can be—comparatively—easier on your body but pretty hard on you mentally. In some ways, you're just waiting to get worse before you can really do anything about it."

"I can relate," my dad chimed in. "I remember the hardest time was waiting for the surgery. Once it happened, then at least I was doing something, even if it was just physical therapy."

"It was like that with my knee surgeries, too," I shared. "I hated waiting for the ACL surgeries because I was just getting weaker, literally atrophying. I was willing to do the pain of the surgery and the hard work of rehab, but I couldn't. This feels kind of like that, but it's my immune system."

"Right. Yeah," my dad affirmed.

"It reminds me of the bad sleep I get before a big climb. Waiting for the struggle to come is the hardest part of the struggle. So, anyway, I've given myself permission to see a therapist. And I think a big part of it, for me, is that I don't want to *fight* cancer."

I was looking earnestly at my parents, into whose faces the entire room now seemed to funnel—there was only the two of them: two people I loved, two people who'd raised me, two people who wanted the best for me.

I really felt that last statement: I didn't want to "fight" cancer. I didn't want to fight with myself. It had been an inkling of a thought before, but I had never really said it to anyone else. And I'd surprised myself when I'd heard my own words.

It didn't mean I was giving up. I would follow the best medical advice and strive for remission when the time was right, but for now, I needed to not resent myself and the slowly progressing weakness and infirmity that was going to set in. As I waited for treatment, I didn't want my whole life to be about *waiting for treatment.*

I don't remember much else of the conversation. We caught up on Bryan—how he was getting on running a lab and teaching at the University of Florida. In some ways, my brother's research was loosely related to my circumstances. He was using supercomputers to look at the genetic evolution of organisms, including diseases, evaluating which computer models made the most accurate predictions. We also talked about my work, but that didn't seem particularly important right now.

As soon as I'd sat down, I was done omitting the truth. I had kept information from my parents for long enough. But now that we were here and talking about it, the scene didn't just cut away when we were done. We somehow had to navigate the more quotidian parts of life. We ate our food. We talked about other things.

I shifted in my chair and fiddled with my water glass. The cancer patient doesn't just walk off after the speech, with the applause still echoing about the room. He goes home and faces the stark reality of a body that is turning on him. He has quiet moments with his family, and joyful moments, and fearful moments. The blue light and the clanking silverware were the only things ringing around the room. There was no soft dissolve or fade to black to spare us the awkwardness of our halting conversation. There was no uplifting orchestra music to escort us off the stage.

*Marianne, engaged with her students, in one of her elementary school classrooms.*

CHAPTER EIGHT

# Failures?

At least once a year, I make a pilgrimage to the Uncompahgre Gorge and the rather renowned Ouray Ice Park in the San Juan Mountains of western Colorado. The Ice Park is a cooperative enterprise between a nonprofit organization, the town, and the mining interests in the area. They collaborate to release water every winter night through an extensive irrigation system; 250 spray nozzles create more than 100 ice-climbing routes. As I write this, the park has plans to expand in the coming years. When I was an instructor, my trips typically coincideed with my teaching the basics of ice climbing to High Altitude Mountaineering School (HAMS) students through the Colorado Mountain Club (CMC).

My wife unwittingly started the tradition by, in February 2011, getting the two of us professional instruction in ice climbing from a local guide service over my extended birthday weekend. On day one, we both scratched and clawed our way up water ice in the narrow, shady canyon before Kristina decided that the seeping cold from "waiting your turn" didn't sit well with her. So, on the subsequent days, I received one-on-one coaching, which let me see marked improvement compared to my previous mentored or self-taught excursions.

I had always loved ice climbing, and had actually began

technical climbing (using ropes) on ice before I ever started technical rock climbing. There is something deeply meditative about ice climbing for me.

Rock routes are often referred to as "problems." It makes sense; you need to find the right sequence of holds and foot placements as dictated to you by the rock's features. Ice climbing isn't like that: within the bounds of safe practice (avoiding rotten ice and small bulges that may shear off, etc.), you are free to swing your picks in and kick your feet wherever you see fit.

I also like the rhythm and the sounds. Swing a tool from a raised elbow and with a flick of the wrist and you'll often hear a deep, satisfying *thunk* as the pick sinks into the ice. You then extend your arm and hang from that tool, sitting your butt down to get your hips away from the ice like you were sitting in a chair. Now, from the knees, you make a toe-up kick with one foot, then the other. Two more satisfying *thunks.* Stand up, bringing your hips into the ice. Arch your back to free up room for the next swing, and now whip the other tool into the ice. *Thunk.* Repeat.

Of course, there are terrain features that dictate that you move more sideways than purely vertically, and there are infinite nuances to refine within this efficient movement pattern. But the basics remain constant, which helps cultivate a rhythmic meditation.

As I improved my ice climbing over the years, I began to turn my attention to mixed climbing. Mixed climbing means climbing on routes that combine rock, snow, and ice. Now you are reintroducing that puzzle of rock climbing in which the terrain dictates the sequence but adding in the disadvantage of not being able to directly feel the rock. On the plus side, though, you are wielding a tool that grips miniscule divots and seams in the rock better than your hand ever will.

Down near the lower end of the gorge, as it begins to widen and open up into the town, you get more sunlight, which means melting and therefore more rock and less ice. That's where I found my first "test-piece." It was a 100-foot mixed climb named *Le Saucisson,* with a continuation onto the ice-and mixed route *Aye Laddy!* The linkup began on a 30-foot-high face of vertical to slightly overhanging rock before climbing over a shallow ice roof and then finishing up on a mostly ice-covered arête with a few intermittent rock moves.

A typical trip to Ouray would now involve a few days of teaching, dialing in my ice movement, and then giving some attempts on this route before heading back home, at a full day's drive.

The first time I tried the route, on toprope—with the rope secured above, so any falls were miniscule, letting me figure out the moves safely—I could barely get my feet on. I slotted my pick into a crack to my left and found a deep left foot that would take the front point of my crampon. This left me out of balance on my right foot, as the steel on that foot creaked and squealed against the rock, flailing for purchase. As I scratched and slipped, scratched and slipped, I was still so low that, really, I was just jumping off the wall to the ground. The rope didn't have time to come taut.

On subsequent attempts that day, I moved around to the right, more onto the face, where a series of precarious hooks and toeholds made me feel less secure but with a sequence I could follow. As I climbed, I looked down at my crampons, a solitary orange spike jutting from the toe of each boot. I just didn't know where to place this small piece of metal on the rock. I didn't know which gashes, dimples, and spots of texture would support me and which wouldn't.

The following year, I made it to the top of the route, but I would hardly call it an ascent. I hung on the toprope a lot, resting between moves, taking a long twenty minutes to reach the anchor. This time, the issue was my core strength. Placing a crampon point into a small scar in the rock, I'd tighten my core muscles and stretch up to find the next tool placement: perhaps a delicate hook of a small ledge. After exhausting myself searching for that placement, I completely relaxed my core, hanging on the tool, but also the rope.

A year later, it became an issue of grip strength. I had focused on core and body-tension exercises over the year, so I could keep my core more engaged, but I could not maintain the grip on my tools for the duration of my molasses-slow ascent.

Then, a "gap year," as I did little climbing due to a third ACL reconstruction on my right knee. (A simple approach hike with an ill-timed heel slip under a heavy pack had sent my upper body sideways and my lower body in the other direction.)

After the tear and surgery, I was unable to focus on mountaineering endurance until my knee was stronger and stable. So, I rotated knee-rehabilitation workout days with more mixed-climbing-specific upper-body work.

Finally, in the subsequent 2015 season, I was ready to make a lead attempt on the Ouray route, bringing the rope up with me and clipping it to the bolts in the rock and placing my own ice screws to safeguard a fall. The focus on technical-climbing strength, rather than mountaineering strength, had helped me become a competent, if unspectacular, ice climber and a serviceable, but marginally worse, rock climber: I could lead with a modicum of comfort on intermediate routes up to water ice 4 (WI4) where we may have vertical ice with good, intermittent rest stances, and up to Yosemite grade 5.9 (and the occasional 5.10) on rock, which by modern standards sits squarely at the weekend-warrior level of competence. On ice, I could work around my week right knee, making extra foot placements, but on rock, if the route demanded a high right foot, there was sometimes little I could do if another sequence wasn't available.

The route climbs a near-rectangular, rocky buttress that juts from the cliffside in two tiers, the first rising thirty or forty feet at a slightly overhanging angle through a maze of blocks, depressions, and sometimes ice meandering through a seam. The second tier rises another 60 to 70 feet to the cliff top, at an angle well short of vertical and which maintains a wash of water ice, looking like a cake with melted frosting.

That day, to reach the base of the climb, I wandered around to the right of the buttress. All but the top of the face was dry. As I evaluated the route for my lead attempt, I couldn't help but notice that the ground to its right rose along with the route's rightward traversing start. That meant the possibility of the rope stretching and me hitting the ground wasn't necessarily any less the higher I climbed. That had been fine when I was jumping back to the ground from the first two foot placements like on my earliest attempts. But the thought of falling off at twenty feet onto the rising slope was way less inviting.

As per usual, I was down in Ouray with our HAMS students, helping them immerse in the basics of ice climbing, for use on short, technical pitches on higher summits. A group of four of the better ice climbers had just finished trying out their "day two" skills on a water ice four (WI4) around the corner when I asked them to pull the toprope down so that I could tie in.

"You sure?" one student asked.

"You guys are done, right?" I asked, not wanting to cheat the students out of their time.

"Yeah, I think so."

"Cool—would you give me a belay?"

"Yeah. Sure will," the student said, and then yelled, "Rope!" as he pulled the toprope down. We both watched it slither to the frozen gorge floor with a whistling hiss, and then I carried the morass of rope around the corner to my project climb.

"Let me see your knot," the student said, after I tied in and got ready for my lead, racking my ice screws onto the clips hung on my harness.

I spun around to face him.

"Looks good. The rope is through the device and is locked; you're on belay," the student informed me, clicking the locked gate of his belay carabiner so that my ears could validate what he was telling me.

"Climbing," I replied.

"Climb on."

Placing the front point of my left crampon into the deep pocket that made the first foothold, I hooked a small ledge with my right tool. I stood up.

I was keeping a very straight, downward pull on my tool, so that it wouldn't spin and dislodge. I kicked my right foot out wide, my toes angled toward the rock. I slotted my right front point into a small depression along the edge of a rock bulge and pressed outward, locking in that foot. In rock climbing, we are often trying to pull in with our feet, recruiting our hamstrings and glutes to bring our hips into the wall. With mixed climbing, we are often pushing away, because a well-placed crampon point can withstand huge forces that friction, alone, cannot. I clipped the first protection bolt, dragging the line of neon-orange rope upward.

At the second bolt, the crack turned vertical. I swung my right leg wide, again, to give me some opposition to balance into. I placed my left tool over my shoulder, temporarily stashing it there, and then grabbed my right tool with my left hand. Next, I removed the free tool from my shoulder with my right hand, allowing me to hold my rightmost placement with my left hand while seeking a new handhold out right with the right tool.

Thirty feet higher, after more delicate but strenuous mixed climbing, I came to the first stretch of ice—the cruxy ice roof capping the lower tier. Driving my hips in, arching my back, and orienting the pull on my right tool (the more secure one) downward, I reached high with my left tool and gave a feeble swing. My shoulder was tired from my efforts thus far, and the high-pitched tinkling of small, falling ice fragments confirmed that I had not made a good placement.

I refocused, drew my elbow into my side, and then raised it again carefully, keeping the weight of my tool in a straight line directly over my shoulder. This made it feel lighter. I swung. *Thunk.*

A cold drop of sweat dripped down my temple and around the corner of my eyebrow; the sun beat down and created shimmers of silver on the ice above me. I heaved myself over the roof, the hardest climbing now below me. Five minutes later I was at the top anchor bolts, having made quick work of the final, less-vertical ice to complete the lead. Below me, the group of students decided their day might not be over, and waited their turn to scratch and claw and flail up the route on toprope, just as I had done all those years earlier.

As I was in the throes of anxiety between my initially discovered high white-blood-cell count and getting to a definitive diagnosis, Kristina and I were also having Kade and Connor tested academically. We presumed the boys were "gifted and talented," and the earliest the battery of tests could be administered was at age four.

It wasn't just that the boys were using complete sentences almost as soon as their first words were spoken. It wasn't the endless building of the next cardboard vehicle or fortress. It was beyond that. There was something in the way they thought: they were endlessly inquisitive and constantly searching for systems and patterns as they learned how the world worked.

We brought the boys to a contracted testing center with a waiting room that was split into three functions: a large and arcing reception desk, a series of low tables and equally low chairs with all sorts of three-dimensional puzzles and other "mind-enriching" toys, and a bookstore that had dense tomes with titles like *The Gifted Parenting Journey, Raising Your Spirited Child,* and *Differently Wired,* about the distinct needs of children growing up with brains that outpace their emotional control.

"Hello!" the receptionist sang out from behind her desk.

She seemed genuinely excited to see us, and added, "Hello, boys—good to see you again!"

We had brought the boys in the week before to get them acquainted with the surroundings and to have them meet the two professionals who would each take one of the boys to administer the testing.

My own testing flashed through my mind. I had been six. It had lasted all day.

I remember holding my mom's hand and climbing up to glass doors, surrounded by a brick façade, all set back from the street by a half-flight of weathered, concrete steps guarded by two metal railings.

I remember reading some paragraphs and being asked questions that demanded inference from the text: 'What do you think Judy was feeling after her conversation with Roger?'

I remember having to guess which shape, number, or picture would come next in a sequence; looking at two-dimensional images of unfolded, three-dimensional shapes and having to decipher what shape would be made when the folds were reapplied; logic problems; and placing odd trapezoidal slivers of wood into a wide-area outline of yet another shape, working until all the slivers fit perfectly to fill in the outline.

My proctor had been encouraging and gentile, in a green, button-down sweater and with brunette hair falling in shoulder-length wavy curls.

We'd stopped for lunch.

As the afternoon wore on, I started to push back on the constraints of the tests.

A green sleeve slid a paper in front of me that had a grid of one-inch by one-inch boxes formed by soft blue lines. On an eight-by-eleven-inch sheet, that made for something like seventy boxes, once accounting for margins. I was asked to draw a picture in each box. Each box had to be a different picture; the pictures could be anything, as simple as a circle.

"After we draw these pictures, we are going to choose one to write a story about. But you only have a minute to draw as many pictures as you can. Are you ready?"

"Yeah."

"Okay, start."

I began drawing a tiny landscape in the first small box. The moon in the upper corner was textured, with shadows. It was no artistic masterpiece but still a decent effort for a six-year-old.

"The time is half up. You really want to draw as many pictures as you can, as the goal of this part of the test is to see how many ideas you can come up with."

Still drawing in the same square, I moved on to a tree, reaching up to the moon.

"I'm kind of a perfectionist. Once I start working on something, I want it to be good." The use of the polysyllabic "perfectionist" was probably a clue as to my giftedness, but that was a consideration for a different module of the tests.

For now, I was staging a quiet rebellion. I was done.

While the receptionist at my sons' testing facility greeted us, I flashed back not only to my own testing but also paid a brief thought to my pending lab results. Already supercharged with my own anxiety, I bore down, trying not to pass it along to Connor and Kade.

I forced myself to look her in the eyes and squeeze out a "Hello."

Kristina moved forward and began chatting. I faded back behind a bookshelf and perused more book spines: *Parenting Gifted Children 101, The Whole-Brain Child,* and *Living with Intensity*. The boys stood close to their mom.

From the back, two women came striding forward. They wore button-down sweaters, just not green this time.

"Hi, Connor! Hi, Kade! How are you boys doing today!?" The boys each gripped one of Mom's legs.

"How are you doing today, guys?" my wife prompted.

"Good," each said unconvincingly.

One of the proctors squatted down to eye level with the kids. "You guys remember what we are going to do today?" she asked.

"Take a test," Connor replied.

"That's right. Take a test. But remember, there is nothing bad that can happen with this test. We're going to keep asking you questions. They will start out easy and then get hard. And if we get to questions that you can't answer, that's okay. We'll just move on to something else. Okay?"

"Okay," Connor replied.

The proctor cast a smiling glance at Kade, who also said, "Okay."

I moved from behind the bookcases to the small conclave happening in front of the reception desk and then lowered into my own squat in front of the boys. My surgically repaired knee doesn't particularly care for squats, but I did it anyway.

"That's right, guys. Nothing you can do but your best. There's no way to get this wrong. And just remember that the tests are supposed to get too hard. It's okay if you find something too tricky," I said.

*Tricky* was one of the boys' words. They used it in place of *difficult.*

"Okay, Dad," Kade responded. He still didn't look too convinced.

We had spent quite a bit of time over the last visit setting expectations around the testing procedures, trying to temper the boys' already-strong perfectionist streaks as we prepared them for the actual tests.

"Okay, Kade. You come with me," said the proctor.

"And you come with me, Connor," the other test administrator chimed in.

"Have fun, boys," I said, hoping that they would. I stood up as the boys marched past me.

My wife and I waved to them as they glanced back over their shoulders. Then we shared a knowing glance.

"We'll give you a call around noon," the receptionist reminded us. "The testing should be over by then."

Neither my brother, Bryan, nor myself followed traditional career paths. We share the same affliction of easy boredom and a desire to push our frontiers, though it manifests in different ways.

Bryan is brilliant. He may change complexion at the mention of it, but it is true. He works at the intersection of biology and artificial intelligence, his career as a university professor having morphed into that of research scientist. He also married seemingly impossibly young, at twenty-one, and he and his wife, Oralia, have been in love ever since. The early marriage along with his being two years older than me meant that his two kids, Istefan and Samara, were considerably older than my boys—already a teenager and a pre-teen, respectively, when Connor and Kade were born.

Bryan is also acutely aware of those moments when his curiosity ends. He once told me that he quit studying philosophy because no one could successfully argue why someone "had to be rational." For him, it was the collapse of this foundational principle that spun the entire discipline into absurdity. That isn't to say that there was no value in philosophical thinking, just that it could no longer serve as the bedrock of his education. Just as Kristina and I had bonded over Descartes' inability to re-establish reality after deconstructing it, Bryan could not re-establish enough virtues of philosophy (for him) after similarly taking it apart. Like a fire raging across the wilderness, when Bryan's curiosity on a topic is reduced to simmering embers, inevitably the embers blow to a new location, igniting a new curiosity about a new topic. Ever the critical thinker, he will then explore it until this newfound fuel is likewise exhausted.

In this way, he is not unlike me.

Bryan had six different majors in college; they ranged from music to the hard sciences. He also attended four different universities, earning two bachelor's degrees and a PhD. And then there were two more universities for three postdoctoral research stints before earning tenured professorship at still another university. Then he set off into government-sponsored research.

As kids, we got into brotherly mischief, of course. That green, clover-splattered lawn in Tennessee was also the site of our "bike jousting" exploits. Take your basic, kid-sized BMX bike, sit a nine-year-old Bryan on his bike at one end of the lawn and a seven-year-old me on my bike at the other, tuck the blade end of a hockey stick into each of our right shoulders like a rifle butt, and now have us both pedal at one another, aiming the stick shafts at each other's chests. That's bike jousting.

We got into fights. There are only two people I have ever been in a fight with. Both were when I was small, about five. Neither fight caused much damage, but both were very much from a place of intent. I knew I was fighting. For the first one, I pushed a bully down while standing at the school-bus stop on the corner down from our house. He left me alone after that. The second was my brother. I don't remember the cause or the resolution. I do remember aiming a flying drop kick at him. I leapt at him with both feet in the air; I was a horizontal projectile, driving upon him feet-first like I was a WWE wrestler. I connected, not to great effect, but enough to stop the fight. I think Bryan was startled more than anything.

But despite the mischief and the fights, there was always an undercurrent of support.

One gray fall day when I was in fifth grade, a few years after we'd moved back to Albuquerque, we were indulging in the tradition of backyard football, which we'd brought back from the Southeastern United States to Albuquerque.

We couldn't fit our games in the city's smaller, walled-off yards and so we would walk to one of the many community parks to play.

I was usually the youngest player. I was slowly starting to develop my "soccer friends" from various teammates in our organized leagues, but our "football friends" were the neighborhood boys from our previous stint in Albuquerque. They all lived about a ten-minute walk from our new location. Those boys just happened to be my brother's age, rather than mine.

That afternoon at the local park, the usual gang was there: the twins Tom and Clint, Ryan and his older brother Jason, and others who have been lost to my memory. Maybe ten kids in total.

The grass was starting to go dormant as the fall watering schedule was kicking in for the parks. Like all New Mexico soil, the ground was hard. I remember the feeling under my cleats—I always wore my soccer cleats for better grip—which hardly dented the ground under my light frame.

One of our regulars, I think it was Jason, had invited a still-older friend, a freshman in high school, probably four years my senior. He played on the freshman football team at La Cueva High School. This kid was trained. He was practiced. And he kicked everyone's butt.

On big fields, with only ten players, there is a lot of space, and his maturing body ate up the ground at a gallop. He was scoring touchdowns, making tackles, and thoroughly dominating.

My competitive reflexes were on high. This was like my soccer mentality: *Don't back down. If I go in soft, that's when I'll get hurt.*

To begin the second half, the team with my brother and I kicked off to the opposition: the La Cueva player's team. Tom leaned into the kick, and I raced down the field. The brown ball tumbled end over end against the light-gray sky. It fell right into the kid's arms. He began racing the ball back up toward us.

Still being unusually fast for my age, I was the first one to meet him. I came in hard, not backing down, not going in soft. The high-schooler extended an arm, bracing it straight and against my chin. Twisting toward me and down, he drove my head into the ground and scampered by. He spun another tackle and outraced my remaining teammates, taking the ball over our goal line.

I sat on the ground, watching the high-fives at the other end of the field.

I wasn't hurt, but Bryan came over and picked me up with an arm under each shoulder, nonetheless.

"Are you hurt?" he asked.

"Only my pride," I said. I still remember that exchange very clearly. It felt awkward coming out of my mouth, like some snippet of cheesy movie dialogue.

Bryan then walked me home. In effect, he declared the game over. He said something over his shoulder to the others as we walked away. I don't know what it was, and I've never asked.

Bryan hadn't even asked me if I wanted to go. He'd just put a hand on my shoulder that felt warm and reassuring on an unusually chilled and gloomy, high-desert day, and he walked the two of us off that green-brown field under a light-gray sky.

I first got the inkling something was wrong when I could almost hear my own pulse. My arteries would throb violently in time with each heartbeat. It reminded me of having head-cold congestion—all the sound from inside my body was echoing inside my skull.

Then there were chest spasms. These really scared me. At first, I mistook them for a heart arrhythmia, which can be anything from an inconvenience to a life-threatening condition.

I was lying in bed, trying to sleep (whenever you have to "try" to sleep, it probably isn't going to go well). I looked at the still fan overhead and studied the curves of the blades. My wife doesn't like sleeping with air flowing around her no matter the season, but especially not in winter. So, except for the vibrations of my own pulse, there was no motion anywhere. A dim light crept in from the streetlamp down the block from our bedroom window. I closed my eyes and immersed myself in the silence and darkness.

In that quiet and dark, I could feel my neck throbbing. Each throb would rock my head ever so slightly, and then the sound of my hair moving millimeters over the pillowcase would scratch at my ears. In the background, a deep, far-off bass-drum sound marked my body expanding and contracting with each push of blood.

I was going to see Sarah, my oncologist, the next day. We were starting to put together a timeline of my changing blood markers. How long would it take for my lymphocytic white-blood-cell count to double? How long until the neutrophils tanked and I would not be able to fight off infection? Were my platelet counts going to drop and cause anemia? My prognosis wasn't bad, but the relative speed of the disease's progression couldn't be abstracted. We would deal in actuals with each new blood draw.

I lay in bed, dreading tomorrow's appointment. I would be worse—that was by definition, as the disease progressed. How much worse was the question. Waiting. Getting weaker. It had now been two weeks since my diagnosis, and we were to have the follow-up appointment on the back of the prognosis phone call I had received in Tenneessee.

*Thump-thump. Thump-thump. Thump-thump.* I was fixated on the rhythm of my body, again. I opened my eyes to find something else to distract me. *Scratch-scratch. Scratch-scratch. Scratch-scratch,* as my head vibrated against the pillow.

Then the center of my chest balled into a knot. Quickly, it released. Well, that's what it felt like. At least now I wasn't noticing the throbbing and scratching anymore.

*Was that my heart!?* I thought. I placed my hand over my heart to see if I couldn't feel an irregular beat. At this point, I wasn't really being rational.

I held my hand on my heart and stared at the ceiling for the rest of the night.

At the following day's appointment, I was brought into the

examination room after the usual shuffle through the halls and stops at various waystations: a stop to get weighed, another to have my temperature taken.

In the exam room, I sat in one of the chairs next to the examination table while the nurse wrapped a blood-pressure cuff around my arm. She hit a button, and the cuff inflated. It exhaled in starts and stops until the device beeped three times and the cuff fell limp.

"145 over 92," the nurse said, matter-of-factly. "The doctor will be here in a moment." And then she left the room.

I had gone from having the blood pressure of a trained athlete to someone who was borderline in need of blood-pressure medication. The stress was omnipresent, and I walked about in a minor fog most hours of the day.

I could focus on tasks from moment to moment, but my brain, plagued by anxiety over my condition, was never fully quiet.

Sarah came into the room and sat down at the computer. "Your blood work looks really good. In fact, your white-blood-cell count is even down a little bit. That's going to happen—it will move up and down as your body fights off little bugs . . ."

"But it will trend up over time," I finished for her.

"Yes. But your other blood markers look great. Your immunoglobulin levels are all great. Your neutrophil and platelet counts all are normal. And, for what it's worth, you've been doing a good job with your cholesterol."

I appreciated this deft touch in her delivery. That last point brought levity but was actually still relevant.

We started talking about the longer time horizons and how much was still unknown. I could be years from treatment, but we wouldn't really be able to tell until we had more data.

"We shouldn't worry too much about treatment, yet. In fact, it's up to you how much you want to talk about it. Treatments are changing so fast, it's hard to know what will be available whenever you may need to get treatment."

I nodded, unsure how much space in my mind I wanted to allow for treatment conversations.

"But once we get there," she continued, "we will be able to talk about all sorts of options. You're young and healthy and will be eligible for all sorts of clinical trials. And you likely would be able to tolerate treatments far better than most; that will also open up options."

I nodded again.

"Have a seat up on the exam table." She pressed on the lymph nodes under my jaw, across my shoulder blades, and under my arms.

"Feels fine. Let's listen to your heart." At this point, I told her about the weird sensation I'd had in my chest the night before. She spent a bit more time listening.

"Well, your heart sounds very healthy. It could just be anxiety," Sarah said as she sat back down at the computer and motioned me back into the side chair.

"Yes, I've had a lot of that. It's obviously been pretty stressful."

"You've been seeing a therapist, right?"

"Yes."

"Well, I'd keep that up. It could also help you with your blood pressure. It's pretty high. We'll want to watch that. If it goes on too long, we may want to think about medications."

This was our second appointment and already the second time

in which Sarah had been reassuring about my physical condition, and how—in particular—my fitness would leave me better prepared to deal with any pending treatment as well as make me eligible for myriad clinical trials.

But now there was high blood pressure, and that could put me on drugs. And each drug I would be on contracted the range of treatment options.

I walked out into the parking lot. The sun danced off the ice crystals scattered here and there on the blacktop, remnants of an early-winter snowstorm. I heard them crunching under my feet.

*The stress is leading to anxiety, which is leading to high blood pressure,* I summarized in my head. And while we all are shortening our life expectancy when any of us have chronic stress, the peril felt far more immediate to me.

Now I was feeling stress about feeling stress.

*The football crew in the years before the run-in with the "high school football player." Jason is front left, facing away from the camera. Bryan is third from the right.*

CHAPTER NINE

# Forgiveness

I had been watching the weather for about three days. The chance of a storm was moderate. Many "moderate" days end up being perfect climbing weather. Now a day out from the climb, I started looking at radar future-casts. Where would the clouds and the precipitation be, and when?

It was early May, 2017, and Colorado was back into its usual monsoon pattern. I was starting to ramp up my snow-climbing outings because a) we were slowly exiting avalanche season on certain aspects, and b) I was now teasing the idea of a trip to the Himalaya with potential climbing partners. This particular trip—to Fletcher Mountain (13,958 feet) again, but this time from its connecting ridge with Drift Peak (13,914 feet)—would be about both. Our objective was to gain the summit of Drift Peak by its northwest ridge, traverse that first summit, make a hard left turn to continue to Fletcher, and finally return via the same route. In snow and ice conditions—and May certainly is still snowy and icy on the high peaks of Colorado—the route would have one short pitch of technical climbing up a roughly 30-foot step between Drift and Fletcher. We'd enjoy getting the ice tools out to hook our way up the rock covered with rime ice and with spindrift flooding the cracks. The route was short, only about 5.5 miles round-trip, which worked well with the tight weather window.

Radar suggested that a precipitation cell would be coming over the mountains at around 11:00 a.m., which is a bit early, with another potential cell around 2:00 p.m. The former was forecasted to stay west of the day's climb, trapped by another sub-range of mountains; the second cell was more likely to hit us.

To be safe, my friend, Dan, and I were planning to head up early, run the ridge, and be back well before noon, before the storm cells hit.

We met at a local park-and-ride and headed up Interstate 70 very early, well before the weekend traffic. I told him more about an unclimbed, 7,000-meter peak in the Himalaya that I was thinking about. I had been internet searching for unclimbed peaks for a few months, now, and had culled a list of four down to a preferred option in the Annapurna Massif north of Pokhara in Nepal—a peak called Gangapurna West. It had been attempted once from the south and once from the north, but with no successful summits. I was thinking about the southern route. By unclimbed-peak standards, there was a lot of information: all of three paragraphs in the *American Alpine Journal.* Having been to the Andes and Alaska, the Himalaya seemed next, plus being somewhere nobody had ever been was very appealing—I've always been drawn by exploration.

Dan is a conscientious climber and very safety minded. At the time, he worked for a manufacturer of protective industrial equipment, and he was a fellow High Altitude Mountaineering School instructor. The lecture he delivered to the HAMS class was on risk management. He also would be my successor to the directorship of the Advanced Crevasse Rescue Seminar, and we were working together to update the curriculum to adapt to modern equipment.

The climb was straightforward at the beginning. Using our snowshoes, we made quick work of the mild approach into Mayflower Gulch We gained the northwest ridge of Drift and then stashed our snowshoes as we headed up steeper and rockier terrain. At this point, it was still winter hiking as opposed to climbing, but steep and over snow-covered boulders.

As we made our way from northwest to southeast on Drift's ridge, the weather was blowing in from the east, a classic Colorado "upslope," and so was hidden by the mountain. Dan and I kept checking in regularly with those portions of the horizon we could see as well as kept up a constant dialogue about conditions.

The sun was breaking through the gray in spots, casting an eerie yellow light onto the white snow.

From Drift's summit, we looked east to the technical rock step. As the clouds continued to darken, we paused to discuss the situation.

"Looks like the weather is hitting early," I said.

"Well, we could just climb the step and head back. That might be all we have time for," Dan suggested.

We moved our way to the base of the pitch and unpacked the rope and technical gear.

I was in the process of handing the rack to Dan when I was hit by a blast of wind. Unable to make myself heard amidst the maelstrom, I slapped Dan on the shoulder and pointed off in the distance, to where charcoal-black clouds bore down on us, pushing a white wall of blowing snow. Despite it only being half-a-mile away, the fast-moving front had already completely obscured the top of Fletcher Mountain, and was consigning more and more of the ridge into oblivion as it moved towards us, swallowing tens of yards of ground per second.

"Woah!" was his reply.

"Let's get the hell out of here!" I yelled over the din.

We repacked quickly and clambered our way back up over the first peak, regaining our ascent ridge.

Thirty or forty feet past and down from our re-summit, all of our metal gear—the ice axes and ice tools, the gear on our harnesses—started to hum and crackle like the noise you hear coming off high-tension power lines.

The static electricity accompanying the storm was upon us, and we were still nearly two thousand feet above tree line. If lightning started, we were very, very exposed.

Dan and I huddled and decided we couldn't stay on the ridge, with its gradual descent. We needed to get down—now.

The northeast face of the ridge would take us down into the basin we'd approached from, but it was still plastered in snow. The southwest side was broken with rocky outcroppings, but it would drop us into the wrong basin, away from our stashed snowshoes. Still, from an avalanche perspective, the southwest side was clearly safer.

Knowing full well that we were abandoning our snowshoes, and so were in for a miserable wallow through deep snow once we were in the other basin, we headed down over the southwest face of the ridge. We moved from outcropping to outcropping, doing our best to avoid sinking up to our knees in the soft snow.

As we lost altitude in big chunks, our gear stopped humming after ten to fifteen minutes. After a half hour more of direct descent, we arrived at tree line, where the shelter of the trees broke up the wind. We could talk more easily.

“I think we made a good decision,” Dan said.

I heartily agreed. We’d taken the least bad of our three bad options, and we were now no longer in immediate danger of being electrocuted.

But I was still nervous. The basin we were in opened up into Clinton Reservoir, and we still had another storm cell coming. Would it arrive early, like the first? I did not relish the prospect of traveling next to, or over, frozen water in a lightning storm.

I kept these thoughts to myself, however, internalizing my worry.

By this time, we were definitely wallowing. The trees around us had kept the snow from melting, and helped catch snow drifts from the more typically prevailing western winds over the course of a long winter. The slope had eased to maybe 20 degrees, which robbed us of enough momentum to consider glissading (sliding down the slope). Dan, a few yards in front of me, took a step and sunk into the snow up to his hip. As he tried stand on his other leg, that foot sunk up to his thigh. He crossed his forearms and tried to create a larger surface area to press up on. His arms sank into the snow. He eventually rolled himself out of the hole, which had now swallowed more than half his body.

And these things, similarly, happened to me. Every two or three steps, I’d sink up to my knee or thigh or hip. Every attempt to climb out submerged new portions of my body. It was like hiking through quicksand.

Even though we were moving downhill, every step was a high step. We had to get a foot above our waist in order to exit the hole the previous step had created.

We stopped from time to time for water and snacks.

“I’m getting worried. Should we call for help?” I asked.

“I think we’re doing okay. It’s hard. I’m tired, but we’re fine,” Dan said. I didn’t mention the second storm cell that was potentially on the way.

After three hours of stepping, sinking, digging, and rolling, I was at an unprecedented level of fatigue. I resorted to feeble attempts at rolling down the hill, trying to spread my weight out across as wide a surface area as possible.

“I really think we might need some help,” I repeated.

“I don’t think so. This sucks, but we can make it out,” Dan said.

I had no doubt that we could, given enough time, but would we have that time? Would the second major storm cell slam us at the mouth of the reservoir, pinning us in place?

Just as I had once done, running through the halls of my house and dodging a maniac’s flashing knife, I was now going to act.

With Dan ahead of me again, I silently wrote a message on my satellite communication device, directed at the members of my climbing community in the device’s contact list.

“Need search-and-rescue support. No injuries. Descending into the wrong basin from our approach in order to avoid lightning. Have no snowshoes. Need flotation.”

I typed and then hit send, pinning our GPS waypoint to the message. But I voiced none of this.

At around 2:00 p.m., we were at Clinton Reservoir. We were now low enough that the tree wells were bare on the east and south sides and filled with snow on the north and west sides. The snow imperceptibly alternated from firm to soft and leg catching as we worked from tree to tree. Soon we began rolling from tree to tree.

Eventually, the earth in front of us was brown, and we walked to the road at the far end of the reservoir.

Overhead, the sky was crystal blue.

At the road, a sheriff towing a snowmobile and a search-and-rescue (SAR) pickup truck were waiting.

Dan was rightfully shocked when they greeted us.

I sheepishly said something, thanking them for meeting us and apologized for wasting their time and spreading their resources thin.

"We'd rather you call us before it gets desperate. We like these kinds of calls," the SAR volunteer said.

They beckoned us to hop into their vehicles and then drove us up the road to our original trailhead and our car.

En route back to town, Dan and I stopped at the "Dam Brewery" in Dillon for a beer and a meal.

"I owe you an apology," I said. "I should have told you that I was calling for help."

"Yeah, I get that we all are going to do what we need to do to feel safe," Dan said. "I would have tried to talk you out of it, but we could have at least had that discussion."

He was right. I had let him down. As I explained my rationale, I omitted my concern about the second storm cell . . . the one which never came and about which I hadn't warned him, even though I knew it was a possibility. I definitely didn't talk about my reflex to act alone and keep my thoughts internalized, both arising from my childhood trauma.

This wasn't a partnership. This wasn't how a team stays safe. This wasn't how you respect another person. Dan forgave me for my transgression, and we continued to partner on the transfer of the directorship of the crevasse-rescue classes. But Dan did not come with me to the Himalaya.

The next week, I returned to the same mountain. Wearing my wife, Kristina's, snowshoes, I slowly worked my way up the snowy slopes, amongst a smattering of trees, to a wind-bare ridge where Dan and I had cached our own snowshoes the week before. Picking up the planes of metal and black plastic, I strapped both sets to my yellow pack and headed down.

I did this alone. That day, the sky was blue but for a few milky drifts of clouds.

Connor was sitting on a stool made from a concave piece of deeply stained wood, about the depth and width of a schoolyard swing. Black iron rose from the ground to meet the seat, positioning the user's arms level with the counter-height kitchen table in matching wood tones.

Kade ran by and gave Connor a shove. Connor flew off the stool and onto the hardwood floor. A sickening *thwack* echoed through the room, quickly followed by a scream and cries of pain.

We were in a rented condo in Durango, Colorado, midway through a summer tour of a few locations in the state that Kristina and I were considering as a potential new residence.

Kade immediately ran into the back bedroom as I stomped after him.

"Kade William!"

"I'm sorry, Dad."

Still venting, I ignored his apology. "Why did you do that!?"

"I don't know."

Calming myself, I simply directed him, "You need to stay in here for a bit."

Kade's response surprised me. He didn't say, "I know," or even shout, "No!" Rather, he asked, "Is Connor really hurt, Dad?"

Not having assessed Connor, all I could manage was a straightforward, "Well, it probably hurt . . . so, yeah."

Kristina picked Connor up and sat him on her lap to calm his cries, but they never really abated; they muted, but did not dissolve the way they usually would. He was antsy and lethargic all at the same time: shifting position on my wife's lap every couple of seconds, slowly folding his chest to his knees and then unfolding again, tilting his head far back and then righting it. My wife spoke soothingly and lovingly to him.

Then, he threw up.

I knew what this meant. I've had four concussions myself, all but one from my soccer-playing days.

As a ten-year-old, I had another player miss heading the ball and head-butt me in the eye socket instead. As a teen, I went up for a header that I never got to because the defender took out my legs, spinning me upside down to land chin-first. (That one ended with seven stitches in my chin, on top of the concussion.) In my twenties, I dribbled past a defender heading down my attacking right wing. Seeing danger in the attack, the defender clipped my feet as he trailed behind me. I spun and landed on my butt but whiplashed the back of my head onto the artificial turf. And in my late thirties, I was training my upper body by climbing the underside of a ladder leaning against my garage wall using only my arms (in effect, "campus boarding," in rock-climbing parlance) when the ladder dislodged. I still don't know how, but it nonetheless deposited me on the concrete with a two-inch gash running vertically down the side of my face along the orbital bone of my right eye (yes, the same one that had been head-butted). That's about all I remember of that one. That, and more stitches.

I'd never thrown up, but I was experienced with concussions and therefore well versed in the potential symptoms.

We got our phones up and started finding local hospitals in our insurance network—something every parent wants to do, first, when the goal is to help their kid feel better.

At the hospital, they decided to run a computerized tomography (CT) scan.

The room was like every CT-scan room I've been in (and, yes, I've been in a few): off-white linoleum that is easy to clean; those same white, rectangular, drop-ceiling roof tiles dotted with tiny holes; and recessed fluorescent lights being the only lighting other than the green and red status lights on the oversized donut that is the CT scanner itself.

It's a painless procedure unless they run contrast dyes, which require an IV, with its irksome feeling of a needle in the vein. Connor didn't need any contrast, but even at age four he knew he felt off, knew he was at a hospital, and knew he was going to be effectively "pinned down" for some procedure.

While in his agitated but slow-moving state, Connor wrestled with the technician, who needed to put him in a brace to immobilize his head and neck.

My stomach turned, a little, out of empathy for my boy.

While I wasn't particularly worried about Connor having a serious brain injury, I had been through enough medical procedures myself to feel the fatherly dissonance of both wanting Connor to simply solider through this pretty mild scan while also wanting to help make his anxiety go away. What's more, we had been through an even worse version of this exact scenario about six months earlier.

We had taken a trip to Westlands Park, in affluent Greenwood Village, one suburb to the east of us, specifically for a treehouse that was there and which we thought the kids would love. Kade had been heading up into a treehouse on something that could best be described as a cross between a ladder and a staircase. It looked like a staircase, with pressure-treated planks suspended from a frame made of two-inch steel pipes. But it was steep like the between-deck ladders on a naval vessel. Kade slipped on a wet stair step, toppled backward down six steps, and halted with a similar *thwack.* The vomiting had started minutes later.

At the hospital, Kade had become so agitated by the prospect of being immobilized and sent into a claustrophobia-inducing tube that he eventually had to be sedated.

So, given my own past experiences, and the experience with Kade, the pit in my stomach grew as Connor resisted the brace.

Kristina and I talked to him, trying to assure him that nothing would hurt, but that he had to be still, "and this brace will help you be still."

As I tried to calm Connor with my words, I was trying to calm myself with my thoughts, but it wasn't working. I was getting agitated thinking about an innocent being harmed. Connor was just sitting on a stool when his brother, as little kids do, thoughtlessly pushed him. When I was a teenager, the family dog had just walked into the back room at the wrong time, getting herself stabbed, her suffering most likely assuring my own survival.

I didn't do a very good job of calming my son, as my internal energy was far from serene. Kristina eventually soothed Connor, who finally allowed the technician to put on the brace and insert him into the strange cylinder that took pictures of his brain from all angles. He didn't require medication. I stepped out of the room and gathered myself in the antiseptic, white hallway.

The CT scan came back clear, meaning we were likely only looking at a concussion. I knew how to handle that. I made sure no screens were on when we got back to the condo. I drew the curtains and kept the lights dim. I shuttled water and crackers to my son, helping him ease his stomach back into order.

I spent the night checking in on the rise and fall of Connor's chest as he slept. In the morning, I made bland toast and spiked a juice with tonic water to further calm his stomach.

Without being asked, Kade dotingly poured the juice.

"What do you hope to accomplish with therapy?"

I was thirty years old, and I was in therapy for the first time in my life. It was early 2007, and mental health care was still far from normalized. For the sake of my appointments, I was commuting from the sleepy mountain town of Bailey, southwest of Denver—where I was living and starting a business after graduate school—into the college town of Boulder—with its high concentration of PhD therapists.

"I'm dating a woman who has an eating disorder. I don't know how to handle it and am not so much worried about trying to help as I am worried about doing things that will make it harder for her."

That's how it started, but this wasn't what therapy would be about for me.

Elyse, my therapist, was a petite woman with straight, shoulder-length hair that she blow-dried up to create volume. She had kind eyes that tilted upward at the corners so that it looked like she was always smiling.

Elyse's office building looked like it had been made from a Hollywood production designer's concept drawing. The complex was inspired by Japanese *shinden-zukuri*—or sleeping-hall—architecture. Small groups of conjoined offices were separated by courtyards with tiny ponds, river rock, and ground-covering vegetation. A lazy creek meandered by. Each complex was made of rich redwood planks stacked horizontally upward from underground parking, elevating the first floors so that each began a half-flight of stairs above ground level. The second floors were narrower than the first floors, with the sidewalls angling to meet pitched roofs, vaguely reminiscent of the Buddhist pagodas in Kyoto. The interior furnishings shared a similar aesthetic: minimalist furniture of carefully honed wood; small, desktop rock gardens; and muted light behind redwood blinds.

"What do you know about your girlfriend's disease?"

"She's diagnosed bipolar. She's gone through phases of anorexia, restrictive eating, and bulimia . . . and she self-harms."

Elyse sat forward slightly. "What type of self-harm?"

"She cuts. A razor blade on her forearms."

"And you are worried about her self-harming?"

"Well, yeah. But it's not the self-harm, specifically. I mean, that's the scariest thing, but all the eating-disorder issues are harm, too—just slower." I sat back and tilted my head up, looking for the right words. "It's that I don't know how to interact with her in a way that doesn't set her off. She's told me that when I am supportive, she wants to prove just how 'sick' she is to me, and when I show frustration, she feels worthless and falls into a spiral."

I leaned forward again, expecting the inevitable, "And how does that make you feel?"

"What do you think your role is in her recovery?" Elyse said, surprising me.

I took a long pause. I had never really asked myself that question. "Well, I don't think I can create her recovery. She has to do that. But I'm here, and even if I don't know how to help, I feel like I can learn how to help—and *should* help."

It was only a few weeks later when Elyse discovered a pattern. In college, ten years earlier, I had moved in with young woman who had a Disneyesque wicked stepmother. Her father had been a caregiver to my girlfriend's mother for the duration of their marriage, her mom contracting Lupus right around the time of my girlfriend's birth. When my girlfriend enrolled in college, her mother passed away from complications. Her father was quick to remarry, and the new couple had "mutually agreed" to cut off my girlfriend financially.

"And is that why she moved in with you?" Elyse asked.

"It was a factor, for sure. Things had gotten bad with her stepmom; plus, she'd quit her job, and her grades were starting to slip. I thought if she could focus more on school, it would remove some pressure. I had my tutoring job, so that helped."

"And you were twenty?"

"Yeah, twenty."

"So, you were taking care of her?" Elyse nudged me.

"Well, financially, yes." I paused. "Yeah, and I guess emotionally, too. But that's part of what relationships are. We *should* be taking care of each other."

"Are they? Do people take care of each other or do they support each other?"

"They take care of each other, sometimes. We all have hard times," I countered.

"For how long?" The question hung in the air.

Now a few months later, the spring blooms had brought pops of bright green to the mature trees lining Elyse's office complex. The low afternoon sun drove piercing rays of light through the half-closed blinds as Elyse called me out: "What are you avoiding?"

"I'm not sure what you mean."

"Well, you seem to spend a lot of time with women who are working on something. What are *you* working on?" She paused. "You had a traumatic event in your childhood, right?" she said, referencing being stabbed.

"Yeah, but it's not like I think about it every day," I said.

"How often do you think about it?"

"I don't know. Not often. I've got a lot going on, and I'm far more worried about her cutting than my fifteen-year-old stab wounds."

"Yes, and how often do you think about being stabbed?"

"I don't know. Every couple of months?"

"And you said she cuts every couple of months?"

"Yeah."

"When she cuts, how do you feel about that? Do you remember being stabbed?" Elyse probed.

"Not necessarily in the moment. At first, it's just triage. It's usually not that bad, but it's been deep enough to need stitches a few times. Maybe after the fact, I might recall being stabbed a bit more often."

"And what do you think about when you think about it?"

"I don't relive it or anything. It's more like a—I don't know—like a physical empathy. It's kind of like I can imagine the steel against the skin, the hot and cold sensations as warm blood releases and hits cool air."

"And that's not reliving it?"

"The emotions don't feel the same, and I'm not hyper-focused like I was then. I'm not running images through my head of being stabbed or anything," I said in my defense.

Elyse came back around to the point: "So, you're not working on processing it? Have you told anyone about when it still shows up in your life?"

"It was fifteen years ago—I *should* be over it," I said. "Besides, I knew that bringing it back up would just be hard for everyone, me, my relationships, my parents, whoever."

"*Should* is an interesting word. You use it a lot. Do you thank *can* and *should* are the same thing?"

"Well, of course not, but . . ."

That day, I didn't have an answer that wasn't literal. Of course 'can' and 'should' are different. But over the course of a few months, I discovered that I liked to ignore myself. I buried my need to heal because I didn't think I should still *have* to heal. This denial manifested in non-communication that made any true partnership hard to come by. In the following weeks and months, I talked to my parents much more about that day, fifteen years ago, and about the subsequent fifteen years, as well.

I met Kristina a half-year later, and we started dating about two years after that. I talked to her about the stabbing early in our courtship, making sure she knew exactly what had happened to me.

Daylight poured through our living-room window, the same one in front of which I had jotted down questions for my oncologist. On the catwalk across from and above the window, I dashed back and forth. First, I was in Connor's room, taking out sets of underwear and pajamas and shirts—so many shirts. Then the same in Kade's room.

I stuffed clothing into two backpacks.

*Oops. Forgot the children's medicines* (acetaminophen, ibuprofen, antihistamines), *just in case.* I glided down the half-flight of stairs to the main level and into the kitchen. The white cabinet door reflected light as I swung it open and grabbed the Ziploc bag we kept stocked with their medicines, ready for travel.

It was Christmas Eve—twenty days, to the day—after my diagnosis, and we were heading to my parents' home, about an hour north of us, across the Denver Metro in Broomfield, where they'd settled after a stint in Oregon to be near my brother, his wife, and his (then) young kids while my brother finished up his first post-doctorate.

Kristina was stuffing bags into the back of the car, moving in and out of the door with our dog, Baxter, the newest member of our family after Ayer had passed away. Baxter was a rescue puppy from New Mexico, an energetic Aussie mix with perpetually shedding brown hair and white, speckled feet like a Spaniel. He was currently leashed to Kristina's waist so that he could not chase all of the bunnies and birds and walkers and . . .

I handed her the kids' backpacks and headed back up the stairs to pack my own bag and get the boys' Christmas presents, which were tucked back in the upper corner of our closet to keep them from the kids' prying eyes. Suddenly, I came to an abrupt stop, frozen mid-stance. I walked over to the bed and flopped down into a seat, sinking in the memory foam.

I just sat there until Kristina came up wondering why the supply train of luggage had run dry.

"C'mon, we gotta go," she said.

I remained seated with shoulders slumped, and then looked up at her, tears starting to well.

"What's wrong?"

"I . . ." I started to cry. "I didn't get you a Christmas present."

And with that, I broke down into heaving sobs. I had not cried since my diagnosis.

Kristina knelt beside me and put a hand on my thigh as my head bobbed up and down, my chest heaving. "It's okay," she said.

"No– it's– not– okay," I replied, still sobbing.

"Really, it's been a lot. It's okay. You're allowed to not have it all together."

"I'm– so– sorry," I said, trying to increase the interval between sobs.

I had done it again. I had been in survival mode for three weeks, and my world had shrunk down to blood draws, doctor visits, and the scrambled contents of my own head. My world had become so small because, despite my best efforts, I still wasn't sharing with those I loved—and who love me. I was sharing information, sure, but I wasn't sharing the experience or my emotions.

"I'm really sorry. You don't deserve . . ."

"It's okay," she cut me off. "Really. Please. It's really okay, Jason. I love you, and I know this has been hard. We'll get through it, and this—today—this doesn't matter."

She stood up and hugged me. I folded into her embrace; my head collapsed on her chest.

I've brought up that Christmas Eve a few times with Kristina. Sometimes I allude to it as I talk about cancer or other mistakes I have made, since. Sometimes I confront it head-on and apologize—again.

Every time, Kristina gives me a half-smile or a hug, followed by a reminder that "Really, it's okay."

I sort of believe it. I absolutely believe that it is okay with her. She forgave me the minute I told her. She forgives me, again, every time I bring it up. I'm not sure I'm okay with it, although I know I need to learn to be.

*Dan climbing out from another post-holed step after the storms had passed and we neared the bottom of our descent from Drift Peak (13,914').*

CHAPTER TEN

# Fear

Most years, the route up the north side of 14,411-foot Mount Rainier via the Emmons Glacier doesn't contain any near-vertical climbing demanding front-point techniques with your crampons. It is, however, heavily crevassed, with Rainier being the most heavily glaciated peak in the Lower 48.

Unlike the crevasse-free snowfields of Colorado, glacier travel typically requires your being connected to your climbing partner(s) by a rope, even for relatively gently hikes up the flanks of a mountain. You stay "roped up" in case a partner breaks through a snow bridge or falls into a hidden crevasse. In those cases, the rest of the teammates drop to the ground, jam their ice axes into the snow, and try to arrest the fall so that the fallen climber—and indeed the whole team—is not sucked into the depths. Then, through feats of minor engineering, the fallen climber can either ascend the rope or be hauled back out.

On moderate glacial ascents, it is typical to rope up into teams of three, or even four, people to create the weight and force necessary from two or three people to stop a single falling climber.

The year Kristina and I climbed the Emmons Glacier as students in the High Altitude Mountaineering School, however, the mountain did have a more technical section that required true ice climbing.

There was a lengthy crevasse, too long to navigate around, bisecting the route about one thousand vertical feet above high camp. This section asked climbers to ascend three stories' worth of 70-degree glacial ice and then take a four-inch-wide catwalk on a leftward and upward traverse for one hundred feet. From there, climbers stepped over the crevasse itself, using a two-foot-wide by eight-foot-long snow bridge.

On our ascent, we did this section in the dark, battered by a driving wind off the top of the mountain.

The day would get harder.

I was the lead climber on the first rope of what were three total teams (or three ropes) of students. In essence, of the twelve of us, I was in front. It was my responsibility to find a safe path over or around any crevasses, avoiding the few seracs.

To be fair, the Emmons Glacier is well traveled, so there was boot-packed snow to suggest the best route. However, routes on active glaciers change day-to-day, so I had to remain focused.

After we unlocked the path over the technical crevasse, the rest of the ascent was fairly uneventful. We zigzagged our way up, alternating between lower-angled terrain and a few sections of compacted and crusted glacial terrain that approached 40 degrees.

As the sun came up, the rising air from the heated ground kicked up the wind even harder. Those of us with goggles pulled them down over our eyes to protect against the wind-born ice crystals. The sun rose off of our left shoulder, bathing Rainier's snow-and-ice-clad upper flanks in a brilliant magenta. I sunk into a rhythm of crunches and squeaks, the snow grudgingly accepting each step of my crampons and each plunge of my axe as we toiled up the giant stratovolcano.

Right about the time my team of four was walking the crest of Mount Rainier's crater to stand on the summit, my radio—strung to the shoulder strap of my pack—crackled to life.

"Rope team one, this is rope team two. We have a climber unable to continue. Can you descend and pick him up? Sharon is going to stay with him, but the rest of us are going to continue on to the summit."

"Team two, this is team one. Yes, we can. We are about to head down," I responded.

We hurriedly took a single summit photo and then began our descent. This is where our group's relative inexperience, including my own, let us down. And as it often does, it all came down to communication.

I figured, given that the rest of rope team two was still headed up, that whatever had happened with the halted climber must not have been that serious. Plus, they had Sharon with them to help. (Sharon was the one instructor with us that day—the eleven other climbers were students. The other instructor on the trip had suffered heart palpitations and a terrible night's sleep while in camp and didn't make the summit attempt.)

We made our way down about one thousand feet, which took about thirty minutes. It would take rope team two about an hour to climb up those same thousand feet, maybe a bit longer with the heavy headwind.

We were just below 13,300 feet in elevation as I headed over a mellow rise and began descending one of the steeper, 40-degree sections. To my right, a massive, triangular piece of rock, called the Steamboat Prow, jutted up from some 4,000 feet below. Our camp was, more or less, right at the base of that formation. To my left, I could see all the way into Puget Sound. The strong winds had blown the sky free of clouds.

Making a switchback turn, I began heading toward a strange snow mound directly in front of my bearing. I couldn't recall any snow mounds from the ascent. This didn't make any sense.

As I came closer, I caught a glint of silver reflecting off an aluminum snow picket. That led my eyes up to a pop of forest-green breaking out from the snow. It was a jacket. The mound was people—two people, Sharon and the student. They were caked in snow on the upslope side, which faced into the wind. Sharon had let the student sit on both backpacks to try to keep warm while she sat on the ice.

"How are you!" I yelled over the wind.

"I can't see!" shouted back the student climber, his breath stuttering from the cold.

"You can't see at all?!"

"Just light and dark!"

Later, we would find out that the climber hadn't worn goggles, and the strong wind and blowing ice had combined to dry out his eyes after a fairly recent laser eye surgery. However, at this point, I thought he was simply snow-blind, a condition in which your corneas sunburn, rendering you essentially sightless for a few days.

"How about you!?" I called to Sharon.

"Ready to get back to Camp Muir!" Sharon replied.

"What?! *Camp Muir?!"* I asked as verification.

"Yeah. How far are we above it?"

Camp Muir was on the south side of the mountain, on the more commonly climbed Disappointment Cleaver route. We were on the north side. Being the instructor on the mountain, she knew that. I concluded that Sharon was at some stage of hypothermia. We had to get her moving. There was no waiting for anyone else to come and help.

Derek was the back man of our rope team, which is where you often put the most dependable and safety-conscious climber when the group is on the descent. He was also a firefighter with mountain search-and-rescue experience. I asked him to help me build an anchor, to which we temporarily attached each member of our team so that we could add new knots onto our rope for our two new members. We would now descend as six instead of four.

We put Sharon in the middle, a position where she'd be supported by the climbers in front of and behind her. We then placed the blinded student at short-rope distance, just a couple of feet, in front of Derek, who would anchor us, and just a couple feet behind Aaron, a sturdy, calm, former military man. They would keep their segments of rope taut to the blinded climber, helping him walk and quickly arresting any slips.

As Derek was clipping Sharon and the student to the new knots, Kristina turned to me and said, "I'm scared."

"Me too," I replied.

That was it. Matter-of-fact.

Kristina and I began rummaging through packs. We redistributed weight from Sharon's and the student's packs to lighten their loads.

Finally, all six of us pressed to our feet and began marching down.

From my position at the very front, I could feel the student stumble, slip, and struggle as he learned to walk without vision, on steep and uneven terrain as well as on the slick glacial ice. I imagine Derek and Aaron were being tugged all over the place. I focused my eyes forward and trusted them with their jobs.

Reaching the significant crevasse from our ascent, engulfed in sunlight rather than shrouded by blackness, I could now clearly see the obstacles for the first time. The first component would be the snow bridge over the crevasse.

I crossed the bridge and decided not to use the four-inch-wide catwalk on the other side. We would walk the very peak of the crevasse's lower edge. This would make a fall more dangerous, as you could theoretically plummet into the crevasse if you fell upslope, but the footing was wide enough for two feet, side by side, reducing the likelihood of a fall.

I placed a snow picket at the end of the snow bridge, clipped my rope through it, and took the left-hand turn along the edge of the crevasse's peak. I placed another two pickets along the peak, about thirty feet apart, clipping the rope through each as I moved. We now had three placements on the rope for the six of us, forming a "running belay." As Derek and our blinded student reached the snow bridge, I came to the top of the seventy-degree ramp from which we would exit this technical section. I stopped and anchored myself in. *Picket number four.*

Kristina drove her axe spike into the ground, providing another anchor point. Sharon did the same, behind Kristina. Aaron knelt on the snow bridge and then turned to face the student and the upslope of the mountain. Derek knelt behind the student. So situated, Aaron and Derek grabbed and placed the student's feet as he took each step across the snow bridge, all the while selflessly courting a bridge collapse from their combined weight.

Making the left turn at the first picket, Aaron managed the student's knot, unclipping the rope from the picket so that he could pass through. Derek stomped the picket, dissolving its bond with the snow, and then lifted it out and slung it over his shoulder.

For twenty minutes the sequence repeated: place your feet along the knife's edge with the crevasse on one side and a seventy-degree slope on the other, manage the ropes, remove the pickets.

Sharon had improved: the work of the descent had sped up her heart rate and returned some warmth to her core and limbs.

Seventeen hours after we'd left, we returned to camp at the base of the Steamboat Prow to banging pots and pans of congratulations.

The student, unable to see a dug-out (and now-unoccupied) tent platform, took his first real fall of the day, three feet down and onto the compacted snow. After he regained his feet, we led him to his own tent and helped him remove his crampons. He crawled inside and immediately fell asleep.

Winter typically comes late in Colorado. On average, the state's snowiest month is March. And so it was in 2020, the winter after my return from the Himalaya. The snow was still lingering on the ground when our state's schools, and our boys' preschool, closed in an effort to help contain the spread of the COVID virus.

Schools were officially closed as of Monday, March 23, 2020. In his announcement, Governor Polis said, "We are acting boldly and swiftly together to protect the health and safety of all Coloradans. The science and data tell us this will get worse before it gets better."

We knew it was coming, and we could tell it was going to be bad. Colorado was a bit behind the schools on the coasts, as the virus made its way from overseas through our costal airports and migrated in toward the center of the country. Atlanta, one of the largest school districts in the nation, had closed a week-and-a-half earlier. Stories of mounting death tolls were already hitting the news. In fact, three days after Colorado schools shut down, the *New York Times* would report the first of the refrigerator trailers arriving outside a New York hospital to store bodies.

Scientists didn't yet know how COVID was transmitted, and in case it was transmitted by touch, doctors were posting videos on how to wash groceries by modifying the non-sterile-to-sterile process used to clean surgical instruments.

Taking cues from other respiratory viruses, like the flu, and combining that with anecdotal evidence that nursing homes were being especially hard hit, doctors and public-health officials were already starting to suggest that those with "comorbidities," a fancy word for other medical conditions, should be more careful. But nobody really knew what "more careful" could or should entail.

The same day that the state's schools closed, the City of Denver issued a "stay at home order." The state would follow suit three days later.

Our family had already been sheltered in place, thanks to a big spring snowstorm a few days earlier that had made the roads difficult to travel. As the storm abated, Connor and Kade had bundled up into their big puffy jackets and snow pants and headed out into the front yard to make snow angels. I went out with them and recorded a few videos.

As they made angels, the bright blue of their jacket torsos burst with color against the pure white snow, which shimmered in the cloud-covered half-light. The legs on their black snow bibs were comically wide, and all the boys could do was roll their toes from one side to the other, rather than separate their legs and close them again. They waved their arms over their heads and back down to their sides exuberantly, until Kade finally sat up and exclaimed, "Phew! I'm exhausted!"

Both boys sat up in the snow, surrounded by their snow angels.

"Are you guys happy about the snow day?"

"Yeah. The snow is great!" Connor replied.

"You guys know that you aren't going back to school on Monday, and that you may not be going for a while, right?"

"Yeah," Kade said.

"Yeah," Connor added on.

"But you know we're still going to work on a little schoolwork, right? Mom has some reading for you to do."

"Yeah, Mom told us," Connor said with a nod.

As the boys shed the wet clothes in the house, my wife was busy organizing folders in the living room.

When the results of the boys' academic testing had come back, revealing that they were, indeed, "advanced," particularly in terms of reading and comprehension, Kristina had taken it upon herself to research preschool literacy programs in order to supplement their schooling.

The boys had also tested as being prone to emotional dysregulation due to stimulation through colors, noise, and transitions in activities. We had had some experiences with a few different preschools, at this point, and it had become clear that a school's ability or willingness to deal with very bright children, who simultaneously struggled with classroom environments, varied.

Now, with the pandemic, it seemed like the least we could do was make sure that the one learning skill upon which so many others depend—reading—would not fall too far behind.

Kristina had ordered a few books and was busily collating worksheets into bite-sized lessons.

"I'm planning on doing an hour-or-so of reading with them before my online meetings start each morning," she said.

"You think that fits in with your schedule?"

"It'll be a bit tricky at first, but it should work."

"If the boys join me for a workout, what time are you going to need them up to do their lessons?" I asked.

"If they're up by 7, we can get them fed and then do some reading."

I watched her slide some worksheets into a red folder for Kade. Then she picked up a blue folder and did the same for Connor.

Looking through the picture window out into our front yard, I saw that the sky had darkened. There was no longer enough light to make the snow sparkle.

"You know, we might not want to send them back," I said. "If Atlanta is any indicator, the schools are going to be breeding grounds for this virus." What was unsaid was: *for me . . . for my safety.* But as I broached the topic, a pit sank in my stomach for the first time, a pit that would haunt me for several more years.

I was about fifteen months post-diagnosis. I was still in the "watching and waiting" phase, having my blood checked every three months to monitor the steadily increasing white-blood-cell count and, thankfully, watch my other blood markers hold steady. Early medical guidance around COVID had already called out cancer patients as a group that needed to be particularly vigilant, but that's because the treatments themselves wrecked the patients' immune systems. Well, what if your immune system wasn't wrecked by drugs but was wrecked because you had *an immune-system cancer*? At this point, no one knew, but the signs sure looked bad.

"We'll see. We've been talking about homeschooling anyway. It's so hit-or-miss with the particular school and a particular teacher," Kristina said.

And there we had it. My safety and the boys' education were likely best served by the same decision of looking inward toward our family and our caring for each other. After all, we knew what was best for us.

But . . . maybe those things wouldn't align. Then what?

Lying in bed that night, I stared at the ceiling, again. I sensed my neck throbbing against my pillow, again. And again, I folded my hands over my chest below the motionless fan, feeling the cold radiate in through the poorly-insulated bedroom window. The darkness rendered the room and its contents colorless. The textures on the ceiling and the folds of the covers that draped my body turned to grays and blacks and deep charcoal tones. I couldn't escape a very specific thought: *it isn't the boys' job to protect me.*

"He'll need to know about this so that he can help manage it. There is no way to monitor everything he eats."

I don't know if that's exactly what my pediatrician said to my mother about my food allergies when I was a kid, but it was definitely the general message.

We discovered I had food allergies when I was two. I have

no recollection of the incident that led to this revelation, and, interestingly, my mom almost always talks about it vaguely. I think maybe she doesn't want to relive the trauma.

Just because I know how old I was, I know we were living in Martinez, California, a forty-five-minute commute north and east of San Francisco, some months before moving to Albuquerque. My mother was cooking something with walnuts; putting a chopped portion against my lips, I immediately swelled up in my face and chest. My mom dashed to get the Benadryl and poured some down my throat, which was enough to get me to the hospital. Once there, injected adrenalin finished the work of returning my body's immune system to order.

We didn't know the name then, but we know the name now: anaphylactic shock. Your throat closes up and you are unable to breathe.

Benadryl—and my mom's quick thinking—definitely saved my life. But on only a couple of rare occasions, my mother didn't stop the story, there.

She's gone on to talk about why there was Benadryl in the house, because there hadn't been previously. This was the 1970s, well before any broader public understanding of severe allergies to peanuts, tree nuts, and the like.

We had Benadryl on hand because Bryan had gotten stung by a bee and had a reaction. My brother, to hear my mom tell it, had never had a reaction to anything up to that point. But on some warm day, scampering about as four-year-olds do, he had stepped barefoot on a bee, which responded by stinging him. His foot had swelled up, painfully, and when my mom took him to the doctor, he'd recommended that we always have Benadryl around for my brother's newfound allergy.

And so there it was, my first near-death experience.

This particular experience, however, never really stopped. It carried on into everyday life. My parents began testing new foods with me very carefully, and we went on to discover that I had less severe but still debilitating allergies to milk and seafood. And all tree nuts were off-limits. Peanuts, being a legume, were okay.

While knowing which foods could harm me was a necessary first step, the real challenges arose as I aged into playdates, birthday parties, and school activities.

Today, for my kids' elementary school, we are discouraged from sending them to school with any foods containing peanuts or tree nuts. For class parties, only pre-packaged treats with listed ingredients are allowed. Back in the early 1980s, when I was in school, moms would send homemade baked goods to class for every occasion. The little, smiling children bringing in paper plates covered in cellophane had no idea what ingredients were in the treats their parents had baked.

I got good at saying, "No, thank you."

My school file was updated each year, upon my mom's insistence, to alert my new teacher about my allergies. I was also encouraged to decline any and all food for which I did not have perfect knowledge of its ingredients.

For a (then) five-year-old, it felt like I was repeating "No, thank you" an awful lot. While all the other kids were enjoying brownies or cupcakes or pie, I would not.

At the beginning, I was just afraid. This stuff—food—that was supposed to nourish me could dramatically do the opposite. Just being around unknown foods caused me anxiety, and I would distance myself from the table of treats.

In class, I'd sit on a miniature blue-plastic chair or on the beanbags, or just stand off to the side, watching the other kids feast.

When I was very small, even the dust from tree nuts could set off an allergic reaction.

I don't recall any one moment, but more a highlight reel of memory snippets. The foil coming off the tray, and me saying, "No, thank you." The serving platter placed on the table, and me saying, "No, thank you." Party balloons in all colors. Streamers and pastel birthday cards. Costumes and Valentines. "No, thank you." "No, thank you." "No, thank you."

It quickly stripped away a little boy's notion of "fairness." Not everyone "gets one." Not all the time, anyway. But eventually the fear gave way to something else, something closer to empowerment: an almost stern resolve.

I moved closer to the treat table. I took part in the sugar-fueled conversations. But I kept my hands off the table. I declined and explained to the teacher that I couldn't help clean up. I moved back when the chewing inevitably began to coincide with the other kids' excited, half-yelled conversations, which sprayed small crumbs all about us.

A practice run? Maybe. It was social distancing, of a sort.

The fluorescent tubes were spasming beneath their opaque ceiling covers as I sat in my oncologist's waiting room on a tan vinyl chair, the kind that always starts out too cold and ends up too hot.

The lights flickered at an uneven cadence, each flicker accompanied by a pitched, electric pinging.

I held my head tilted back, gazing at the light show. I tapped my right foot in a quick and driving rhythm against the low pile of the industrial-grade carpet.

That morning, I had received the results of my latest round of bloodwork, pushed to my health-record app on my phone. Sarah and I were now starting our pattern of checking all of my blood markers every three months. This was to be the first check-up.

My heart was pounding as I flipped my phone over in my hands again and again.

A week before my first scheduled "watching and waiting" appointment, I had gone into my oncology lab for my blood draw. A few days later, with a *happy chime* on my phone, my latest lab results had come back with pretty good indications across iron levels, T-cells, liver function, kidneys, and the like. It confirmed my diagnosis (yet again). But at the bottom of the results, the specialist had written, "Cannot rule out blasts of underdeveloped cells."

In other words, the person who'd read these lab results said they could not rule out that I potentially had a far more aggressive version of this disease than we'd realized. My bone marrow was possibly on overdrive, pumping out cancerous cells that would soon crowd out the functioning cells in my veins. That would demand we completely wipe out my immune system altogether, and replace my bone marrow through a transplant.

Thus, I needed to get some additional bloodwork done *immediately*.

Called back from the waiting room, I strode twenty yards to pass through one of those self-locking, heavy medical-center doors and sat in a taller, but similarly poor-at-temperature-regulating chair. The phlebotomist jabbed a needle into my left inner elbow. I refused to watch (and still do) the blood drain into the vial at the end of the thin plastic tube.

I returned to the waiting room as Sarah ran the diagnostics on these new, latest labs, sitting there in my original chair tapping my foot and watching the lights snap in and out.

I didn't notice the magazines this morning. I didn't wait with a cup of hot chocolate in my hand.

I stopped twirling my phone and briefly depressed the power button. My foot stopped tapping, and I sat still as I gazed at the screen. It had been thirteen minutes since I'd returned to my seat.

I began tapping, again.

The outer door to the clinic opened with a deep-toned, metallic click.

An elderly couple shuffled into the clinic. He had gray hair, full on the sides but with a spotty thatch on top, not unlike my own, minus the gray. It was cut too short to comb over, the man having selected the lesser of two evils. His jeans hung loosely around his legs. In front of him walked his wife; she wore a bandana around her head, covering the hair loss. She was gaunt and walked with a slight limp.

They began the check-in process, signing electronic forms on the pad in front of the receptionist's computer, carrying on a half-whispered conversation with the receptionist, who greeted the couple by name.

The hushed murmuring was broken by another metallic click.

This time, it was the door to the exam rooms swinging open. Sarah strode through quickly, carrying a printout in her hand, clearly eager to deliver some news.

Before I could rise from my now-too-warm seat, Doctor Sarah was upon me. She crouched into a squat at my feet, which I had stopped tapping.

"They aren't blasts," she said very quietly, leaning closer to me.

"We'd be seeing quite a spike in the number of these cells, and we're not," she elaborated, pointing at the paper. "You aren't having any symptoms like fever or chills or anything, right?"

"No," I replied.

"And nothing has changed in the genetics of the cells. Blasts may sometimes present with only one or two of these factors, but you aren't having any."

I let out an audible exhale, flashing back to that anxiety-filled moment of talking through my initial test results on a restaurant patio along the banks of the Tennessee River.

For a moment, I felt awkward about having this conversation in the waiting room. Then, I felt grateful at the urgency with which Sarah had delivered this news.

"They have to do this, you know. They have to write up their findings to avoid any potential misses," she explained.

"I get it. No false negatives."

"Right. No false negatives," she repeated.

"You want to come back and do the rest of the exam?" she asked.

Exhaling deeply, again, I stood up. Sarah got up from her crouch and raced me to the door, opening it for me. We walked side by side down the narrow hall.

Back here, the lights didn't flicker.

*The rope team beginning to snake its way across the snow bridge while bringing down the sight-impaired climber on Mount Rainier (14,411').*

CHAPTER ELEVEN

# Balance

The Flatirons are iconic rock formations that wall off the town of Boulder, Colorado, from the high peaks of the Rocky Mountains to the west. They are lichen-covered, conglomerate sandstone and tilt back and away from town at a seemingly steady 55 degrees for anywhere from 50 to 1,000 vertical feet of gain (depending on which Flatiron you are talking about). They are featured with various large, and often fragile, flakes, almost as if sheet rock had been laid over them.

While the north, south, and west aspects of the Flatirons contain all types of rock climbing, from overhanging sport climbs to class three and four scrambles, the east faces very consistently offer up beginner-difficulty slab climbing on their inclined planes.

Slab climbing is characterized by the need to "smear" one's feet on the rock, trying to get as much of your rock shoe's sole down and in contact with the climbing surface as you can in order to generate friction. There typically are only minor texture ripples, and not the defined good edges into which you would otherwise drive your big toe.

A slab climber needs to learn to trust his or her feet by relying on the sticky shoe rubber and good ankle mobility to keep that rubber on the face. On a harder slab climb with few solid handholds, as you step up, your only true points of contact strong enough to hold your weight are the smeared soles of your feet.

Boulder, Colorado, is also one of the focal points of climbing in America. It is filled with outdoor athletes pushing the boundaries of all forms of climbing. As such, these expert climbers will often free-solo (not use a rope) up these beginner-grade east faces as a matter of course—as a morning or post-workday workout. But many other far-from-elite climbers will do the same, with clubs and meet-up groups and regular parties of friends choosing a line up one of the sizeable slabs to feel the freedom that comes from untied and unfettered upward motion. Given that the rock is only 55 degrees, the likelihood of a fall is comparatively small, but the potential consequences of falling and tumbling hundreds of feet are self-evidently dire.

Given that I lived within a couple hours' drive from the Flatirons, it was only a matter of time until I (being one of the "far-from-elite" types) was invited to try.

It was 2018, and I was about three years out from my most recent, major expedition to Denali. I was still, unbeknownst to me, months away from my cancer diagnosis, and was a couple of years in with working to put a team and a plan together to try the 7,140-meter peak of Gangapurna West in the Nepalese Himalaya. I wanted to test team dynamics and get out with various interested climbers so that we could all get to know each other. For one of these trips, a potential climbing-team member suggested a "scramble" up the First Flatiron, "scramble" being a euphemism for a ropeless "free solo" ascent of a fifth-class rock climb.

Bringing together a group of acquaintances on a climb, rather than a group who had climbed together many times, I suggested we bring a lightweight, alpine rope in case any of us—including myself—decided we needed it.

There were no complaints, and so half-a-dozen of us piled out of our vehicles on the extreme west end of Boulder on a clear fall morning.

The sun behind us was still casting long shadows as we made our way up winding trails of red clay. We told tales of past adventures and listened for responses, feeling out each other's approaches to adventuring in the mountains.

Most of us wore shorts and T-shirts on this unusually warm, autumn day. Through my red-tinted sunglasses, the sandstone formations above us looked deep maroon, like one would imagine the rocks on Mars.

At the base of the First Flatiron, on its far right side, we put on our harnesses in case we ended up taking the rope out. It's far easier to harness-up on level ground, before you want your harness, rather than up on the cliff, after you realize you need it.

We had an experienced guide with us, not as a paid guide but as a potential participant for our trip. He offered to carry the rack of climbing protection and the rope, in case we decided to place an anchor and pitch out any of the climbing.

Each of us took our own line up the arête, the broad east face left of it, or the gully farther left yet, choosing our own adventure. We climbed side by side or catty-corner from one another. No one wanted to be directly above someone or have someone else directly above them: a nod to the seriousness of a fall and the potential to "bowling-pin" your fellow climbers down the face.

The conversations made light of reality.

"The rock is so grippy!" one climber remarked.

"Yeah, between that and the low angle, if you slipped, you could probably just starfish yourself out and you'd stick," replied another. We were three hundred feet up now, the ponderosa looking smaller and smaller below us, town spreading out into the Great Plains behind us.

I was making steady progress, not the fastest nor the slowest of the climbers on the face. I found a ripple of an edge, gripping it with my left hand. Reaching up and right, I found a flake I could pinch from the side. It was friable and could break with a solid pull, but it would help me balance.

The rock felt gritty in my hands. Microparticles rolled under the pressure of my skin—tiny ball bearings. It made me wonder about the security of my feet as I found a dimple in which to press the ball of my right foot; I stood up on it.

I couldn't shake the two climbers' exchange from my head. In hindsight, I'm glad of it.

*But people die from unroped falls on the Flatirons,* I thought. It can happen; in fact, it does happen, seemingly every year. *What if it's not a feet-first slip? What if you spin off and away from the rock?"*

Above, our guide friend, sensing the testosterone flowing perhaps a bit too freely, called out, "If anyone wants the rope, we can break it out!"

He was standing in a large, foot-deep ledge about twenty feet above me, his white helmet and salmon tank top drawing a sharp contrast against the deep-blue sky.

My next thought was, *I shouldn't be doing this.*

It was as clear as any thought I've ever had in the mountains. Behind this thought was a more complex realization: *risk equals probability times consequence*. The probability of a fall was very, very low, but the consequence was obviously super high. So, what was the total risk?

*Who cares?* The real question was, *Is the risk worth it? What do I gain? Is it an unnecessary risk?*

*Yes. For me, yes.*

"I'll take the rope," I called up to him.

"Okay, I'll lower the rope down," he said. He didn't need to hear the rest of my internal monologue.

I tied in and waited as the guide climbed up to a bathtub-like feature a good thirty meters above and seated himself for a hip belay, legs propped against the "tub" lip to secure himself.

"On belay!" was the call.

"Climbing!" I called back.

I moved up, climbing more quickly from the sense of security the rope provided. I began to flow over the rock.

Another climber asked for the rope as well, and so the guide connected himself to the rope's middle and sent the other end down to the other climber.

We whole group now moved like a caterpillar: our lead climber and those still making the ascent free solo would move up to a new belay stance, and then myself and another climber, each on the end of a doubled-over rope, would follow.

The chatter died down as the distances between us expanded and contracted, creating natural barriers to conversation.

No one gave me any grief over using the rope. The group was good to its word—if anyone wanted the rope, we would take it out and use it, no questions asked.

Up on the summit, I stood at the lip where the east and west faces meet, the Continental Divide visible off on the horizon, beginning my rappel over the vertical west side off a massive eye bolt. I held the rope relaxed but firmly in my hand as I slid down.

Touching the ground, I yelled up, "Off rappel," and another climber headed down. As his feet came to rest beside me, I looked him squarely in the eye as he returned my gaze.

"Once, I was up on the north side of Rainier, up on Emmons . . ." I began.

As spring 2020 wore on, warmer days dominated, and the occasional snowfalls were melting out in hours. The ground radiated heat. The grass turned green. The towering, mature oaks sprouted green-yellow buds that made the arches above the sidewalks seem almost neon, like a welcome sign.

Colorado's governor, Jared Polis, had let the "stay-at-home" order expire, moving to a cleverly coined "safer-at-home" policy. Bureaucratic tasks like notary services, marriage licenses, driver's licenses, and the like could all be performed online. Businesses could allow limited in-person staffing, but no organization could compel vulnerable populations to come into the office.

A few months earlier, as the pandemic was first impacting America's coasts, I had left my job to start my own consulting practice, helping healthcare organizations and small banks develop more mature analytic capabilities. With physical contact limited to only the frontline healthcare workers—who were receiving spontaneous rounds of applause as they headed in to work each day—using data (rather than anecdote) to make decisions was suddenly at a premium. Doing so with a workforce that was no longer co-located was a new challenge. My nascent consulting practice was thriving due to mere circumstance.

But the movies were closed. The mom-and-pop shops remained closed (some would never recover). And restaurants were effectively only serving up delivery through a newly marshalled army of drivers who used to work customer service in those same shops and restaurants.

Our local trail, just steps outside our front door and which wandered its way to a pond and bird sanctuary, became a human sanctuary. With outside activities suddenly, and paradoxically, safer than going to the coffee shop, scores more people were treading on the clay, leaving dimpled footprints whenever they headed down the trail too soon after a snowmelt. A metal, a-frame-style sandwich board had been repurposed at the trailhead, reminding hikers to remain "six feet apart."

Since the new year, stories coming in from Seattle, San Francisco, New York, and Boston had shown us that this virus wasn't something to be trifled with. The evidence was mounting that I, in particular, was at risk. People with immune conditions and respiratory diseases were not faring well; there was now a platoon of refrigerator trucks filled with bodies in New York. Cancer patients and organ-transplant recipients were proving to be more vulnerable than almost anyone else. Even the nursing homes, the sites of so many deaths, were starting to segregate residents into those with and without "preexisting conditions." Well, I had asthma and a blood cancer that was a cancer of my immune system. So, other than that . . .

The schools were closed through the end of the school year,

and Kristina and I had begun to ever more seriously investigate homeschooling our boys. That coming fall, Connor and Kade were supposed to be enrolling in first grade, a year early, having "tested out" of kindergarten.

"Maybe this will force us to try out this step of educating our boys ourselves," I mused while chatting with Kristina one day. "We would have been too scared to do so, otherwise."

Both public and private schools used to in-person learning were scrambling to invent an online-learning model in just months. We decided to enroll the boys in a dedicated "alternative" school that had been providing online-only schooling for a decade. We thought that, while we would be responsible for the day-to-day lessons and support for the kids, we could at least have the lesson plans spoon-fed to us, the de facto teachers. We could follow the curriculum at our own pace, and the school was practiced at offering well-honed technical and curricular support from afar.

Given that both Kristina and I were working from home, all while facing a long summer that would be devoid of get-togethers and play dates, we started the kids' lessons as soon as the materials arrived from the school, even before summer vacation truly started.

The boys were racing through their first-grade curriculum. Building from the schedule to work on reading with the boys that Kristina had created when the schools first closed, we broke the subjects into blocks to be delivered on the days the schools suggested. Some lessons happened every day, like math and reading; others, like science and history, were broken into alternating days.

In essence, Kristina managed the everyday lessons while I took on the alternating-day lessons. Sheepishly, I was aware that there were more daily lessons than alternating lessons, but my consulting practice was burgeoning to the point that I had to bring on outside help. My wife, an economist by training, was understanding and helped tweak the schedule into a morning and afternoon routine so that I could come back and revisit a few more lessons as the curriculum expanded along with the boys' abilities.

Conor and Kade would eventually race through the first-grade curriculum in a couple of months and start second grade early on in what was supposed to be their first-grade year. But in this late spring, we were still just getting our feet wet and were marveling at the flexibility of homeschooling.

That flexibility let us also keep physical health at the forefront in a way that traditional schools had not been doing for a while. We took the boys out on hikes and strider-bike rides, and they continued to join me for many of my morning workouts. It wasn't so much about what we did as it was about developing the habit of doing something physical.

We were managing. Maybe we were even doing well, all things considered. But we were highly, highly isolated. As groups began to self-select into "pods" of like-minded people who viewed COVID risks with similar levels of severity, we remained a singular pod of four.

"We went to the park today while you were in your meeting," Kristina told me one afternoon.

"Did the boys have fun?"

Kristina sat on the same couch where I had crafted my notes and questions for my oncologist. Now, though, boxes of textbooks and workbooks made end tables. The far end of the living room also had a desk and a filing cabinet. The desk was some cheap thing ordered from Amazon, about two feet deep and five feet wide; it was plywood with taupe veneer, the kind that peels up at the corners after a year, and we were sure the kids would destroy it in short order. Subdivided crafting-supply containers, sitting at the back end of the desk, were filled with scissors and tape and crayons and pencils. The filing cabinets were the old, industrial, metal kind, standing nearly as tall as my chin. Every time we opened or closed a drawer, a deep note resounded from the flexing steel. Inside were file folders organized by subject and by child.

I backed over to the desk and hoisted myself onto it, sitting with my legs dangling.

"When we got there, there was another mom and a couple of kids at the playground. The boys just didn't want to go over," Kristina said.

"Yeah, I get that."

"Eventually, Kade went over and played a little . . . sort of near-ish to the other the kids. But you could tell that he was keeping his distance."

"I guess that's good . . ."

". . . I guess," my wife cut in, "but it wasn't like this was some crowded place. It was two little kids. He seemed hesitant."

I nodded.

"Connor wouldn't go over. We sat under a tree. Eventually, the other kids left, and I asked Connor if he wanted to go over and play. He wouldn't go. We sat and talked about how they're learning that the virus is spread through the air, but he said he didn't want to touch the playground equipment. He just refused."

"I guess we need to keep trying. I can come along next time."

"This isn't healthy for them, Jason. I know we have to take this virus seriously, but we can't have our kids scared of everything, either."

"The quarantine ended not that long ago. People are just getting back into the world. It's going to be weird, sure. But we just need to give them more opportunities," I tried to reassure her.

My seat on the desk proved uncomfortable; the solid surface dug into my haunches and my hamstrings, and I shifted from side to side. The side window was agape, letting in a cool breeze. It was soundless outside. No traffic. No children running and playing. No cranking of a bike chain as someone pedaled by.

"It's just such terrible timing for them, though, this point in their development. You should have seen Connor; he was almost in tears," Kristina said.

"Well, they just announced they're working on a vaccine. Science is going to catch up," I said, maybe more for myself this time.

The conversation just faded away: empathy and concern, but no resolution.

"I haven't been at altitude for months." I told Kristina this with the same emphasis and implied shock one would use to speak of not bathing for that long, as if my very health and wellness were at stake.

"Well, we can't just hold every weekend, waiting for the right weather," she retorted.

As the fall of 2017 was closing out, and with winter looming on the horizon, I was starting to worry about getting fewer and fewer good-weather days in the high mountains. It had been eighteen months since I'd returned from summitting Denali, and I missed the feeling of mental, emotional, and physical exertion.

I was determined to stay in shape. Getting in shape is such hard work; staying in shape is always easier. So, I had been feverishly working out each morning. Long runs, interval sprints, and heavy-pack "hill days" were on daily rotation, while every other day I was targeting legs, upper body, and core to get my body ready for the abuse of pack straps on my shoulders, tens of thousands of steps on uneven terrain, and the grip and calf strength needed for vertical ice. But there are only so many ways to simulate altitude—the easiest is to just go to altitude.

Toward what end? I didn't yet know. I was in the early stages of planning a trip to the high Himalaya. I'd been higher than 6,000 meters several times by now, but expecting a few, isolated peaks, there was only one range on Earth to get higher than 7,000 meters. Being heavily drawn to self-reliance, a habit perhaps ingrained by trauma, I was also looking for a peak about which there was limited climbing information. So, I was looking at a number of potential objectives that had either only been climbed a few times or that offered a first ascent—the first known climb of a peak.

The boys had just turned two, and so I also wanted to ensure I was getting quality time with the family. I sincerely wanted to spend time with them at home and visiting museums and quietly reading in the public library. And we did do those things.

But at least once a month, I wanted to get out and do some climbing. I wanted to feel my body strain against the thin air in the heights of Colorado. I wanted to be rooted firmly in the present, my friends and I fully reliant upon each other for safety. And I wanted to take purposeful steps toward the next big climb.

The problem was, weekends needed to get scheduled out well in advance with a busy family life, and the weather tended not to give a damn about when I was free for mountain climbing.

The narrative that I had told myself, "It'll be fine, just fine, if I can get up and do something fun every month or so," had morphed into an expectation.

It wasn't that Kristina didn't want me to get out and climb, either. This wasn't an argument. It was a realization that, with two-year-old twins at home, everything had to line up—my schedule, my climbing partners' schedules, the weather, the snow conditions, all of it—for me to get my fix.

So, it was this one particular evening, when Kristina and I were standing in the kitchen, that I told her I just wasn't climbing enough anymore. As I shifted back and forth from one locked leg to the other, the hardwood floor creaked, the sound echoing through the beams each time as the heavy sole of my boot came down.

The lights from inside our kitchen, unable to penetrate the evening darkness, bounced back at us from the window over the sink. Glancing at the window, I only saw a reflection of myself, an agitated form surrounded by four yellow orbs from the kitchen lights laid against a black background.

"I know. But it's frustrating," I replied.

My wife was visibly mustering her patience. "And HAMS is starting in a couple of months, right?"

In about two months, I was scheduled to begin instructing with the High Altitude Mountaineering School again. That would be a weeknight lecture, with a weekend field day every week, for about two months.

"Yeah." I was now staring sheepishly at my feet.

"I know you were wanting to get out tomorrow, but you are going to get out a lot more."

We stood in silence. I was thinking of all of the things pulling on me: a climbing goal, climbing instruction, all of the training and planning, work (which was energy-sapping in and of itself), being a father, being a husband.

"I was just looking forward to it."

"I know. I'm going to go to bed." Kristina turned and left the kitchen, going up to check on the boys one last time, her bare feet almost soundless on the hardwood.

I was left staring out the window, which only reflected inward.

The coming winter ended up being the last season I formally instructed with HAMS. And the expedition in the Himalaya would have to wait for two more years.

Sarah's oncology practice moved to an adjacent building, her new office's first-floor windows facing out into the parking lot. The windowless third floor and the old building had been left behind.

When I first received the mailer giving me notice of the move, I was mildly troubled, mostly just because it was another change. I had certainly experienced enough changes recently.

I didn't realize how beneficial this change would be until I stepped into the new waiting room.

As I opened the glass door (as heavy as the old wooden door) at the entrance, I was struck by how foreign the new waiting area looked.

I went up to the reception desk. There was black-and-white, checkboard tile along the desk front, a far cry from the familiar margarine-colored paint. I provided my name and electronically signed the myriad consent and notification forms.

Behind the reception desk, the handcrafted note thanking the office for their caring for a departed family member had been replaced by a less somber, but also less heartfelt, piece of manufactured wall art.

I spun to my left as I turned to leave the desk. This opened me up to the length of the waiting room, which was about fifty feet long.

The coffee station sat at the far end. The machine may have been the same as before, in hindsight, but it looked new, perhaps because of the fresh-looking art deco storage containers filled with single-serving coffee pods. I certainly didn't recognize the machine at the time.

I moved toward the seating area, appreciating the muted, white morning light coming in through the windows, as opposed to the queasy yellow of the old fluorescents. I took a chair with my back to the windows. At angles, the light flared off the tiles on the base of the reception desk and again from its laminate top. It bounced off the storage containers for the coffee pods. There was a glint from the doorknob, which beckoned for a twist and a walk back to the exam rooms.

After the scare of potential "blasts" of cancerous cells, I had stopped reading the lab results on my mobile phone prior to each appointment, which made the week between the blood draw and my appointment a stressful one, full of anxiety. At least the weeks no longer started with my phone's "happy chimes" serving as an unwelcome starting gun, though; I had turned off notifications.

I knew that if anything urgent popped up, Sarah would call. So, it wasn't as if I spent one week every few months feeling like I was in mortal danger. But still, with a slow-moving disease, it was always a question of, "How much worse has it gotten?"

Most appointments brought a bit of progression in my condition, and so each appointment was measured in degrees of disappointment. It wasn't always great disappointment, but it was disappointment, nonetheless. It had reached the point where I started to notify work about appointment dates, informing them that an "oncology week" was approaching.

Those weeks began with the blood draw. When I was at the old office, it started with opening the great wooden door, treading over the low-pile carpet, and taking in the familiar fluorescent lights and yellowing walls. I would announce my arrival at the desk, and then head back to the phlebotomist once she called my name.

After getting my blood drawn, I would return to the waiting room where I would sit anxiously, foot tapping or fingers tapping or trying to read a book on my phone.

The oncology weeks ended, after my appointment with Sarah, with me leaving through the same big door, after the second round of waiting and yellow light and magazines with inspirational smiles gracing their covers.

Today, in the new office, my hands were calm. My phone sat in my pocket.

My breath moved easily and evenly. I had made a habit of checking in with my breath, to help wrestle with the anxiety. Today, my breath felt light in my belly and full in my chest. I held my back straight and my chin up. I panned my head easily, taking in my new surroundings.

The air I was breathing hadn't had the time to build up that sealed-building staleness. I smelled a hint of fresh paint and mortar, of sawdust and varnish.

Over time, those smells eventually went away. I didn't notice anything during future visits; the powerful HEPA filters did quick work pulling particulates out of the air. But the new office never smelled like the old one, and my memories of visiting the old clinic faded along with the new clinic's odors of construction.

Not quite two years later, I ran into a physician friend of mine, Mike, while I was out on the trail with my boys and my wife. We were descending from Mount Sniktau, above Loveland Pass, the boys' second-ever Thirteener. The early-summer sun shone brightly through the thin atmosphere. Rays of light danced off the remaining snow drifts at 13,000 feet, sun pockets on the white surface bouncing the light in many directions. While Mike's climbing partner, Steve, another friend of ours, chatted with Kristina and the boys, Mike asked me about my health and how I was handling "the PTSD of the office visits."

"I honestly hadn't ever thought about it in those terms," I replied. "But it makes sense."

"Yeah, this is very common in oncology—kind of a continuing trauma going back to the place they were given this terrible news, time and time again," he said.

Mike stood in a classic mountaineer's pose, the uphill leg bent and the downhill leg straight, bearing his body's and backpack's weight. Though Mike's stance was strong, he looked at me with very soft eyes.

"You know . . . thanks for asking, Mike. It's interesting, a while ago my oncologist changed locations. It's not like my appointments are fun or anything, and a clinic is still a clinic, but I don't carry all that emotional baggage into the place. It looks different. It smells different . . ."

"You know, smell is heavily linked to memory," Mike interjected.

"Yeah. Exactly. I don't get worked up about the appointments just walking into the place."

"That's great," he exclaimed with a smile.

"I mean, I still have cancer, and as you know, it could mutate and get worse or whatever. I wrestle with that."

"Sure," he said, his face turning serious again.

"But I'm still in the 'watching and waiting' stage, and I'm out doing this stuff; so, it could be worse."

"Yep."

The boys and Kristina started to pivot away from Steve, signaling the end to their conversation, so I shouldered my pack, too. Taking a few steps down, I told Mike, "But, to your point about the appointments, honestly, now I'm doing okay."

*Connor and Kade at the beginning of homeschooling during the first summer of the pandemic.*

CHAPTER TWELVE

# Exploration

We were heading out a bit too soon in the season—early April of 2014—for the snow to be consolidating, but my anticipation was high and, I guess, infectious. The mellow Quandary Peak (14,271 feet) is one of the most popular Fourteeners due to its gentle east slope, which rises at fifteen to twenty degrees for three miles straight from a county highway. For those same reasons, it is often a person's first "snow summit." It also makes a popular first "couloir" climb, ascending up a snow-filled gully, as the south face has a thirty-five-degree line that is fairly non-taxing. But we were here to try something different. I'd talked three partners into coming along on what was to be my first truly challenging climb following my third ACL replacement on my right knee.

Matt was close to my age. He was a rock-climbing instructor, but a former student of mine on excursions to the high peaks. We had similar backgrounds—with fairly demanding jobs, a love of the alpine, and kids, though he and his wife had managed to have their kids just one at a time.

Steve was ten-odd years older than me, and it was he who would be chatting with Kristina and the boys years later on Mount Sniktau while our friend Mike asked me about oncologist-office-visit PTSD. Steve was calm and rational and exceptionally good at communicating. He was my role model when it came to making group assessments of conditions and being open about discussing them, a lesson that is forever needing to be reinforced in the backcountry.

John (along with his wife, Debbie) was the director of the High Altitude Mountaineering School for which I instructed. He and Debbie were my HAMS instructors the year of the Rainier rescue. They were not on that Rainier trip with me and Kristina, but they were very much a part of the outcome. It had been their careful tutelage that readied us for that event. Over the years, I'd spent hours with them tied to each other's ropes or talking through student needs, crafting lectures, and planning out field days. More than any other climbers, it was John and Deb who'd taught me the foundations of technical systems, situational awareness in the alpine, and team dynamics. My first half decade as a climber was inextricably entwined with them and their partnership and mentorship.

Through long-established trust, Matt, Steve, and John were willing to support me on a climb that would help me test out the new parts in my right knee and the severely atrophied muscles around them.

I knew that, even with deep snow still on the high peaks, there would, nonetheless, be a small army of people on the mountain heading up the east ridge along the firm, boot-packed snow that so many feet had helped create. The sheer volume of climbers on Quandary keeps the snow dense and passable, often without snowshoes.

We would instead be gaining about 1,000 feet via a snow-covered road that passed under the south face. From there, we would continue around to the peak's southwest aspect, where a set of broken buttresses, divided by deeply cut couloirs, combine to make a winding route that corkscrews north and then east to the top.

I had spotted the line on my first climb after the surgery, when I'd been climbing a nearby lower and mellower peak.

Over the next month, I spent about ten hours online and in the climbing library at the American Mountaineering Center in Golden trying to find any reference to anyone climbing up the southwest aspect of Quandary. I couldn't find anything.

While the indigenous and mining history of Colorado make it unlikely for any mountain terrain to still be untrodden, there was at least no record. We had the opportunity to put up a new route, a rarity for any major peak in the state, let alone one of its most popular.

As we passed the frozen lake below Quandary's south face, it was just becoming light enough to see. We'd be in the shade for most of the climb, which was the point. We needed the snow to stay frozen and firm.

We moved up into the basin, the mountain towering to our right, and started to approach the couloirs.

The air was brisk but not cold, and we had worked up a little heat from the approach.

John stepped out into the more deeply snow-filled basin, placing his feet lightly to avoid sinking. As I followed, I suddenly plunged down to my knee. I felt the cold around the bottom of my pant leg, a sensation that seeped up to my shin.

As I strained to lift out my leg from the posthole, the extra pressure on my other foot was enough to drive it down and into the snow as well. Now I stood with both feet sunk up to my knees.

I dropped my hands to the snow, spreading my weight out over four limbs, and crawled away.

This repeated. Every so often, I would punch through the snow's outer crust and drop one of my feet, or occasionally both, into the cold.

Steve and Matt, behind me, suffered the same fate.

As we began up the first section of the couloir, the snow proved to be far worse: unconsolidated and sugary. For about five hundred vertical feet, we took turns wallowing in the lead, making a trench for the three other climbers to follow in.

Up in front of me, Matt stepped to his right so I could pass when it was my turn to break trail.

I brought my right knee to my chest, my foot now above the snow level; as I dropped my foot down, the snow gave way. The entire column of white collapsed, and my foot dropped back to its starting point.

I tried the left foot. Same result.

The granular under-snow left an even coating around my boots. The snow's crusty rim, however, remained at thigh level in front of me.

I placed my forearms on the rim, feeling a dull cold move up my arms. As I shifted my weight forward, the snow under my arms sheared off and dropped to my feet, as well.

I could now inch my feet forward into the trench I was digging. The rim of snow was higher now, up to my waist, as the couloir tilted upward to steepen.

I resigned myself to swimming through the deep snow and cycled through a process of jamming a knee into the snow in front of me, which would break off the snow below it, and then slapping my arms down on the top of the snow, which would remove the snow above my original knee placement. The cold powder now continuously dusted my feet.

After maybe a minute of this, a trickle of sweat moved down my left temple, and my back felt sweaty where my pack pressed into it.

I was beginning to pant.

Eventually, one of my knee thrusts did not result in a cascade of white. Optimistic, I bent at the waist and placed my chest and arms down on the snow above the trench.

The snow held.

I swung my right leg up and out of the trench. The snow held.

With a roll, I was able to get my left leg out as well. And though I was on my back, I was finally on top of all that snow.

The snow continued to hold. I rose to my feet.

“That– was– fun,” I spurted out between pants.

Matt laughed. I was maybe three feet in front of him.

The snow would prove to be relatively consolidated above us, and it continued to improve as we climbed higher and into colder temperatures.

Moving to my feet, I kicked steps only as deep as my shins, and we approached a natural resting point at the top of the first couloir. Here, the angle softened to ten degrees as the route bent right, traversing to the next, steeper section. The team followed in comparative ease behind me.

Turning eastward, John took over and, with his superior fitness, made quick work of the next major section of couloir, another four hundred feet up a forty-five-degree slope.

There was a boulder the size of a food truck in the middle of the couloir, and we paused under it for drinks and a discussion.

I was feeling good. My knee felt fine, I mentioned to the group, and my temperature had regulated now that I wasn't laboring like a salmon swimming upstream.

I looked back at our footprints in the snow below and then away to the mountains behind us, on the horizon and across the basin. The sun, blocked by Quandary, left us in the same shadow that cast a long, gray cone across the basin floor.

I turned my attention back to the route, scanning the terrain above us.

I had been the one to study potential routes and variations from photos I had taken on that previous trip and as I researched previous ascents. "The more we move right, the more snow climbing we'll do before we reach the top of the west ridge. If we stay left, we'll end up well left of the summit. Of course, we can just follow the top of the west ridge for as far as we want," I told my friends.

"I'm enjoying the snow, now," John said.

"Yeah, this is good climbing now that we are out of that sugar snow," Steve agreed.

"Let's cross over this low hummock and join the couloir to our right?" I asked. "Looks like that second couloir extends pretty far up."

Nods and words of assent came from the team.

Matt led us away from the boulder on a gentle rightward traverse. We gained maybe twenty feet of elevation on a low rib that separated us from the next couloir.

As the day wore on, the sun arced across the southern sky and moved from more in front of us, hidden by the mountain, to off of our right shoulders. The rocks to the right of the second couloir kept the right flank of snow in shadow. The left side was cast in a golden light, turning the snow from a stark white to a warm, wheat color.

The sky above us transmuted from a pale purple to a deep blue.

At this point, the couloir branched both left and right. John eyed the rightward line. "What do you think about heading over there? It's steeper, but it's narrow and shaded," he asked.

"Yeah, that looks like fun," said Steve.

"Looks good," Matt said.

I nodded at John.

As we hugged the rock wall on our right, the snow stayed firm, and the steps John kicked, out in the lead, made perfect and secure platforms for our feet.

At each resting point, John let fly his predictable but endearing exclamations over the beauty and the good fortune we shared, being blessed to live in such a grand place.

While the climbing was physically taxing, it was secure. And while we didn't know exactly where we were going or what terrain we would encounter next, my mind was strangely quiet, not silent but focused. I was neither hot nor cold. I was exerting myself but not exhausted. I moved with purpose but, in turn, stopped to survey the potential hazards in our wider environment.

I was present, wholly present, on one of the final climbs before our kids were born. Kristina was recently pregnant, and we had yet to learn that it was twins.

We stopped at a few more decision points, having crisp discussions about the tradeoffs of one potential path over another. At each stop, the basin below us would visibly recede. From its trough, the far side of the basin rose sharply to a wide bench half-a-mile wide and a quarter-mile deep, rounded in white. It was the bench where my students and I would someday stop when the howling winds and biting cold made further progress an untenable risk. Beyond the bench and against the skyline was a similarly half-mile-long connecting ridge, rounded and corniced but for one technical ice and rock pitch at its left terminus. That ridge, between Drift Peak and Fletcher Mountain, was where—in the future—I would fail my partner Dan, and myself, by succumbing to an anxiety-induced call for rescue, but without consulting with Dan.

The snow lost its golden hue as the sun moved higher in the sky.

The air grew warmer against my face.

We topped out right where a group of climbers were staging to make a ski descent down a northern couloir, on the flip side of the ridge.

Our two groups exchanged pleasantries and a few brief stories of the day's adventures so far, each of our groups having climbed from the opposite sides of the same ridge and each the only group on its respective line.

The skiers dropped in, leaving us standing on the ridge alone. The summit, with its crowds of those who'd ascended the standard route, was a hundred-or-so yards away. The wind was whipping but not ruinous. It tugged gently at the folds of my jacket. I raised my voice to be heard above the sound.

"Thank you, guys," I said.

When I was a child, my family would go camping—national parks and national forests made for cheap, family-friendly getaways. But as a teenager, the thought of being separated from my friends and away from soccer practice made these "dirty" excursions seemingly intolerable. Later in life, as I returned to the outdoors, I simply tolerated camping; it was a means to an end. Some snow climbs require that we set out before sunrise, ensuring firm snow and comparatively easy travel. And some big climbs simply demand multiple nights on a glacier or a mountain's flanks—hence camping.

Kade and Connor have always loved camping.

Of course, I couldn't have known that at the beginning, so we began in our backyard the summer after they turned four. Given the complete lack of wilderness around our suburban home, I chalk up their initial fascination with novelty. It isn't like we saw any wildlife or views; in fact, we heard traffic going by from our tent.

However, they loved the process. They loved trying to blow up the inflatable mattresses; they loved having me do it, eventually, on their behalf. They loved the sleeping bags and their "human shape." They loved watching the light change through the tent walls from white to pink to red to black, as the sun went down.

So, in the first fall of the COVID pandemic, about two years after that first night camping in the yard, we decided that taking the boys camping was as good of a way as any for Kristina and me to celebrate our tenth wedding anniversary. We certainly weren't going to a restaurant or a fancy hotel, so why not go the other direction and sleep on the ground?

A few weeks before, we had scouted a rock formation jutting from an aspen grove in the remote Lost Creek Wilderness southwest of Denver. The rock meant we'd have something to do when our family visited as a "pod of four." I had found a walk-up on the side of the six-story-high monolith, which would allow me to traverse out onto the face and place an anchor so that we could hang a toprope for the kids.

We parked at the trailhead and slung our packs on our backs. The brilliant blue and red of the boys' respective packs jumped out against a sky flooded with light from the low-hanging October sun. Golden aspen leaves shimmered and danced on the trees, while their fallen compatriots made a golden carpet for our walk to the campsite, framed under "archways" of slender white aspen trunks. The air was cool and breezy, with just a crack of autumn.

My wife's pack was bulging with the tent and a couple of sleeping bags. Mine was stacked with supplies, so that its contents protruded well above my head. And even then, another pack sat in the car waiting for our second haul, full of water jugs, as it was too late in the year for there to be any runoff water at the campsite.

The boys packed in their climbing harnesses, sleeping pads, and changes of clothes, each leaning on a trekking pole for support. Mom marched in front, leading the way, while I swept behind, ready to nudge along any stragglers.

However, there were no stragglers. The boys were pulled like a magnet to the rock face, pointing their poles in excitement and chirping about possible climbing routes. The trail rose to meet the rocks at a small platform, maybe fifty square yards in size, encircled by the same sentinel aspens we'd just hiked through. Here, we shrugged off the heavy packs with a thud, and Kristina fished the tent from her pack. The boys began organizing the camp.

Kade called out, "This tree is for our trekking poles! All the trekking poles should be on this tree. Look, you can hang the straps over the little branches!"

"Yeah! Yeah!" Connor said, bouncing around with manic energy.

"And this tree is for our packs. We should put all of our packs on the ground here!"

"Our climbing gear should go here, at this tree!" Kade said.

Kristina looked up and said, "Okay, boys, but your dad and I need to get into our packs for our camping gear, first. And could you guys make sure you get your sleeping pads out of your packs, too?"

Kristina and I staked down the corners of a pyramid-style tent, ten feet on each side. Then we raised the center pole, maybe six feet high, and the tension held it in place.

"Okay, it's time for those sleeping pads," my wife directed.

The boys scooped up their packs like grocery bags and then carelessly swung them down near us before dashing off.

"Close enough," I said to Kristina with a wry smile.

The boys ran about the campsite, sitting on every downed tree, every stump, and every boulder, searching for the perfect thrones.

"Stay out of the fire ring!" my wife called out.

"The *what?!"* Connor said as he looked up from the ring of stones someone had built however many seasons ago. His hands, face, and chest were already blackened with soot.

"The fire ring, Connor. The place where people make fires. It'll make you . . . it's already made you filthy!" Kristina said with a sigh.

Connor cackled, and Kade joined him in the laugh.

Evening was approaching fast, and I reminded the boys to put on some layers, as it's "easier to stay warm than get warm." Then I headed back to the car to portage back the several gallons of water, enough to last for our three-day trip. As I marched past, Kristina was connecting our camp stove to the fuel.

Upon my return, the boys were sitting around the stove with their mother. They had facemasks and gloves on, not for the germs this time, but to protect against the crisp fall-evening air at 10,000 feet. I placed the water jugs on a large rock near the fire ring, completing our camp kitchen.

"Can we go see where we might be climbing tomorrow, Dad?" Kade asked.

Kristina looked up at me from her seat on the ground, minding the stove, and nodded.

"Yeah, let's go look at the rock face," I replied.

Connor and Kade scampered behind as I ambled up to the rock, making lazy switchbacks as we gained elevation so that the boys could follow my lead and avoid a slip.

"How about this as a first route?" I asked. We were now touching the granite, and I pointed up at a water-stained runnel, streaked black and pocked with features where millennia of cycling snow, snowmelt, and runoff had shaved off layers of rock. After about twenty feet up the runnel, the rock plateaued, turning into a ledge maybe five feet deep, and offering a good position to take a rest, before the climb continued another twenty or thirty feet up a fist-width crack.

I took a video with my phone, panning up the potential route.

"That looks like a good one!" Kade exclaimed.

Connor, ever more cautious, asked, "How are you going to make an anchor?"

"I hiked around to the top the last time I was here. There's a place I can put in some cams"—spring-loaded camming devices, a common form of climbing protection—"and make an anchor. It'll be just like your first outdoor climb we did a couple of years ago. Do you remember that one?"

"Yeah," Connor replied, "I remember it some. We didn't have

climbing shoes, yet."

"That's true. Your feet were still too small, but you both made it up!"

With a laugh, Kade jumped in, saying, "Yeah, we did!"

"Hey, Dad?"

"Yeah, Connor?"

"Are you going to make that YouTube channel we've been talking about?"

Connor had first broached the topic of making a YouTube channel not long after the pandemic started. With the supplemental teaching we were doing at home, Kristina and I were leaning more and more from YouTube searches as we looked for reputable summaries of topics on which we were not experts. I found it particularly good as preparation for some of the elementary-school-level science experiments we'd be attempting.

I think Connor mostly liked the idea of "being on TV."

"I'm thinking about it, Connor."

"Well, I noticed you're filming."

"Yes, Connor."

I wasn't really sure I wanted to do it. There was something about the exposure that felt uncomfortable, especially now, with the health issues and all of the uncertainty surrounding social media. But, on the other hand, I had been taking videos of my climbs for years, and I had also started filming some of our family hikes and little adventures. It was more of a home-movie vibe, but I loved watching the footage with the boys and seeing their eyes light up and toothy grins emerge.

"You know, Dad," Kade inserted himself, "it would be really fun to film all the cool adventures Connor and I go on."

"I do that already, you know."

"Yeah, but we could share them with people. I think people would like to see little kids doing all this cool stuff."

"Yeah, they would!" Connor piled on.

"And, you know, you could teach people all the things we do to make sure we're safe," Kade finished.

That caught my attention, and I felt a little of my resistance melt. I had the start of a thought, not fully formed until a few weeks later: *in the midst of the pandemic, discovering the outdoors is sanctuary; we can all do with a little more "outside."*

I'm not sure what I was expecting. My parents told me that the landscape was rolling hills and cider-apple groves and berry farms, but I still wasn't imagining something quite this pastoral. On the way to our vacation rental, we passed strip malls and gas stations, taking a right at a perfectly ordinary stoplight, and then headed east across the bridge from Quebec City and into the middle of the Saint Lawrence River. Once onto the Île d'Orléans, we were quickly immersed in French-Canadian farm country.

Kristina and I had brought Connor and Kade, who were almost four years old now, managing the full day of air travel, ground travel, and border checks all with our mostly-well-behaved toddlers in tow. My brother, Bryan, and his wife, Oralia, brought up their teenagers, Istefan and Samara. My parents flew out, as well. It was a family vacation, with all of us there, like we hadn't had for many, many years.

We'd rented a home near the island's east coast. The water lay just on the other side of the two-lane country road that circumnavigated the island.

My parents had discovered the location while researching their genealogy, tracing our French-Canadian ancestors back to the original French settlers of Canada. This included long-ago relatives who'd founded Quebec City and whose "noble" blood allowed them to be placed in charge of such an enterprise. So, the family had congregated to spend time in this magical place and learn a bit more about our history. We had trips planned to Old Quebec City and museums on both the mainland and the island, along with one or two restaurant reservations. But much was left unplanned; we would also be taking the opportunity to slow down.

On this first morning, I stepped out the sliding-glass door onto the back patio and moved across the rolling lawn at a quick step. My running shoes receded into the soft, water-laden grass.

To my right, in the far corner of the immense yard, was a small airplane; not a functional one, but a frame-only playground version about the length of a horse, made of welded yellow, blue, and red steel bars. The boys had discovered it the previous evening, upon our arrival. They had not yet dragged my father out to climb and teeter with them, but that was coming.

Reaching the road, I turned left and broke into a jog up a hill and toward the village center. My feet smacked against the concrete sidewalk until it ended. I hopped down onto the asphalt, passing stone cottages and wooden-gabled Quebecois-style homes. The road was still wet from the morning's sprinklers.

A bit of gold sunlight reflected from the pooled water at my feet.

The first available crosswalk came into view at the foot of the

Catholic church. The crosswalk stretched in front of the church from the cemetery, which extended to the near corner of the plot. Time-worn, centuries-old headstones tilted slightly askew, moss covering their northern aspects. It was here that I ended my run and examined my options: I could fork right around the church and head down to the water; or I could head left and cross the street, above which sat a manor-style structure on a knoll, stately brick with a gabled white roof. In front was a sign for La Boulange, the name both an homage to artisanal pursuits meaning "the craft of baking" and a simple, informal declaration: "The Bakery."

I took the crosswalk and headed up the stairs, climbing the knoll to the bakery. As I walked, my heart started to settle.

The bakery's front patio had two wooden, park-bench-style tables and two wrought-iron café tables. I turned, looking back down to the road and across the church cemetery to the water, where small waves lapped against the shore. There on the patio, enjoying the midsummer sun that had already risen well above the water, patrons of all ages sipped coffee or peeled apart croissants or Danishes. Not being a French speaker, I didn't understand much of their conversations.

I stood patiently in line, taking in the smell of coffee, the whir of the espresso machine, the background hum of a dozen conversations, and the light pouring over the patio and through the front.

My heart rate continued its descent. I had nowhere I needed to be, at least not urgently.

I don't typically drink coffee, but we were on holiday. In stuttering French, I ordered a small macchiato and a gorgeous, flaky croissant. The croissant sat, bronzed, in the middle of a white plate, and I carried my coffee and bread to a corner of a less-occupied table.

*"S'il vous plait?"* I asked, gesturing at the bench.

An elderly man nodded his approval, and then turned back to a man and a woman sitting across the table from him.

I spent a good amount of time on the patio. Out on the water, the morning sunlight jumped and oscillated and exploded into flairs. I thought ahead to my day. We were going to take the boys strawberry picking which, therefore, dictated tonight's dessert of angel-food cake with strawberry topping.

Maybe after fruit-picking we would try out any one of the local bistros for lunch. My parents could fill up on the East Coast seafood delicacies of their youth, culinary fare that could not readily meet their expectations when sampled in the Rocky Mountain West.

In the evening, we would all pitch in and cook for the ten of us, making do with the groceries we could find. Our boys had already shown quite an interest in the kitchen, and hovered under the arms of whichever adult chef would let them.

That was it. Three things. That was our plan for the day. I initiated another conversation with myself in my head:

My life, these days, felt harried—from preschool drop-offs to lunch meetings to reading those missed emails on the commuter train home. Each day was packed with scheduled conversations between work colleagues or with customers. Chores waited for me each weekend, competing with the desire and time needed to get out and do something as a family. Somewhere in there, Kristina and I would squeeze in the odd date night, letting one set of grandparents or the other take the kids.

And while no vacation should be mistaken for day-to-day life, the reality was that I had been choosing this pace. Perhaps there could be a happy medium, something between the slow pace of our agrarian vacation and the minute-by-minute, scheduled life back home: *Where in my life was the time to take the leftward path on the crosswalk and up the knoll to the bakery? Where was the time to sit on the patio and be alone with my thoughts? Further, what were Connor and Kade learning from watching me?*

I finished my coffee, bused my dishes, and made my way back across the crosswalk to stand, again, at the foot of the cemetery. The sun on the water had turned from gold to white.

Keeping my chin up and my eyes level to the scenery, I broke back into a jog. It was downhill now, and I opened up my stride to get back to the rental home more quickly.

As I approached, there were the boys with their grandpa. Grandpa was in the back of the small plane. The boys sat in the first two seats. The kids' eyes were alight with joy and possibility, imagining themselves soaring high over the water.

"Dad!"

"Hey, boys!" I jumped on the back of the plane.

"Make us lean right!"

I moved over to the wing, and the frame settled as the right wing dipped.

"Now we're heading over the mountains!" Kade called out.

Over those two weeks surrounded by fields and farms, Kristina and I talked a lot about slowing things down. We talked about the need to reevaluate our lives' trajectories. We began a more conscious assessment of what spontaneity and adventure and the space for it all meant to us.

Most of our vacation days were filled with only three things: a morning at the bakery; a midday dedicated to one particular aim, such as a cider tour, a visit to a national park or museum, or window shopping in the various boutiques that dotted the coastal drive; and an evening meal. There was time to see where the hiking trail led or linger in the stumbled-upon shop or at the sidewalk café for a bit too long.

Just a short five months later, I would walk into the doctors' office for a routine physical and walk out with cancer.

Pat was the CEO of a local credit union, and he had an ask of me.

I was a member of their volunteer board of directors. My work with the credit union had started back in 2007, when I purchased my first home in Highlands Ranch—a rolling sea of homes densely packed in, like those in the inland suburbs of Southern California—a few years before my wife and I started dating. The credit union was a keystone institution of the community, established when Lockheed Martin was the only major employer in what was, then, still an undeveloped region south of Denver. I was first brought in by recommendation of a local landscaper for whom I streamlined inventory-carry and route-planning, resulting in reduced gas use, less pollution, and fewer trips back to the shop to pick up supplies.

While still grappling with my new diagnosis, I was also in the final stages of planning that attempt on Gangapurna West when Pat asked me if I'd be willing to speak at the upcoming board retreat. It was now the summer of 2019, and while we had, by now, determined my specific form of cancer, we still didn't have enough history of my disease's progress to get any sense of a long-term prognosis. There was plenty of reason for optimism, but there was real uncertainty, too.

Rhetorically, I asked Pat whether my story of climbing, cancer, and family would be appropriate for a board meeting centered on planning out a strategy of mindful dedication to creating community and helping the less fortunate. I really wasn't sure how to stitch this all together into a talk, but maybe there was an angle.

Pat knew of my health status, but the rest of the board did not. I wasn't fearful of trusting any of them with this information, but it would still be a shock, and I did not want it to distract from the real work that needed to be done at the retreat.

But I also knew that stories matter. The credit union very much was wanting to engage those with difficult life stories, ones perhaps buried in shame or uncertainty: teen suicide; food insecurity despite living in the suburbs; debt crippling parents' ability to provide for their kids. These weren't just abstractions, rather very real travails at the intersection of finances and life. If the credit union was going to engage with the community on a human—rather than transactional—level, telling hard stories needed to be okay. It needed to be safe.

So, that was the rationalization, but for reasons I couldn't quite pinpoint, I also felt personally compelled to share my story.

On the last day of the three-day retreat, I was scheduled to speak. We were set up in a rustic-chic conference room at a luxury ranch, tucked under the western slopes of Colorado's Continental Divide near Winter Park, the northernmost major ski area in the central mountains. The roughly thirty-by-thirty-foot square room stood on a peninsula jutting from the main lodge's huge terrace. Picture windows looked out in all directions.

The typical summer thunderstorms were rolling in over the mountains, and we could watch the sky slowly darken as the hours ticked by.

Muted light fought its way through the clouds. The board and credit union officers filled the room, along with their life partners.

I stepped to the front, controller to my slideshow in my right hand, notecards in my left.

I began by telling my colleagues and friends about what we were going to try in a few months: a previously unclimbed peak in Nepal's Annapurna Massif. I described the sparse three paragraphs and one photo we had by way of information about the peak, emphasizing the unknown nature of this climb's particular risks. Our prospective route ascended the wall of a moraine to a snow perch on the peak's southeast spur before gaining a ridge endlessly crenellated by fluted snow.

Then I talked about my family, who would be staying behind. I asked myself more than the audience, "Why would you attempt a dangerous climb like this?" I called out, explicitly, the fact that my family bore both the unseen cost and unseen benefit of these climbs. The cost was their uncertainty and worry while I was up in the mountains. The benefit was whatever lessons I could pull from my climbs that helped me be more selfless once I came home.

In other words, all of my climbs were selfish and needed to be redeemed with selflessness upon my return.

I asked the audience, "Would you go on this trip?" And then I asked, "What if you had cancer?" letting the question hang in the air.

I broke into a series of adventure tales, describing the climbs and peaks which have had the greatest impact on me. The audience nodded with interest when I talked about climbing Longs Peak with my dad and attempting to share these experiences with him and my wife. "How does someone get into this weird hobby, anyway?" I asked, then answered.

The nodding heads stopped, and faces leaned in and forward, as I described bringing a blinded climber down from near the frosty summit of a windswept Mount Rainier.

And then I talked about some of the lessons I had learned on my climbs, and I talked about my earnest desire to impart these lessons to my boys.

"My boys are very bright," I said, choking back tears and then clearing my throat.

"And one of the issues with bright kids is that they move toward success. It's a reinforcing loop: 'I'm good at this; I'm going to keep doing it.' And what happens is that they sometimes stop being willing to challenge themselves. I want them to challenge themselves."

I paused again, gathering myself.

"So, maybe I can take back to them a lesson of *go to an unclimbed peak in the Himalaya*—I would rate our chances of success at maybe 25 percent. But I'm doing it anyway."

I talked about the support and love that I'd received from my family which had always given me the necessary foundation to take meaningful risks.

And I talked about how we all need that support and love anyway, because, in life, there will *always* be risks, even if we don't actively seek them out. "Risk finds you," I said. "It's the kind of thing that can show up in a doctor's office on the Tuesday following

Thanksgiving."

At this point, my world had turned inward. I was talking to the room, making good eye contact and engaging with my audience, but I only know this because I've seen the video. I don't remember anything outside of the rush of my own, turbid emotions.

It seemed like the opposite of an out-of-body experience. The faces around me disappeared. The clouds and darkness rolling in over the mountains no longer captured my attention. I stopped feeling the hardwood floor push up at me from under my trail shoes. I shifted my weight from leg to leg, but I felt none of it. It felt like walking through the pitch-black darkness of a moonless night on a trail with only the small circle of headlamp-cast light around my feet. My world had shrunk to only what was immediately around me.

"I don't know how much more time I have to bring these lessons home," I concluded, breaking down in front of the room. "But I'm going to go, and I'm going to try to climb this unclimbed peak . . ."

The metaphor was cliché, but it was all too real to me: ". . . and we'll see what lessons I can bring back."

***Kade approaching the camp site the family made, celebrating Kristina's and Jason's tenth wedding anniversary and which spawned the start of the family's YouTube channel.***

CHAPTER THIRTEEN

# Achievement?

"We should climb Denali."

That's how my friend, Chris S., brought up the idea while we were standing in the bottom of Ouray's Uncompahgre Gorge teaching new climbers how to climb ice on an early February day in 2013.

It was almost two years before Kade and Connor would come into the world. And it would be six months after their birth when Chris and I, along with a team of four others, finally set foot on the mountain.

A little short of five months after our initial conversation, I tore my right ACL for the third time due to a simple slip while on the approach to the Kautz Glacier route on Mount Rainier. It was the graduation climb for a group of High Altitude Mountaineering School (HAMS) students and my first such trip leading as a senior instructor. Having far fewer functioning nerves in my right knee due to the previous injuries, and an awful lot of scar tissue, I wasn't positive I had torn it again. And with the sincere desire to give the graduating students a climbing experience, I continued up Rainier for about 6,000 vertical feet to Camp Hazard (11,300 feet), from where we would attempt the summit. My contracted and tense leg muscles, as needed for an uphill climb, kept my knee stable. But it was on the way down, muscles fully extended, that I felt the severe instability and resultant bone-on-bone contact. It was a torturous descent that was further complicated by a whiteout (a snow- and/or windstorm that creates very low visibility) that had mandated our retreat from Camp Hazard, having climbed no higher.

After my third ACL reconstruction on that knee, I proceeded to train for Denali in earnest. The climb provided a goal around which to structure the endless hours of physical therapy. Countless squats and lunges were designed to help me move uphill under a heavy pack. My teammates and I hauled sixty-pound sleds up the slopes of local Fourteeners, and I even managed to put up a seemingly new route up Quandary Peak, corkscrewing up its southwest couloirs.

It was nearly two years following that surgery that I was with five others, making our summit push high up on Denali's West Rib. We were on the West Rib Cutoff route, taking the standard West Buttress route up to 14,400 feet and then turning southwest to the West Rib where the standard route turned north up Denali Headwall.

It was a far less traveled route, and we later discovered that we were one of only two teams who'd selected it that season. It was somewhat shocking to the system to move from a well-guided stream of humanity, with climbers numbering in the hundreds, to being completely on our own on this glaciated giant.

I was the expedition leader, having put together the plan, the logistics, and the team. We were moving up the mountain as two teams of three: Chris S., Sally, and I were on the first rope; Chris K., Aaron, and Pat were on the second rope. Most of us knew each other from the Colorado Mountain Club, and particularly the HAMS courses. Chris S., Sally, Aaron, and I had co-instructed. Aaron was also on my rope team that had helped bring a blinded climber down the northern flanks of Mount Rainier. Chris K. was an uber-fit cyclist and former HAMS student. Pat was Aaron's regular climbing partner.

The terrain was broken up, with outcroppings of steep boulders bracketing prolonged sections of steep snow ramps. Chris S. was in the lead, placing the occasional snow picket or slinging a boulder to clip our rope through in a running belay, like I had done on the Mount Rainier rescue three years earlier.

In the thin air around 18,000 feet, a bright light drove ferociously through the wispy clouds, bringing a harsh glare to the metal protection Chris S. was attaching to the mountain. My eyes' only relief from the incessant reflections of light off the snow, ice, and climbing protection was my tinted sunglasses, designed especially for the UV radiation at altitude.

The sun's radiation bounced off of the snow on all sides, effectively putting us in one, large reflecting dish. The effect was heat, and we sweated through our layers, despite the ambient temperature being below zero (Fahrenheit). So, we stopped every hour or so to take in water and reapply sunscreen.

The heat also softened the top layer of snow, turning the upper inch into something the consistency of a corn chowder, layered over a substratum of rock-hard snow that made it difficult to hammer in pickets.

We moved comparatively quickly over the rocks, our crampons making high-pitched squeals and squeaks as the steel grated on the granite. While some sections of rock were steep and merited protection, most of the ground was class 3 or class 4 climbing, with sure placements for our hands and feet.

The snow conditions, however, made for long sections demanding continuous protection. The soft top layer made footing mildly treacherous, the snow balling up in our crampons, eradicating their ability to penetrate down to the harder snow. And that hard snow, underneath, was too hard for an ice-axe pick to penetrate with any ease, which made our position on the fifty-degree slopes even more precarious—should any of us slip, it was unlikely that we'd be able to arrest our fall through the standard practice of jamming our picks into the snow.

When on snow, then, Chris S. would hammer in one of our six pickets and clip his rope through as he moved past. The rest of us would pass our rope through the same picket, except for Pat, who was at the rear of our small column. His job was to extract the picket and sling it over his shoulder, collecting them. Once Chris S. had placed all the pickets, he would anchor himself into the mountain and wait. We would each come up to his position, coiling our team back together like a compressed spring. Pat would come last, and hand over all the pickets to Chris S., allowing the procession to start again.

This process significantly mitigated the consequence of a fall, as each rope team was continuously anchored to the mountain, but it also slowed our progress significantly. Stopped at a granite boulder the size of a dining room table at 19,150 feet—per my altimeter—we paused to discuss our predicament.

"We're moving slow," Chris S. commented to me as we waited there for the rest of the team.

"Yeah, we are. But I don't think we can move much faster."

We talked about abandoning the running belay and unroping altogether. The thinking was that, if we were tied to each other but without any gear placements between us, then a fall by one of us would potentially yank everyone else off, too.

We ruled that out as being beyond the comfort zone of several of our teammates.

"We have about thirty-six hours until it's supposed to get bad with wind," I told the team as we all gathered at the rock. We weren't in immediate danger, but we also weren't going to make the summit at our current pace. We had been on the move for about 12 hours and were still somewhere around 1,000 vertical feet short of the summit.

We could climb through the night. We could reverse and head back down to our high camp at 16,300 feet. Or, because we were in the midst of a "carry over," ascending the West Rib route and then descending the standard West Buttress route, we could potentially make a new camp; we were carrying all of our overnight gear.

"We just need to keep our bodies in good enough shape," I cautioned to silent nods of affirmation.

"I'm about out of water," Chris S. finally said, the only climber to speak up.

That ruled out climbing through the night; we needed to stop to melt snow into water. And heading down would likely take nearly as long given the need to place pickets.

The sun had dropped low in the sky, casting our long shadows onto the rock bench and across the nearby snow. Behind us sat East and West Kahiltna Peaks, just above and just under 13,000 feet, respectively, their summits now a vertical mile below. The east fork of the Kahiltna Glacier sat behind the peaks, and a maze of crevasses surrounded basecamp, now more than two miles below alongside where the bush planes drop you off and then pick you back up at the climb's end. Farther out, jagged teeth and spires of black granite jutted up in an endless array.

I had come to recognize, from my nearly two weeks on the mountain, that the sun would not drop much further. We were near the Arctic Circle, and it was early summer; the sun would never quite set. With the sun being so low in the sky, it must have been late. I took a look at my watch: 11:00 p.m.

Here, above 19,000 feet, we'd reached the highest we had yet been, and sleeping at your high point doesn't usually make for good acclimatization. It is, instead, normal practice to "climb high and sleep low," allowing your body to adjust by exposing it to doses of thinner air while climbing and then dropping back down to richer air to sleep.

Nonetheless, setting camp seemed like the best option. We could sleep for a few hours, melt snow for water, and then either cut the corner off our route and just head down on the standard West Buttress route or continue on to the summit, if we all felt up to it.

I knew we were somewhere just southwest of the Football Field, the broad plateau a few hundred vertical feet below the summit where our route and the standard route converge. I marked our position on my GPS device and then shut it off. I wanted to conserve batteries in case the next morning demanded any type of rescue.

Stepping off our rocky perch, we flipped our ice axes over and began digging a tent platform. Using the adze—the blade on the back of the pick—we scraped off the surface layer of soft snow and then began hacking into the hard snow and ice underneath. We would take turns, each member of the team staggering away from the worksite in gasping pants due to the lack of oxygen.

After about an hour, we declared the platform "good enough," and we pitched camp.

Each rope team was in their own tent, and a voice called through the nylon, "Are we going to get out of this?"

"We're fine," Chris S. replied.

"Weather kills on Denali, and our weather is good. Let's just see how we're all doing in the morning," I joined in.

I slept fitfully, my sleeping bag making a slow migration to the foot of the tent, as our insufficient hacking job had left the ground still sloped a bit too steeply. I woke up early, curled in a ball at the foot of the tent and with cold feet where they pressed against the tent door, compressing the down of my sleeping bag.

I was uncomfortable, but otherwise fine. I checked my pulse oximeter, making sure that I was within tolerances for blood-oxygen saturation. Low readings were an indicator of a heightened potential to experience severe altitude sickness. Mine read 73 percent of what I would expect to see at sea level, which was well within the corridor of "normal" for being above 5,800 meters.

We passed the pulse oximeter around and checked the team's levels. We talked about symptoms. Of the six of us, I was the only one not experiencing a mild headache, but we were all in pretty good shape.

Regardless of what we did from here, head up or head down, we would need water, so we set up our two stoves to begin melting snow. However, we couldn't get one stove to light. Thus began a long process, six hours, of melting enough snow on one stove so that six people could hydrate, which would combat the headaches.

We sat and ate snacks and continually assessed our bodies. With the light activity, peoples' symptoms and oxygen numbers were both improving.

I powered up my GPS device, and given the need to navigate by it—as we were slightly off-route—I took the first position on the first rope as we did our final safety checks. Then I announced, "Well, gang, it's been a pleasure. One last push." Turning my body sideways across the steep slope, I crossed one leg over the other and began sidestepping up. Every so often, I would rotate my steps and face the opposite direction across the slope, putting more strain on one calf muscle and less on the other.

Our route and the standard route intersected at the base of a prominent fang of snow-covered rock called Archdeacon's Tower, at about 19,600 feet. There, we dug a shallow rectangle and cached our camping gear, making us lighter for the summit push.

Now on the flat, quarter-mile-long Football Field, the punishing, late-afternoon sun demanded we strip down to just our base-layer tops. Sweat dripped down my temples from underneath my helmet.

"Enjoy this, gang!" I yelled back to the crew. "Not everyone gets a summit day like this!"

The forty-degree slopes of Pig Hill made up the bulk of the climbing that remained. I moved into a rest-step, pausing to weight my straightened back leg with each step forward, taking in a breath each time. Even so, every hundred vertical feet or so, I'd have to stop in my tracks and pant for a few moments before resuming the plod onward.

The snow was hard here—no soft top layer. My crampon points dug in well as I pointed my toes outward allowing me to engage all but my front points, reducing the strain on my already-tired calves.

We topped Pig Hill at the Kahiltna Horn, another snow-covered rock spire—not unlike Archdeacon's Tower—that marked the exit point of the alpine classic Cassin Ridge, with its narrow chutes, exposed arêtes, and hanging camps. There were a few other teams around us now, heading across the final summit ridge or returning from the top.

I decided I wanted Chris S. to take his position back at the front of the rope. He had done so much solid leading for so long, and navigation was no longer an issue. He and I changed positions.

"Good job, Jason," Chris K. called out to me.

"Thank you!" I said, somewhat weakly due to my oxygen-starved lungs.

Clouds had started to roll in from the east, but to the west the view was clear. My eyes stretched out into the distance, watching the ground peel away and descend, turning from shades of white to an emerald green. Even lower, a vast river wound off into the distance, meeting the horizon.

The sun, reflecting off the Football Field below us, gave the air a glassy look, with ribbons of color playing games with me as the light refracted across my sunglass lenses.

My axe was in my right hand, upslope from our position just below the peak of the ridge, and I drove my spike into the snow in a purposeful and methodical cadence that became a mantra: *Axe, step, step. Axe, step, step.*

Then the rope dragging in front of me made a right-hand turn. Following it first with my axe placement, then my feet, and then my eyes, I looked up to see Chris S. and Sally stopped and facing me. With each foot placement I made, Sally brought in a length of rope, shortening the lifeline between us.

I joined the two of them on the summit. Sally and Chris came over, and we all embraced.

"Good job, Jason," Sally squeezed out.

"Thank you so much for making this happen," Chris said.

"Good job," I half-spoke and half-exhaled in relief.

Our other rope team followed quickly behind, and all six of us were on top in moments. We took out snacks, sipped our hard-earned water, and passed around cameras for photographs. The gathering clouds prompted us to add layers, and we donned our thick, puffy parkas.

It wasn't long, however, before we started thinking about the need to descend to high camp on the standard West Buttress route before the weather moved in.

"If you are feeling tired and a bit weak, that's normal," Chris S. reminded us.

"I need to start moving," Sally said.

We reversed our path across the ridge. As I was on the back of the first rope, Chris K., who was the lead climber on our second rope, was right behind me.

The conversation grew light. "I think we should glissade this mother," he joked, referring to using a "sliding-down-the-snow" descent technique on the steep, hard-packed Pig Hill. "Might be a little hard on the ass, though."

I laughed and mimicked the sounds of stuttering breath being forced out by a potential washboard descent.

Turning my head up from the snow and back across the glassy air over the Football Field, I thought about digging up our supplies, the traverse across Denali Pass (the site of many accidents due to a steep slope under it and fatigued climbers crossing its precipice), and our need to set up camp. Farther yet, I looked down to the Kahiltna Glacier towards basecamp and then traced the glacier south to where it twisted and extended its way nearly fifty miles into a wash of green in the lower elevations.

Our path home was laid out in front of me. Somewhere at the end of that path was the start of the path to the next climb, and a twinge of bitterness penetrated the joy I felt over our accomplishment.

And then I had another thought, a reminder: *we still have half the expedition in front of us, and it stands between me and my wife and boys.* I ended the banter and shrunk back into my mind: *Axe, step, step. Axe, step, step.*

We had just passed through the second winter of the pandemic and the second wave of COVID. Spring 2021 was upon us, and we had still managed to keep COVID out of the house. The virus was better understood, and we did things to avoid airborne transmission. Receiving groceries on our doorstep now felt safe, and we took other matters on a case-by-case basis. Service contractors coming to the home (which we did allow to happen) or trips to the dentist (which I didn't do) all became cause for relative risk assessment.

Kristina and I got our first vaccines, with me getting an earlier window of availability due to my immunocompromised status. (I wasn't in the first wave with the elderly but was in the third wave.) While the vaccines were promising, and indeed incredibly effective for most, we began to see early signs that the vaccines were not as effective for those with immunocompromising conditions.

Patients with Chronic Lymphocytic Leukemia, in particular, are notoriously bad at vaccine uptake. Flu vaccines, for example, have seen "normal" immune system responses in only ten to twenty percent of CLL patients. Vaccines work by teaching your immune system to mark and attack the bad cells. Well, CLL affects the very cells that are supposed to do the marking, the B-cells.

The Leukemia and Lymphoma Society (LLS, and as of 2025 called Blood Cancer United) began to conduct clinical research on COVID vaccine efficacy for those with differing types of blood cancer. Upon getting my vaccine, I volunteered to be a part of the LLS study and have my body's response to the vaccine measured. After one shot, I had essentially no response. After a second shot, I had a mild response, showing antibody levels about one-tenth of those found in healthy adults.

LLS accumulated more information as the pandemic wore on. At that point, some studies were showing near or even above 50 percent of blood-cancer patients who contracted moderate to severe COVID died from it. And of all the blood-cancer types, those with my particular version had the worst response to the COVID vaccines.

I, however, was in a gray area. I had an immune system that was "better than" those with advanced stages of my disease or when compared to those who had undergone immune-system-wrecking cancer treatments. So, my probabilities were going to be a bit better than those in the study.

But how much better? Better than an exceptionally at-risk group isn't really saying much. The advice from physicians to those in my circumstance was, "Get vaccinated. Act unvaccinated."

And so I began to agonize.

A third vaccine dose produced a better response, but my physician team continued to caution me, "You are at higher risk; you need to act like it."

I could get past not going on climbing trips with friends. And I didn't feel any particular loss from being out of an office setting.

In fact, getting more time with my boys was part of what the revelation in Quebec had been all about. But my condition wasn't just demanding that I isolate myself; it demanded that my family isolate themselves, too.

The darkest moments, the time when the tears came, were when I contemplated the sacrifices made by my wife, my kids, my parents, and anyone else who wanted to spend time with me without putting me at risk. They avoided get-togethers of all kinds: weddings and funerals, playdates, clubs and camps, the normal things in life.

Also at this time, third-grade-level work began for the boys, and it challenged them. When the boys completed their second-grade studies within the second semester of their first-grade year, they'd completed two full years of schoolwork within nine months. Now, doing third-grade work while still only six, the age of kindergarteners, they'd gone from turning in work that was largely affirming to seeing mistakes that needed revision.

The need to revise was new to them, and they experienced it as criticism—emotionally, they were still so young. Moreover, they had very limited social contact, no real peer group, and parents who loved them but who now were seemingly constantly correcting them both domestically and scholastically. Resentments surfaced. Tempers flared. Between tantrums and work interruptions, the three hours of schooling a day often turned into seven, eight, and nine hours.

"Connor, you have to get this done. Please," I pleaded. Connor sat on a kitchen stool at our breakfast bar, math worksheets laid out in front of him. "I know it's frustrating, but we can work through them together."

My wife was in the living room, sitting next to Kade on the couch, both of them staring at his red clipboard. She was making a similar plea.

Almost in unison, both boys screamed, "I'm not going to do it!"

My wife tried to deescalate with Kade: "Honey, it's just eight problems. We can find one you think is easiest and start with that."

I was starting to fray: "Connor, I have a meeting in twenty minutes, and we've already been at this for thirty. I just need you to do the darn problems."

Connor slammed his pencil against the counter, and it bounced down to the floor.

"Connor! Pick up your pencil!"

From the other room: "No! I'm still not doing it! It's stupid!"

"Kade, baby, please."

"No!"

"Kade, I can't do this right now."

"I'm not going to do it!"

Meanwhile, back in the kitchen . . .

"Connor, the whole reason I'm here is to help, because you and your brother have refused to do this all morning with your mom. I need you to pick up your pencil and do it!"

"No!"

Connor folded his arms across his chest, tilted his chin down, and dropped his brow over his eyes.

The boys' first reaction to an assignment had become to stomp away and scream about "not doing it!" A delicate dance of coaxing compliance or threatening punishment would ensue. Time ticked away from those finite windows dedicated to schoolwork that we'd carved from our own work calendars. Falling behind on one lesson meant starting the next one late, and we invariably had to be done by X-o'clock because both Mom and Dad had "a video meeting to get to" or some such.

We tried star charts. We talked about our roles contributing to the family. My wife and I took days off from work and tried to depressurize things. Depressurizations didn't last. We could turn the tension in the family down a notch, but over time it would rise back two or three notches.

And neither Kristina nor I were taking care of ourselves—or each other.

We were also in the midst of selling our house, getting ready to move closer to the Rocky Mountains but while still remaining in the Denver Metro—we'd decided we couldn't be that far from definitive medical care. That is the one thing we *had* promised ourselves after our Quebec trip—a quieter life, closer to the hills.

Our current house had boxes filling up the garage, and we were living in classic "staged-home" style, with only the absolute necessities on counters and in cabinets, to make the home look positively spacious. The downside, of course, was the constant need to find the box in the garage that had the thing we thought we wouldn't need but which we did, in fact, now need.

I lost sleep from anxiety.

Kristina was losing sleep from the stress of being a mom, a professional, and—now—a teacher, not to mention the spouse of a person who was consistently at risk.

That evening, I found her sitting in the chair tucked into the corner of our living room. The boxes of textbooks and workbooks held their places as end tables, but now we shuffled them back and forth to and from the garage when we had a home showing.

The sun was sinking, and the light was faint as dusk filtered through our east-facing picture window. She had taken a pause from filing the day's schoolwork records, and loose worksheets were scattered on the floor and on the couch. The boys were upstairs, getting into their pajamas.

"They need to go back to school. I need them to go back to school," my wife said. She looked at me with sunken eyes. Her back was caved, and her neck arched forward. She looked tired, deeply tired.

"I'm not being a mom when I'm being their teacher. This can't ruin our relationship." She sounded desperate, pleading with me. "I know we're worried about the virus and the *potential* of that, but this *is* happening, and it is happening now."

"I know this can't go on forever," I said. "If it was going to be forever under these circumstances, we would stop and adjust. I want the kids in school, too. I don't know—if it's just a few more months before we can get them vaccinated, should we wait for that?"

"I need them to go to school *now*, Jason!" She wasn't screaming, but she was emphatic. And my wife, who rarely cries, started to well up.

"If I just knew how long this would be going on, this would be easy. It's tough when we don't know how much better it will be in the future or when 'better' will start," I said, referring to some future world in which the virus was more under control.

We were both losing a war of attrition.

A perverse relationship had started to form, one in which my kids were paying the cost of keeping me safe. Inverting the parent-child relationship was a regular topic of my ongoing therapy sessions. And this concern wrestled for space with the struggle of being consistently at risk in a way that was easier to control at home but difficult to control anywhere else.

Our pod of four couldn't continue with these tension-creating entanglements and our swapping of the familial roles.

The boys were more than two grades ahead of their age, academically, but it was clear that this situation wasn't working.

I bought my first guitar in the Danish-themed Central California wine town of Solvang, just north of Santa Barbara—the iconic location in the movie *Sideways*. I was twenty-four and in Solvang on a family vacation with my parents and my brother. I had just determined to leave behind my attempt at a professional golf career upon being offered a fellowship to the University of Maryland, where I would pursue a master's degree in public policy.

Between beer and Scandinavian pastries, I wandered into a music shop with my brother. He was an accomplished musician, with perfect pitch. He'd formally studied music while at university, somewhere along the line in his progression of majors. I was not a musician. But I saw an Ovation acoustic/electric guitar with strings close to the neck that would accommodate my short fingers. It had a good tone, bringing the high-pitched notes out clear and resonant. The lower notes were still a bit crisper than I wanted but were warm-sounding enough. Along with the guitar, I bought the softest set of strings I could find, to help mute those lower notes, and placed them in the storage compartment in the guitar's hard case.

I also looked around at some guitar-tab books. My brother had suggested that I first learn to play songs I was familiar with; I would be able to hear the differences between my playing and what was embedded in my mind from years of hearing the songs on the radio. I picked up some Bob Dylan and U2 and Counting Crows songbooks. I also bought a picture book of chords: "over 2,600 guitar chords," the book's cover proudly proclaimed.

I didn't do much with the guitar during the rest of the vacation. My family and I were there to wander the shops and eat too much and chat over iced tea and lemonade.

I had a few months before heading east to school, and a lot of free time, so I was determined to learn five chord voicings a day. I started at page one: C major.

At first, my fingers just didn't do what I wanted them to do. In particular, I had a hard time getting my left ring and pinky fingers to work independently. They felt fused together somewhere in the back of my hand. I would bend my ring finger down toward the guitar's neck, and my pinky finger would follow despite my desire to place it elsewhere.

I pressed my index, middle, and ring fingers all the way down, pinning the strings into the guitar's neck at the first, second, and third frets, respectively. I overcompensated, and forced my pinky to jut partially outward, like an upper-class snoot holding a teacup with "sophistication."

The next sensation was a mild, but uncomfortable, pain. The soft pads of skin on my fingertips revolted at the impertinence of the bronze-wrapped silk pushing back against them. On my ring finger, the outer corner of my fingernail dug into me, heightening the pain. I was still years away from climbing rock, working on finger and forearm strength while grating my skin with regularity over sharp granite or quartzite—I'd later be more than used to such digital discomfort.

Doing my best to ignore all these new and unpleasant sensations, I dragged my right hand down over the strings. The pick, which I had pressed between my thumb and my curled index finger, called each of the six strings to action, and the familiar sound of a mid-octave C major wafted from within the guitar.

I already knew this voicing. I had messed around with some of my brother's guitars, long ago, as he showed me the fundamentals.

Looking at the pictures of alternate voicings, I wrestled with my uncooperative left hand. I moved up the neck, placing my index finger at the third fret, and then a new voicing at the fifth, across all the strings at the eighth, and then a more comfortable triangulation of finger positions beginning at the twelfth. Each new chord began with halted fumbling as I contorted my hand into the proper position.

When I eventually arrived in College Park, Maryland, moving into a split level, four-bedroom house with three other graduate students, I was through the C chords and almost done with the Ds. This included chords predominately used in jazz, like "D-flat dominant seventh with sharp ninth." These were not the type of chords I'd heard Bob Dylan or U2 play, for sure. In addition, I found I had a difficult but manageable time spanning my hands across four frets; getting across five felt impossible.

Around College Park, I was seeing flyers for guitar lessons—not uncommon in a university town. I pulled one partially cut tab with a phone number from a flier and tucked the slip of paper into my pocket.

Back at home, sitting on my bed as light dimly flowed through the garden-level window of my lower-floor bedroom, I thrust my hand into the front pocket of my jeans. The now well-worn calluses of my fret hand fished for the scrap of paper. I brought it out, looked at the number on the paper, and then placed the scrap on my nightstand.

Sliding off the bed, I knelt and pulled the hard guitar case out from under the bed frame. The brass fixtures along the side of the case made a satisfying snap as I unlatched them. I wrapped my hand around the mahogany neck and lifted the guitar from its molded seat.

I stood up, did a half-pirouette, and sat again, the mattress sinking beneath my weight. With my heel, I pushed the guitar case back underneath the bed.

Eschewing the pick, I flicked my right middle fingernail across the strings. My left hand found its place on the frets. The strings felt cold, having just come out of hibernation. Strumming with intention, now, my left hand moved in time:

D major . . . D suspended fourth . . . D suspended fourth, D major, D suspended second.

"She's a good girl. Loves her mama. Loves Jesus, and America, too." I whispered the lyrics to Tom Petty's "Free Fallin'" as I played.

For three and a half minutes, I just strummed and whisper-sang in my off-tune voice.

It wasn't that I was too busy with school and making new friends to really pursue the guitar. After all, it was never a bad thing to be able to pick up a guitar and play a song in order to attract people over. It was that I'd decided I wasn't going to push this hobby.

I had spent the last two years traveling from state to state and town to town with golf clubs in the back of my Volkswagen Jetta. It was all the same guys in each town, playing one- or two-day mini-tour events with prize money so small it often didn't cover the costs of our entry fees, food, and hotel.

To this day, I have never worked harder than I did on the competition golf circuit. Fourteen-hour days were not unusual. Finishing a competitive round, I might assess that I was fighting a push to the right or had struggled from down-sloping lies in fairway bunkers or even just needed to keep my chipping feel in shape after a good day of ball striking. There was always some skill to improve or maintain.

We'd double up in rooms, sleep across the backseats of our cars, and tell the same stories of "that putt I missed on sixteen." We didn't play guitar, and there certainly weren't other people around who would have cared anyway.

After I finished the song, the strings felt warm under my skin.

I gently rested my Ovation on the bed next to me. Reaching toward the nightstand, I lifted the paper with the phone number and then dropped it into the waste basket next to the bed.

I was talking to Pat over the phone.

Pat is somewhere north of ten years older than me. Yes, he was the CEO of the credit union for which I had volunteered and served on the board of directors. Beyond that, though, he was and is a friend. Until I moved hours away, we'd get together once a month for breakfast to talk about credit-union business but also about the mosaic of life.

Pat deeply desires to help his community. It had been Pat's vision that the credit union move to a more inclusive model of lending, with financial packages designed to help individuals ladder-up from securing basic needs, to coming out from debt, to planning for the future. He is also a connoisseur of stories. He believes in the power of real, honest human stories to move and motivate. He made stories the centerpiece of his community-engagement strategy, calling out people's real needs—and our ability to meet them.

My energy this day was a bit frenetic. We were entering the second winter of COVID, expecting the next "wave" of cases to flood through our cities and towns. We knew more about transmission, and avoidance was possible at a cost, but the first vaccines—while they'd been announced—were not yet available.

The conversation with Pat started as I stood in the basement of our suburban brick home, down where Connor and Kade had bounced up and down with me while counting jump tucks. The can lights we had installed in the exposed joists of the low, seven-foot ceiling bathed the concrete floor in white light, drawing out each imperfection in the fifty-year-old slab.

Over the previous weeks, I'd been trying to convince Pat that the internet marketplace we were building to bring well-off credit-union members into contact with struggling members needed to be launched with capital injection, despite holes in the financial forecast. The whole point of iterative design, I argued, was to quickly pivot what we built. Venture capital knew and would accept these risks, as long as we were honest about them. If we waited until we had a finished product, we would be past the time when a capital injection could really help.

The intent wasn't my problem; how I'd delivered the message was. I had stepped pretty hard on the CFO while making my point over the last months. I was talking to Pat both to underscore my earnestness but also to apologize. Like we always did, however, we turned to the intersection of life and business—something I found refreshing.

We were talking about fear. I had come back from the Himalaya transformed by the experience of attempting a first ascent on a remote 7,000-meter peak all while wrestling the demons of my blood cancer and my mortality. For over a year, now, I had been trying to avoid a virus that was killing off people like me with ruthless efficiency.

I admitted that I wanted things done fast these days, and that it was hard to separate my desire to speed along the credit union's business changes from the anxiety caused by my personal circumstances.

"I am afraid every single day, Pat. I wake up afraid. I go to bed afraid," I said. I was pacing up and down the half-flight of stairs that connected the garden level of our tri-level home to the basement. The white paint on the wooden steps was slowly flaking off under the years of footfalls.

"Well, we try to not make decisions out of fear."

I didn't respond for a few moments. But my pacing stopped. I flicked off the light switch at the top of the stairs. The colors of my climbing gear, neatly organized on metal racks lining the walls, immediately faded to black as the basement went dark. Closing the door behind me, I took the next half flight of stairs, moving from the garden level to the main level, arriving in the kitchen.

I swallowed. "I can understand that," I choked out, despite how inapt I thought his statement to be in my case. Plus, like most mountaineers, I appreciated fear; it kept us alive, helping us make rational decisions in the hills based on circumstances our very fear had helped us identify.

I moved around the granite counter and stood at the kitchen sink. The sealant coat on the black and white granite reflected the sunlight in splashes; here and there, the glare made it impossible to see the marbling and miniscule threads of red and gold that wove through the stone.

The white kitchen cabinets, gray-white subway-tiled backsplash, and white plank-wood floor only bounced more light. The black trim of the appliances was washed out. I was indoors but squinting.

I brought my gaze up, looking out the window into the backyard. With Colorado's extended falls and late winters, the grass was still deeply green, contrasting against the brown fence in the yard.

"You know, Jason, it's okay. You have a lot going on."

"Yeah, but that doesn't mean I don't want to help make this work."

"It's okay, though. You may be at a point where you are just going to be less useful. That's okay. I mean, in your career, and professionally. That doesn't mean you aren't important. To your family. To your friends."

What Pat had said was said out of concern. It was said to provide me with a different perspective. It was said to provide me room to make other choices. I've never doubted his intentions.

I thanked Pat for his time and promised to be back in touch in a few days. But I ended the call quickly. I was fuming.

I slid open the patio door and stepped from the black-and-white kitchen onto the back porch. A year later, we'd be gone, out to our home nearer the hills, leaving the cold sterility of black and white for mess and vibrance. Outside, I exhaled deeply. The not-yet-dormant, fall grass felt cool against my bare feet, and I was bathed in rich color where the green bushes and brown tree limbs, and even the occasional yellow-flowering weed, danced beyond me in the gentle breeze sweeping the yard.

*Teammates on the descent, looking back down the standard route on Denali (20,310') towards Mount Foraker (17, 402').*

CHAPTER FOURTEEN

# Journeys

We were about six hundred feet off the ground on a 1,500-foot rock climb called *Royal Flush* when we heard the telltale cracking of thunder. That was unusual, as the mid-fall weather is normally stable in the Colorado mountains. Looking southwest up the canyon past Officers Gulch and toward the Copper Mountain Resort, we could see dark rolling clouds rolling toward us. We had minutes until the skies opened up.

"We should head down," my friend and mentor Fabrizio Zangrilli, a top guide and alpinist, said. Not waiting for my reply, he began laying strands of rope into his hand, readying it to toss down from our bolted anchor.

"I agree," I replied as I clipped my rappel device into a loop of Dyneema fabric, a pliable weave that is stronger than steel and which was tethering me to the bolted anchor.

This is part of what we were up here for, anyway, doing multiple rappels down an alpine wall. It was 2017, and I was two years out from my trip to the Himalaya, early in the planning stages but also making sure I had the requisite skills for heading into the unknown. Yes, we would have liked to have climbed a little longer, but nature had spoken.

The sudden loss of light, as the clouds moved quickly above us, turned the granite from a light gray to a dark gray, muting the rock's splashes of tan and green lichen.

As Fabrizio and I double-checked our systems, making sure the rope was running through our devices correctly and that the carabiners holding those devices to our personal tethers were all locked, the first rain started to fall. We had six rappels to do, so diligence would be the name of the game. The drops began almost spittingly, with the wind from the front pushing them nearly sideways onto us.

Following Fabrizio's lead, I rappelled to the next anchor: two more bolts driven into the rock offering exceptional security. Fabrizio had already threaded one strand of rope through the new anchor point and tied it off to one bolt. I quickly attached myself to this new anchor and removed myself from the ropes as Fabrizio began pulling the rope from the tied-off end. When the neon-green rope shook loose from the higher anchor, thirty meters above, he called, "Rope!"

Green coils tumbled towards and then by us. While the twists of rope were still settling, I was already pulling again from the tied-off end, making a great loop of our rope until the black-painted middle markings came to rest at the center of our new anchor. I untied the secured end, retied a stopper knot in it (something our rappel devices would jam into should we ever lose control, keeping us from rappelling off the ends of the rope), flaked enough rope into my hand to create mass, and then gave it a firm throw down and away from the mountain, similarly calling, "Rope!"

Two anchors later, and still two rappels off the ground, we ran into another team of two climbers. By now, things were truly wet. The skies were free of life-threatening lightning, but mud was accumulating on my climbing shoes as we stood below another two-bolt anchor on an ample ledge.

"I dropped my rappel device," one of the two climbers said, with a hint of desperation.

"Well, can you do a Münter rappel?" I asked, referencing the hitch you can use to belay or rappel, in a pinch, if you don't have a device.

"I know what it is, but I've never done one for real," was the reply.

"Here, take my device," Fabrizio said calmly, and handed his rappel device over to the climber.

"Thanks!" said the climber, giving a broad exhale of relief.

As the other team was heading down, we waited, so as to not cross ropes and create chaos. This gave us time to dig into our packs and throw on rain-shell jackets.

"You should go down first. This Münter is going to twist the heck out of the rope," Fabrizio told me, as calm as ever.

It was a testament to Fabrizio's instruction that I, too, felt composed during our abrupt departure. I had years of climbing experience at this point, and we had gone over multi-rappels before, about a month earlier on this same wall, to work on efficiency; time standing around is dangerous time on high, cold mountains.

Heading down this penultimate rappel, my feet skidded and swam over the saturated surface. The brisk alpine air combined with the water to chill my feet, sockless in my climbing shoes. I slipped a few times, banging one knee and then the other. I brought my legs higher in front of me, more perpendicular to the rock. Pushing off the wall with them, I focused on moving the twin strands of rope through my friction-hitch backup, which grabbed the rappel ropes at waist level. The extra slack in the rope, in turn, threaded more of itself through my rappel device, lowering me some more.

As luck would have it, this was not the first bail Fabrizio and I had executed.

I'd spent two years, upon my return from Denali in 2015, working with him on, roughly, a monthly basis, learning the finer points of high-altitude climbing. I now knew enough to not only apply but to teach some of the finer points.

Fabrizio is an accomplished expert, having been one of a cadre of intrepid souls who traveled across the globe, from range to range, following weather windows as they appeared in new locations with predictable, seasonal regularity. While balancing making a living by guiding clients up 6,000-, 7,000-, and 8,000-meter peaks, including the first-ever commercial expedition on K2, he had put up first ascents in Alaska and Queen Maud Land, Antarctica. He had also rescued climbers on Pumori and K2—the latter from above 8300 meters, one of the highest successful rescues ever recorded. Fabrizio was much larger than me, a powerful climber with a dark, Mediterranean complexion in stark contrast to my slight and Slavic features. He is direct and gruff in moments of focus but also filled with empathy and with a strong humanist bent.

At this time, he was also at a new point in his life, being a fairly new father—which we had in common—and in a position to only take on the work he wanted, not needing to guide an endless parade of clients up the same routes on the same mountains.

So, each month we would attempt a new climb or go over a new set of skills, sticking close to home and our children in Colorado. Not necessarily having the luxury of traveling great distances, and also needing to schedule our weekends well in advance, we'd hit bad weather or bad conditions more than a few times.

On one occasion, we hiked into the western (back) side of Grand Traverse Peak in the Gore Range above Silverthorne only to determine that loose snow and loose rock made our springtime ascent plan foolish. We postholed through thigh-deep snow into another couloir that wasn't our original objective, finding snow conditions no better than on the approach, despite the higher elevation. Another time, we hiked into a rock climb only to find that the cracks the guidebook had labeled as four inches wide were actually five or six, which we hadn't brought cams for. Unable to safely protect the climb, we bailed after the first pitch.

The failures were largely mine; I was planning the objectives, but Fabrizio also knew that failure was a good teacher. He was there to make sure I survived my failures as well as to turn each outing into a learning experience. We'd deconstruct what happened, address the lessons of the day, and still find something productive to do, like improving my gear placements on a traditional lead or working through how to communicate when we were separated by a rope length and couldn't hear each other.

We did accomplish some climbs, though. We turned a rock climb into a mixed climb during a mid-fall ascent of Mount Toll on the Continental Divide. We flowed up ice pitches—well, Fabrizio flowed. I learned to loosen my hips up and approach something closer to flowing, allowing me to climb far higher in a single push than I ever had before. And we got up rock pitches that forced me to stop my habit of always climbing directly over my feet by applying a broader range of techniques and more-gymnastic movements.

However, getting to the top of things wasn't really the point. We covered movement, mental, and system techniques. I learned the fundamentals of aid climbing, breathing rhythms when I was on the sharp end of the rope, and, yes, how to most efficiently perform multiple rappels in sequence.

Mostly, though, what I was learning to do was assess. Of all the skills fundamental to high-altitude climbing, this was maybe the most important one and also the hardest to teach. You simply can't know the conditions up high on big peaks, unless perhaps you're on a busy mountain like Everest. And I was planning an attempt on an unclimbed 7,000-meter Himalayan peak. By definition, there was no one to talk to about snow conditions, avalanche danger, the right gear to protect a pitch, or safe places to set a camp.

The boys call them "date days," and they will usually declare their desire for one-on-one time with either me or Kristina by stating, "I want a date with Mom," or, "I want a date with Dad."

That's how this outing with Kade started in early December 2021. He came barging into my office, flinging the door open. The spring doorstop at the bottom of the wall reverberated with the impact.

"Hey, Dad!" he said.

I was sitting at my library wall, which had a small desk jutting out from the middle, soaking in the light from the two upper-floor windows that overlooked our driveway.

Kade walked across the room and positioned himself in front of, and framed by, the far window. I whirled my seat around and stood up, reaching my arms wide to hug my son.

"Hi, Kade," I said as he pressed his head into my belly while wrapping his arms around my waist.

"I want a date with you. Can we do something together next weekend?" he breathed into my stomach.

We had been in our new home, in Longmont, for about three months. As I stepped back from our hug, I could see, above Kade's head, the Front Range extending north into the distance, culminating at the pronounced flattop of Longs Peak. The mountains were shimmering white under a deeply blue sky that belied the coldness of the air surrounding the summits.

"Yeah, we can take a look at the weather as we get closer to the weekend and find something good to do. What do you feel like doing?"

"How about dry tooling!?"

Kade and I discussed heading out to Saint Mary's Lake, a remnant of a great glacier that had carved an easterly descent from the Continental Divide thousands of years ago. There, we would see if we couldn't find some rock onto which we could hook our tools. Many of our initial High Altitude Mountaineering School field lessons began at that accessible location, which is just a half-mile hike from the trailhead at the extreme eastern edge of the James Peak Wilderness. I knew the area well—where the snow slopes got steep, which ones presented avalanche danger, and where the rock faces shed boulders. I could choose a relatively safe location that would be within Kade's climbing abilities.

While mixed climbing combines rock climbing, ice climbing, and mountaineering tactics on routes that have—not surprisingly—rock, ice, and snow, dry tooling is the practice of using ice tools on dry rock, and it allows you to use mere millimeters of metal in the picks to grab the tiniest of rock features. However, unlike standard rock climbing, there is the added danger of your tools popping off the holds and potentially rebounding back and hitting you. But the medium of rock, itself, can be more reliable than ice, particularly if taking a fall in which massive forces are applied to the protection.

I had just bought each boy a small ice axe, a version made specifically for ski mountaineering. These axes were short and light, making them easier for the boys to manipulate, fitting the boys the way a standard axe would fit adults. However, their shafts were mostly straight, without pronounced curves—as ice tools for waterfall ice and dry tooling usually are—meaning the kids would have to work harder to hang onto their tools.

One of my first home-improvement tasks in the Longmont house had been to put up a twelve-foot-high bouldering wall in the second, single-car garage. It was eight feet wide and canted at thirty degrees overhanging, complemented in that garage by the storehouse of family adventure gear: clothes, camping equipment, rock protection, ice tools, harnesses and helmets, ropes—a multicolored bonanza of equipment, accumulated over the years, that could outfit a family of four or an expedition to Denali or the Himalaya.

I had placed climbing holds on the home wall specifically hardened to withstand metal picks, allowing me to practice dry-tooling techniques. Seeing me at it one morning, Kade simply had to give it a try. I made him put his helmet on, added some clear safety glasses, and duct-taped foam over the integrated adze on the back of his and his brother's ice axes, so he'd have two tools. And up he went. Showing good, natural form, he hung from the tools with straight arms (which conserves energy versus pulling in using your biceps), and then shifted his feet until he could reach with one axe or the other to the next hold. Again, he shifted his feet. Again, he made another reach.

"That was really fun, Dad!"

"You liked that, huh?"

"Yeah!"

"I like dry tooling, too."

I grinned down at my son as he asked, "Have you been dry tooling, Dad?"

"Of course. That's what we're doing today, isn't it?"

"I mean, outside. Have you gone dry tooling on a mountain?"

"Yeah."

"I would like to try that!" Kade said as he pulled off his helmet and safety glasses. His eyes were alight and dancing. He looked back up at the pink plastic holds he'd just climbed and pronounced, "Dry tooling is cool! Can we try taking our axes on one of our rock climbs?"

"Well, you don't use tools at climbing areas. They can damage the rock. So, we'd need to find a place to climb that isn't developed."

"What does 'developed' mean?"

"Well, you know how the climbing areas we go to have bolted anchors at the top? And the rock doesn't have a lot of loose dirt or plants?"

"Yeah."

"Well, someone has to do all that work, putting in anchors and cleaning the route for the first time. Doing all that stuff is called 'developing' the route."

"Oh."

"So, we don't want to damage the route and ruin all that work."

"Okay. So, is there someplace we can go, Dad?"

"I'm sure there is, but I'll need to think about it some, maybe do some research. We need a place with decent rock, but which isn't really used by rock climbers. We also will need some way for me to put in a toprope for you. That probably means someplace in the mountains."

On the morning of our "date," Kade got up and pulled on his black base layers; black-and-gray-striped socks; gray underwear with red stripes; black, waterproof pants, and a sweatshirt with a charcoal-colored chest and upper sleeves along with a cherry-red hem and forearms.

On the way out the door, we checked the weather again, and we saw that it was going to be unseasonably warm near the lake at 10,500 feet. As Kade climbed into his car seat, I stuffed his red-orange softshell jacket into the pack before loading it back in the car.

At the Saint Mary's Glacier trailhead, Kade put on his Microspikes (his feet were still too small for crampons), held fast to his hiking shoes by stretchy green silicone. As he sat there tugging at the spikes, I noticed how brightly the sun was shining. Kade's softshell jacket was still in his pack. The jacket would be too warm for the uphill trudge in front of us. So, with no hood, his face and head would be fully exposed. I plucked my sunhat from atop my head and pulled on a thin beanie in its place, plopping the sunhat loosely over Kade's head and then cinching up its chin strap. The sagging brim was as wide as his shoulders, and its blue color seemed out of place on this particular child, Connor being the one who usually self-selected into blue.

"Sorry it's a blue one, Kade. I didn't think you wouldn't have your outer jacket and hood on."

"It's fine, Dad. Thanks for letting me wear it."

It was completely cloudless and windy. The trees creaked, and the breeze echoed through their branches as we hopped from patches of icy, compacted snow to rock to frozen mud and back to icy snow again. Kade didn't talk much. He simply commented, once, about a group of preteen kids who passed by toting sleds.

Eventually, the trail began to widen, and the dense trees spread out, the ground becoming bare and dry. The wind was whipping at our clothing. Kade tugged the chin strap on his borrowed hat a bit tighter.

"Should we take off your spikes?" I asked.

"Sure."

Kade found a small stone to sit on and pulled off one green band and then the other.

"Can you get my tea out of my pack, Dad?"

"Sure."

While Kade sipped his orange-spice tea, which gave off a waft of cinnamon as the stiff breeze pushed steam by my face, I stuffed his Microspikes into his pack.

After our pause, we moved a few hundred yards further up the trail, coming upon Saint Mary's Lake. The water was frozen and a muted blue. Over the past few months, ice fishermen, shuffling in ice cleats, had created pockmarks and scrapes of brilliant white that looked almost like swirling snow but for being unmoved by the wind blowing across the lake's surface.

We took a seat at a log on the lakeshore as I told Kade, "Why don't you wait here? I'm going to check out those rocks and see if they might work for us."

"Which rocks? Those ones?" Kade pointed to a gray granite crag that stood two stories high by fifty feet wide.

"Yeah. I want to see if I can get up alongside and put in a toprope. Why don't you have a snack, and I'll go check it out?"

"Okay, Dad."

I crunched over frozen dirt to reach a snowy slope with straw-like grass protruding, into which I kicked steps as I moved up the hillside.

As the slope steepened, my feet began to slide, so I made my way onto the rock face. Finding small ledges, I tiptoed my way up another body-length or so before the face drew blank. Finding no more foot placements, I reversed my path back to Kade. He had some energy beans poured into his hand, plucking one from his palm and popping it into his mouth.

"Is it any good, Dad?"

"I don't think I can get up there." Kade was too small to belay me on a proper lead climb. So, any rock feature we found would need to have an easy route around the side and up to the top, where I could set an anchor.

Kade looked at me as he plucked another orange bean from his hand and placed it in his mouth.

"I think those rocks," I said, pointing away from the lake and toward the peak to our north. "The ones at the bottom of that peak."

Kade spun around and took a look, asking, "How far is that?"

"I don't think very far. Maybe a third of a mile?"

He tossed another orange bean into his mouth.

"Okay."

We picked our way through head-high willows up a drainage to snow-covered talus below the rocks. I placed each foot with intention, trying to avoid sliding between the buried stones. I took small strides, and Kade followed foot-placement for foot-placement.

As the slope steepened, the snow dissolved. The south-facing slabs rose up to the sun, and the rocks radiated heat.

The crag was a yellow, vertical band of rock sitting between angular granite boulders rising three or four stories high. The yellow rock leaned back at a welcoming angle: maybe sixty or seventy degrees. I dropped my pack at the base, and Kade came up to join me.

Opening his bright-red pack, Kade pulled his body harness out, untwisted it, and pulled its loops up his legs and around his shoulders. Young kids are top-heavy, their heads making up a disproportionate amount of their total body weight. Their climbing harnesses, then, wrap over not only their hips but also their shoulders, preventing them from potentially banging their heads against the rock or even spilling out of their harness in an upside-down fall, as could happen with a seat harness.

Meanwhile, I scrambled up the granite slabs to the right of the yellow band, bringing some slings and an orange rope up with me to set up a toprope off a handy tree.

By the time I had scrambled back down, Kade was tied into the rope and had his tools in hand.

I ran the rope through my belay device, clipped the device to my harness, and called out, “On belay!”

“Climbing!” Kade replied.

Kade reached his right tool above his head, hooking a deep ledge at a full arm-plus-tool length. Then with his left tool, he found a knob of textured rock. He pulled up and placed each foot, in turn, on the rock face. Now reaching wide right, he found a side pull and leaned left, away from the hold. He then walked his feet up higher. Still pulling against the wide-right tool, Kade raised the shaft of shimmering orange in his left hand and hooked the black pick at its tip into a vague crack just wide enough for the pick to slide into place. Continuing this way, making technical moves with a natural ease and grace, he reached the top of the fifty-foot route in only a couple of minutes.

"Take!" he yelled.

"Gotcha!"

"Lower!"

"Lowering!" I eased rope through my belay device as Kade walked backward off the cliff.

"Nice climb, Kade!" I gushed as he reached the ground.

"Thanks, Dad!"

Fighting the wind, I asked, "You want to go, again?"

Kade did about five laps on the climb that day, trying new movements until he found his most efficient pattern for every sequence.

After we packed up and headed back down through the willows and past the lake, Kade was more talkative.

"What was the name of that peak Connor and I wanted to climb?"

As soon as I'd gotten back from the Himalaya, a little more than two years ago, now, both Connor and Kade had peppered me with questions about my climb before we could even get out of the airport.

They wanted to climb in the Himalaya, too. They wanted to know which climbs would be hard for them but within the realm of possibility. We had settled on Island Peak in Nepal, a climb that was regularly guided and of comparatively low altitude for the area, at 20,226 feet, but still just a few feet shy of Denali, at 20,310 feet. Despite having a comparable altitude, Island Peak was far less difficult of a climb, often taking a day and a half—after acclimatization—as compared to Denali's average of more than two weeks on the mountain. We had also decided that the boys had to be around twelve before attempting such a climb. (Eventually, about five years later when we began truly researching the climb, we learned Nepal was seeking support from the climbing community to enforce a rule prohibiting the issuance of climbing permits to those under the age of 16. So, we've since turned our attention to peaks in neighboring countries.)

Pausing among the high branches of the willow bushes, I faced my son. "Uh, that was Island Peak."

"Do you have to dry tool on Island Peak?"

"I guess it's possible, if conditions are really dry, but I think that's unlikely."

"But dry tooling is a good skill to have, right?" Kade asked as he sought affirmation that his newfound love was truly useful.

"Yeah. It helps if you are confident on lots of different terrain."

"Yeah. I want to be good at all different types of climbing."

"Well, we can certainly do that. I guess you liked dry tooling?"

"Yes! And I want to keep training for Island Peak."

"Did you know that there are dry-tooling competitions? Well, a combination of ice climbing and dry tooling."

"There is?!"

"Yeah. The US is kind of new at the competitions, but there happens to be a gym where you can train for it not too far from our house," I said. "It's a little warehouse called the Ice Coop, in Boulder. It's kind of run-down and not very tall, but the climbing team sets their own routes and do lap after lap on the traverses to get fit."

"Really?!"

"Yeah."

"Ooohhh. I want to go there!" Kade said, his smile broadening. He was incandescent.

I was getting sweaty, my back pressed against the hard plastic of the seat. It was morning, but the New Mexico heat was already starting to build as the late-spring sun continued its ascent above Sandia High's infamously windowless classrooms, which had been constructed this way, in the 1950s, to keep kids focused on their studies.

The mood was light, and there was a constant murmur of whispered conversations. Finals were over, and all the kids, similarly sticking to the red seats fastened to the hardwood desktops in the hot, red-brick room, were anxiously waiting out the final two days of the school year.

A voice crackled from the canvas-covered PA speaker in the upper corner of the classroom, blurting out various events for the final days of the year. Nobody paid much attention.

". . . and the class rankings for sophomores, juniors, and graduating seniors are posted outside of the main office in the Administration Building."

It had never occurred to me that there was a class ranking, until now. It also hadn't occurred to me that a class ranking mattered . . . yet.

I had pieced together a pretty good sophomore year despite

having been stabbed just before school began and then sleeping with my bedroom door locked for half of it. Academically, I was doing quite well; I knew I had made As. The soccer season resulted in a state championship. I had just started playing golf; I was still bad at it, but I had a natural talent that I could focus on and cultivate. I had grown pretty close to quite a few people: Gary and Rici, who had just started dating; Amy, to whom I gave rides home from school; Ian, who sat with me talking philosophy during coffee-fueled late-night Denny's sessions; Sonja, who pushed a quiet and confident feminism into my consciousness; Susanne, who reminded me to find unabashed joy in things—a lesson I sorely needed at the time; Brandi, who shared a similarly-needed kinship of trauma; and Chad, who was simply my best friend.

The announcements barely registered. The year was almost over, and I was looking forward to getting on the golf course and deeper into the club soccer season, with its summer travel schedule. I already held my sophomore year in my rearview mirror. In class, we were given something close to free reign for signing yearbooks and indulging in a sort of short-term nostalgia as we recounted tales from the past year. Between classes, moving from one set of campus buildings to another, we kids filled the cloudless deep-blue sky with light, cheerful banter and the crafting of summer plans.

That day, as I came back from lunch and was about to enter the locker hall, my friend Gary caught me up with me.

"Hey, Jason!"

I stopped and turned. Gary was a bit bigger than me, because—well—everyone was. But he was a bit smaller than everyone else, it seemed, despite being a wide receiver on the JV football team. He was also a fellow blonde, but not quite as fair-skinned as I—another low bar.

Gary had confided in me when a family member had fallen ill. He knew that I still struggled in the aftermath of the stabbing, empathizing with my avoidance of violence in movies; but just like everyone else, he was unaware of any other remnants or aftereffects, because I kept these hidden. He had started dating Rici that year. (To this day, they are still madly in love and happily married.)

"Have you seen the class rankings?" he asked.

"Nuh uh."

Gary and I took a sharp detour leftward, away from the locker hall, leaving its Columbia-blue doors behind and heading for the Administration Building. Inside the foyer, columns of white paper reflected the muted desert light back at me. Three columns were taped next to the inner doors, each for one of the three classes that had been ranked. Each page had two columns of names, and the pages were mounted one above the other, several feet high, to make room for the roughly 350 kids in each class.

Gary pressed a finger on the top left corner of the top page of the leftmost column.

There sat my name. There were no names above it.

"Huh," I commented, quizzically, before we pirouetted back out of the building.

Back in the locker hall, I looked at Gary. He leaned in as I spoke with a voice too quiet to be overheard above the din, saying, "Great. Now it's mine to lose."

I was pretty tired of weighty decisions and consequential actions. When I got back from my month attempting to summit Gangapurna West in the Nepalese Himalaya, I was tired. I was tired of living one-day-at-a-time. It had been a year of grappling with what "living with cancer" was supposed to mean. After that long year, there was a month of making sure food and sleep and falling stones were all managed for our team of seven while living on the side of an enormous peak. I was tired of thinking about death, and I was still—unbeknownst to me—three months out from trying to navigate "living with cancer during a pandemic that kills people with cancer."

And, I had stopped writing.

Part of my post-diagnosis therapy included a little journaling every night. It wasn't about the journal, per se. It was more about having a dedicated time, every night, to process what I was feeling. It was about observing my emotions so that I could experience and work through them rather than letting them fester.

I kept up my journaling habit rather religiously until about midway through our attempt on Gangapurna West. I paused during that trip because I didn't want to carry the journal up to the higher reaches of the mountain. What I ended up doing, however, was breaking myself of a positive habit.

My friend, Marisa, who'd come on the trip to Nepal, was helping me think through a potential short film about my experience on that mountain and its echoes throughout my life. She was just breaking into nature and adventure photography and had also done a few small pieces of directing and cinematography, such as a short film about a figure skater attempting to skate a series of frozen alpine lakes in Colorado. Together, we were working on a narrative arc, and I had a homework assignment, into which I launched one morning during my light-rail commute to work.

That day, I took a seat on the train as the doors chimed and the PA warned not to block them. The molded-plastic seats and thin fabric did little to pad my hip bones. Similarly folded into nearby seats, or standing with one hand grasping a chrome pole, fellow commuters in dress shirts or pantsuits or pencil skirts stood with sunglasses on and earphones inserted.

The train lurched forward, wheels creaking, before settling into an accelerated pace, headed for the downtown Denver business towers starting on the horizon. As we hurtled along, signposts along the tracks flickered shadows into the train car through my east-facing window.

I slid my laptop out of my backpack and then tucked the bag under my feet, opening the screen with a soft click. I double-tapped the matte touchpad and brought up a spreadsheet.

Marisa had laid out some words in three columns: "VO" (for "voice over"), "Shot List," and "Jason Notes." In the VO column, she had put down some opening words, about forty lines' worth. Above that column she had noted, "put into your own words."

I began reading.

> There are only a few things in life we can control. We can train and plan and hope for the best. We can find joy in the in-between moments. But when it really comes down to it, it's what we do with the moments that seem the most chaotic, the most unknown—those gut-churning, fear-soaked moments—that speak to our essence as people.

Pondering all this, I found my eyes drawn to the rooftops outside my window as the sun climbed above them, turning the sky from orange to yellow to white as the train rocked and bobbed along the tracks.

I turned back to my computer. The screen glowed intensely. The heat from the computer's wires and drives and chips was starting to ebb through my dress pants.

"Excerpt or statement about how it feels in the uncertainty," was spelled out in antiseptic characters, too neat for the chaos.

I moved my cursor to the "Jason Notes" column. The pipe cursor blinked at me, expectantly.

I began to type. The sun reflected off my screen, projecting my face back at me. My red beard stood in contrast to my blue shirt. The keyboard thudded under each keystroke. My fingers moved swiftly and forcefully as I typed:

> *No parent wants to hurt their kids. In any way. Ever. But here I am. One day, I'm going to begin treatment. And it may work. But it may not. And that uncertainty is going to be scary. And it is going to be really scary for kids who see Dad as an indestructible superhero. I am going to hurt them, and I don't know when. I want them to know how much I hate this. How much I already regret it.*

A tear rolled down my cheek. Pulling my glasses off, I dried my cheek on my shoulder.

The VO column prompted, "thought process of teaching sons."

In response, I typed in a question for myself:

> *If I could give them one more set of lessons, one more example of Dad trying to really live in the middle of an often-messy life, what would I do? What would those lessons be?*

The piped cursor blinked. I didn't know where to begin.

*What would I wish to tell my boys if I wasn't there to tell them?* I thought.

Occasionally, the train screeched around a soft corner, clacking along the narrow-gauge tracks. The accordion center of the train car would stretch on one side and contract on the other in the turn, almost as if the train was breathing.

And then I realized that beginnings make self-evidently good starting points, and I, the narrator, gave way to I, the father.

> *You guys were born early. Too early, to be honest. You've been fighting since day one. Ever since, I've wanted to protect you. Make it all okay. In my head, I've always known that, to some degree, that was impossible. My heart hasn't quite learned to let go of the hope.*

As we approached the university stops south of downtown, the dress shirts and pantsuits and pencil skirts gave way to jeans and T-shirts. Gone were the sunglasses and earphones, replaced by strongly voiced conversations that rose above the train's mechanical groanings.

More rows on the spreadsheet sat blank, begging to be filled in with whatever lessons I thought worthy to impart. The white space was daunting.

Gradually, I began to move my hands across the keys again, the keypad letters pushing back against my fingers. The blinking pipe cursor moved its way from left to right, and the white space began to shrink as characters flowed and bent and shifted from one line to the next.

The horizon was gone now. Steel and marble and concrete towered outside my window, while bleating car horns interrupted the train's electric hum.

I slid my fingers across the matte touchpad until an arrow

hovered over the icon of a disc. I double-tapped, and the computer flickered. I scrolled the page back up.

Questions and declarations. Urgings and invocations. Sentences divided by the all-too-tidy lines of demarcation defining the spreadsheet's cells. Scanning the cathartic words, I thought, *Maybe this isn't a movie. Maybe this is a book.* Standing to exit the train, I closed my laptop on sixteen neat rows for sixteen messy chapters—a first attempt at explaining a life.

**Kade, on the unseasonably dry approach to some dry tooling at Saint Mary's Glacier, wearing his dad's hat.**

CHAPTER FIFTEEN

# Heirlooms

I held the four scrolls of canvas and rolled them neatly, stuffing them with newspaper scraps so that they wouldn't flatten. They went into my jade carry-on duffel, surrounded by the traditional Buddhist prayer scarf, or *khata*. The scrolls and the buttermilk hue of the scarf were almost identical, and they formed a massive, off-white rectangle at the top of my bag.

Later that day, in early November 2019, I flew west from Kathmandu to Denver, heading back after over a month in Nepal. I was limping and exhausted, and I very much wanted to be home. I wanted to talk to my wife and to my boys. I wanted to see how this last month had changed them. I wanted to know what new adventures we would share together. I wondered what was next.

Our attempt on Gangapurna West (7,140 meters), also known as Lachenal Peak, in north-central Nepal's Annapurna Massif, had started beating me up almost from the outset.

I had been on the mountain, away from the comforting yellow tents and camp kitchen of our basecamp at 13,250 feet on the dusty, boulder-strewn moraine, for all of about seven hours, and I was already emotionally exhausted. The first two of those hours were spent hauling a heavy pack filled with fuel and spools of static line to the base of the tunnel-like feature we sardonically dubbed "Hell's

Gates." I wobbled under my seventy-pound load for about two miles, moving north over polished boulders comprising the west bank of a fierce tributary at the extreme northeast headwaters of the Modi Khola.

The farther I headed up-river, the more in-cut and severe the canyon became. On each side of me were 500-foot vertical walls that then laid back into lower angles as they stretched even higher. On my left, the slopes above rose sharply for 4,000 feet. On my right, they towered upwards for 5,500 feet, stretching eastward to eventually become the south ridge of 7,555-meter Annapurna III.

The cream-colored, vertical cliffs were pocked with conglomerate rocks ranging in size from a fist to a van, the sun glinting off them as if to highlight their menace. The cliff walls were seemingly randomly disintegrating, sending down a little cascade of small stones and dust over here, and a little over there, slowly exposing more and more of the larger boulders to the pull of the void. The hiss of the river and the periodic echo of rocks crashing to the ground in some unseen part of the canyon added sonic chaos to the otherworldly views of the grand Himalaya.

Above me, the disintegrating cliffs eventually gave way to illuminated white snow cut at intervals by ribbons of gray stone. The summits seemed steeper, more pyramidal, and more impassable than any I had seen, let alone come into contact with. Elongated clouds passed thousands of feet below the summits, marching down-valley to cover the terrain below basecamp in a white carpet.

Eventually, the western, left wall of the canyon broke into a notch, with the vertical cliff faces tapering toward one another. At the base of the notch was the tunnel: here, the walls and half-frozen boulders had been carved by a rushing torrent. The base of the tunnel was wider than the top, so the walls curved overhead like an awning to form Hell's Gates.

The route now demanded about seven hundred vertical feet of ascension, over little less than two-tenths of a mile, alongside something steep enough to be a low-angle waterfall. Half-frozen, half-exposed microwaves and coffee tables and passenger cars of rock menaced overheard. Shale disintegrated into sediment around them.

This day, half of our seven-person team would move gear from basecamp to a cache just below the Gates, while the other half would take one load each from there up the Hell's Gates gully and then another 1,000 vertical feet beyond. Up at 16,300 feet, we'd planned an intermediate camp, the launching point from which we'd climb to advanced basecamp (ABC) and the ridge that opened access to the upper mountain. That thousand-foot climb was across a somewhat flatter half-mile over scree and disintegrating rock.

A sharp right-hand turn to the east from the cache at 16,300 feet would take us under and past three rock towers, maybe 300 feet tall each, of shedding sandstone. From there, heading back left and north, a loose gully would bring us to a small plateau below the southeast spur, a rock buttress jutting out nearly a mile from the summit plateau. We would then need to scramble up another gully, maybe 60 to 70 degrees and filled with a mix of snow, ice, and rock, to gain the southeast spur. At the spur, snow finally accumulated, and we would be donning our crampons. The initial, gently angling march up the spur led to a headwall, 1,700 feet high, of corniced avalanche chutes. If we could surmount the headwall, we could follow a semi-circular ridge sharply upward to the summit ridge and its 50-meter-tall, snowy summit pyramid.

Our lead team was pushing hard to move gear up that extra 1,000 feet, as per the plan. Noah was the youngest, in his mid-twenties, almost too big and strapping to be a high-altitude climber but who'd made the transition from the flatlands to the Colorado mountains with aplomb. A few years later, he would make the US Ice Climbing Team. Lee, about my age, was uber-fit. He was an accomplished adventure racer, comfortable in all kinds of terrain, from whitewater to slot canyons to high peaks. His bald head seemed to just make him faster, like it was the final step in paring unnecessary mass off his lean form. Keegan was a bit older than me, a child of the 1980s metal music that he kept pumping through his earbuds when trekking or climbing didn't require intense focus. He said "dude" a lot and told off-color jokes, but in an endearing way.

That day, the trailing team included Matt—the same Matt from our ascent up the southwest couloirs of Quandary Peak. His kids at home, like mine, pulled hard on him, and he was the most likely—along with me—to be the one making a satellite-phone call home when the twelve-hour time difference made sense. Steve was the oldest member of our group and had also been with me on Quandary. His open communication style set the bar for me, even if it was a bar I didn't always reach. And Marisa was the budding photographer and cinematographer. She was endlessly optimistic and humble, preferring to let her camera capture others in action, passing on the glory, even though she had to be in those locations herself to get the imagery.

The seven of us had all met via the Colorado Mountain Club, but the team hadn't really come together until after my cancer diagnosis. Pre-diagnosis, it had been hard to find the right group of people with the skills, time, and money to make the trip, let alone the mentality to want to attempt something with such a high likelihood of failure.

I had invited the potential team to come along to the Leukemia & Lymphoma Society's Denver office, where I was going to pitch the trip as a fundraising effort for cancer research. Waiting for our appointment in the lobby, sitting on golden vinyl seats, I broke down a bit when I told them about all of the uncertainties in my life: we didn't know how quickly the cancer would progress; we didn't know if it would mutate into something more virulent; we didn't know if other symptoms would present; we didn't know if my ability to athletically perform would be impacted; we didn't know if something else—infection or the like—might threaten my life.

But I also told them about my hopes for my kids and my desire to demonstrate to them boldness in the face of uncertainty, whether on a mountain or in life. The team coalesced around the mission; in preparation, they got fit and practiced crevasse rescue and emailed contacts to help with our cancer research and patient support fundraising.

We would need multiple trips over the initial days to ferry our equipment up to this staging area at 16,300 feet. But on this day, my job was to fix our first line in the initial gully that took us upwards from the moraine and Hell's Gates. The climbing was easy, just a scramble, but we would need to haul heavy loads up this route multiple times and, due to the ever-present rock fall, would need to move fast.

Carrying a pack with three coils, each coil being two hundred meters of fixed line still in its packaging, I hunted and pecked my way over the conglomerate surface and through shallow pools of spray water. The roar of the neighboring waterfall washed out all other sound until the occasional rock landed close enough to shock me with a *crack*.

At the top of the gully, as the bottleneck opened up and the terrain eased into a boulder field, I stopped next to a rock the size of an economy car rooted in the slope. I took out the three spools of rope and placed two to the side, later to be hauled further up the mountain.

I began to cut the shrink wrap from around one bundle of rope, but the coil immediately fell apart, with a good portion of it cascading back down the gully. The zip ties that had held the rope coil together had broken, and now I had a real mess.

I looked down at the tangled ball of rope and then began to haul back the portion that had slid below me. We would need to put more rope in place higher up, where the altitude would complicate those tasks, so I saved the two still-intact coils for those fixed lines. I began stuffing the white tangle of line into my now nearly empty pack, leaving one free end.

I made a somewhat loose and treacherous circumnavigation around the boulder on a mix of shale and sand, and then tied a bowline knot in the rope, fixing it to the boulder as the anchor point.

I hauled out line from my pack until a bird's nest of rope appeared at the pack's top. I then took my pocketknife and severed the rope at the knot. I spent a few minutes unthreading the knot until I had another long span of free rope, which I carefully stacked into a neat pile back in my pack.

I took out my shimmering sapphire-blue rappel device, attached it to the rope anchored to the boulder, and then started to back my way down the roughly thirty meters of rope that I had freed by cutting the coil where it was knotted.

The rock under my feet was dusty in places, covered in remnants from the crumbling walls around me; it was wet in other places, spray from the water lashing whole sections almost continuously. Either way, the footing was less than ideal. More than once, I lost traction as my boot slid over dust or swiped over water.

Checking below me to find the next anchor point, I came to another boulder, about half the size of the first. I made another circumnavigation and tied another bowline, leaving an ample tail of free rope at the end

I then crouched downslope and behind the boulder and shrugged off my pack. My movements were oddly soundless against the dominating flow of water, which frothed up white.

Taking the tail from the rope on the now-fixed anchor, I measured alongside it the rope end coming from my pack. Matching the strands together, I gave the two ropes a twist, and then ran the twin ends through, tying a flat overhand to marry the ropes. I twisted and ran the rope ends through, again, stacking two of the same knot.

A few small fragments of rock cascaded over the top of the boulder and dusted the route behind me. I peeked over the boulder like a soldier in a trench.

To my right, on the gully wall, water trickled out from midway up the cliff of what appeared to be dirt and rock and boulders. I wasn't on the dust and stone of a mountain; I was at the extreme toe of the glacier. These rocks weren't cemented to the wall in compacted dirt; they were frozen into the moraine.

Frozen things melt.

I continued my descent, rappelling on my newly placed strand until I was another thirty-odd meters farther down the gully.

Another tangled knot constricted at the top of my pack. Pulling lightly on the rope, I pumped my legs forward, heading back up a few feet to look for another suitable anchor point.

Looking up as I climbed, I caught movement out of the corner of my eye. From the left, a suitcase-sized stone had detached and was hurtling toward me. It skipped over the ground and took unpredictable sideways zigs and zags when it bounced.

I leaned back on the rope, letting my device and harness take my weight while pulling the fixed line taut. I watched the projectile clatter down until it took a bound a few-tens-of-feet in front of me, crashing close enough to me to be heard over the water. Now able to judge its airborne direction, I jumped to my left, penduluming on the taut rope.

The rock shot past me on the right as I came down awkwardly on my left foot. I collapsed, banging my right knee into a boulder.

Exhaling forcefully, I reascended my lost ground and took shelter behind a rock, my blue helmet bobbing up and down as I worked to make an anchor here.

My radio, strapped to the upper portion of my pack, crackled with static. It was the first sound I heard that wasn't water or rockfall.

I slung my pack off, again. I grabbed the gnarled rope, again. I cut the rope at the knot, again. I made a dash around the boulder, again. I tied a new knot, again.

My mind was fully awake, and I discovered that I was panting.

As I began to unthread the next mess of rope in order to free a new length, I muttered, "Slow is smooth, and smooth is fast." I repeated the mantra. I quieted my voice, but the words continued to march through my brain: *Slow is smooth, and smooth is fast.*

I was in the gully, repeating the sequence and under occasional, random fire from an unfeeling enemy, for four hours.

At the bottom of the gully, I radioed my teammates that I was at the river and heading back to basecamp. As the adrenaline subsided, I began to feel my surgically repaired right knee. It was bruised pretty badly, and the swelling pressed on the hardware contained in it, which—in turn—radiated pain up my leg.

I rested in basecamp for two days, my right foot elevated, before I headed up again. I wasn't done with my climb. I had been planning this thing for three years. My entire climbing career had pointed me to this opus. I had gone through countless potential teammates committing and then backing out. I had cried with my teammates, shortly after my diagnosis, when I'd told them that I "didn't know what the arc of my disease would be, and that I hoped to leave one last lesson for my boys about following dreams." They'd stuck with me and helped will this expedition into existence. *What was that lesson I hoped to teach? Isn't it time to live that lesson?*

Three days after I put in that fixed line, I began hauling a week's worth of previsions, along with all of my personal gear, back up the mountain, solo. I was going to catch back up with the team at the now-established ABC, two camps above me on the snow at the bottom of the southeast spur, just above 18,000 feet.

One day later, I was leaving our intermediate camp, 1,000 feet above Hell's Gates, when I tethered myself to another fixed line; this one had been put in by Noah and Lee with one of the spools I had left for them. The line skirted the base of a 300-foot cliff band of red-tinted flakes and splinters of rock, eventually rounding left to meet the last fixed line, which gained the snowline and advanced basecamp.

I didn't see the rock this time. It came from the top of the cliff, flying, soundless. I noticed it only when a loud crack announced its presence. One bounce, and it was on me. I jumped, the fixed line holding me fast. The rock careened into the inside of my right leg, above the knee and along the hamstring and groin. I spun in the air and landed on my butt, facing downhill.

My leg instantly went numb. My first thought was, *Is my leg broken?*

I stood up, pushing on my left leg and using the rope as a fulcrum. Upright, I put my right leg down and weighted it. I still couldn't feel my leg, but it supported my weight. I checked my pants for blood, but there wasn't any.

I sat back down, fixed my pack to my ascender, and then took down my pants to examine the damage. I had a Y-shaped gash, but it wasn't profusely bleeding. My entire inner thigh was pink with a rising bruise.

It had been a well-enough-timed jump, and a solid-enough fixed rope.

After resituating my clothing, I tugged on the ascender and continued to head up.

I slept two nights at advanced basecamp. On the day between, I headed out with Noah and Lee, taking the sharp end of the rope to break trail up a snow-covered ridge and along a snowline traverse above a sheer band of rock. I was enjoying movement for the first time since the trek into basecamp, despite the throbbing pain in my leg. Out on the peninsula of the southeast spur, there was nothing above me except the sapphire sky. My boots sunk into the snow with cushioned steps, the only sound being the familiar jangle of the gear racked on my harness. For once, no hazards—crumbling cliffs or loose stones—loomed directly overhead.

Eventually, though, my leg just stopped working. Limping, I rallied Noah and Lee, and I let them work past me and beyond to a point where they could eye the next camp placement.

Back at advanced basecamp later that afternoon, I told the team I had to go down. I couldn't keep up with our two strongest climbers; I would be holding them back, and I would be putting them and myself in danger: "I have to get home. I have boys who are depending on me. And you have to get home safely, too," I told the team. "A weak climber puts everyone at risk."

"I didn't even know you were hurt," Lee responded.

"My knee always hurts. I wasn't sure how bad things were until now."

Most of the team only nodded in affirmation.

"I'll carry a load down as I descend," I promised.

Noah and Lee climbed for a few more days, reaching a high point at around 20,000 feet, at the base of the headwall.

Eventually, the expedition just became a matter of attrition. We had lost Steve on day two, helicoptered out with heart palpitations. Marisa never intended to go beyond advanced basecamp and supported the team well from there. Keegan's toe, sore before the trip, became unbearably painful; once finally back home he would learn it was a bone infection. I could be of no help. I could barely move myself let alone carry sufficient equipment to aid other climbers or support a rescue. Matt, meanwhile, couldn't match Lee's and Noah's pace, and we had to decide if a three-person team or a fast moving two-person team stood the best chance. We chose the latter. Eventually, Lee became ill, and the two-person team, now high on the mountain, was down to one.

With bad weather arriving in a matter of days, discretion won out as we communicated over our radios.

Two days after we called for a retreat, I was helicoptered out from basecamp, unable to cross the treacherous terrain that stood between there and the comparative safety of the Annapurna trekking route. In Pokhara, after I was released from the local hospital with a favorable diagnosis, I had a few days to kill while the team trekked out.

Hobbling along the town's rows of shops, I found four paintings. Three depicted sections of our trek into the Annapurna Massif. One scene we would recognize as we crossed the Modi Khola. Two paintings were of Machhapuchhare, the last major peak we'd passed en route to basecamp. Two captured images of the Annapurna Massif itself, but from the north side. A painting for each member of the family.

I tucked the paintings carefully into my suitcase, my hands moving deliberately as I stuffed the rolled treasures and nested them with the khata, just as purposefully as my hands had moved over the tangled ball of rope not so many days before.

At Denver International Airport, my boys were all questions. "Where did you go, Dad?" Kade asked. They knew, generally, that I had gone around the globe to go climb in the Himalaya, but the range was just a name, and the details remained fuzzy to them.

After big hugs, I took Connor's hand while Kristina took Kade's, and we marched over the cold tiles to baggage claim. The buzz of the airport matched the boys' energy. The concourse was alive and bright. DIA's circus-big-top ceiling (supposed to be representing Colorado's mountains) was diffusing light to seemingly every corner. The boys had taken off school to come pick me up, and I didn't try to contain my smile even though I was dragging a sore right leg. The indecipherable hum of hundreds of conversations filled the vast hall.

"Remember, I went to Nepal/ I was climbing in the Himalaya."

"What were you climbing in the Himalaya?"

"A mountain called Gangapurna West."

"Was it like Everest?" Connor chimed in.

I laughed. Every climber gets asked about Everest: *Have you? Do you want to? Would you ever?*

"Kinda, but kinda not. It's tall, like Everest, but not as tall. Climbers don't need to use oxygen tanks where I was. But they do need to climb really carefully because there is no one else there. If anything goes wrong, they have to handle it themselves."

"Did you have fun?" asked Connor.

"Yeah, was it fun?" asked Kade.

I paused, thought a bit, and then said, "Yeah. It was fun."

"We want to climb in the Himalaya, too," the boys said, now in hive mind.

"Okay. Maybe one day when you get older."

As we arrived at the car, I mentioned, "I have presents for you."

"Can we see them?" Kade blurted.

"Yeah, but then I need to repack them so they don't get damaged."

"Are they fragile?" Connor asked.

"Yeah. Not like, 'Don't drop them or they'll break' fragile, but they are handmade."

I slid my duffel and gear bags into the hatchback of the car and then opened my duffel, pulling out the canvas scrolls.

"Now, there is one for each of us." I unrolled the first one. "This is the Annapurna Massif . . ."

Slowly, over the months that followed, the boys' plan started to take shape. First, they wanted to climb "the hardest peak" in the Himalaya. I calmly informed them that it's hard to know what the hardest peak is because there are so many different styles of climbing, "and besides, there are climbs that kill lots of people, and those climbs must be hard but don't seem quite worth it."

"What makes a peak hard?" Kade asked.

"Well, it could be the altitude, like Everest. It could be how hard the climbing moves are, like Meru. It could be how bad the rockfall or avalanches are, like Annapurna. It could be the logistics."

"What's 'logistics'?"

"Logistics is about getting you, your climbing team, and all of your stuff to the climb."

"You can have hard logistics?"

"Yeah, some places are just hard to get stuff to. Mountains and cliffs in Greenland, for instance, are pretty hard to get to."

Kade and Connor sat on that information for a while. A few weeks later, I was informed that, because the Himalaya are so hard, they would climb a mountain there sometime around 2026.

"I think we could go to the Himalaya when we are, like, nearly twelve or something," Kade said.

"That will give us lots of time to train, right, Dad? Seven years?" Connor asked, grinning.

"Yeah, we could find a way to get ready by then."

Half-a-year later, I was standing with a cup of water in the kitchen on a bright midmorning amidst the early pandemic lockdown. Kade had just finished a protracted battle with my wife regarding the week's spelling list and upcoming spelling test. I was wearing my workout clothes, having just done some "gym class" with Connor. The dried sweat felt uncomfortable on my skin, and my shirt hung heavy.

Kade came into the kitchen, his deep-red shirt popping against the white of the room.

"Dad, what's the hardest easy climb in the Himalaya?"

"Well, there are peaks called trekking peaks that are below 6,500 meters, and then there are peaks taller than that. Both types of mountains can have harder or easier climbs."

"How tall is 6,500 meters?"

"Over 21,000 feet. That's like taking the altitude we're living at and stacking it up four times."

"That's pretty tall. How tall was your climb on Denali?"

"Denali is just over 20,000 feet, so about a thousand feet shorter."

Kade gazed past the dining table at the photo of the south aspect of Denali that I had bought in Talkeetna upon my return from its summit. "Could we climb Denali?" he asked.

"Well, Denali can be pretty hard because you have to carry all your own equipment. You can't hire people to carry your stuff for you. Well, you can go with guides, and that can help, but you need to carry a lot of your own stuff."

"Other people can carry your stuff in the Himalaya?"

"Yeah, if you want them to. We didn't have anyone help us beyond basecamp. We had a company help us get stuff to basecamp and then work in basecamp for us, but we carried all of our own gear above basecamp."

"So, is there, like, an easy but hard climb?"

"Well, there are peaks that are pretty tall, like Denali tall, but which get a lot of climbers on them. Like Island Peak and Lobuche East."

"Are those hard peaks?"

"They are pretty hard. It takes about three weeks to do the whole trip, but you're only on the mountain for a few days."

"Which one is taller?"

"Island Peak is taller and a little more technical."

"I think we should climb Island Peak."

"Yeah?" I asked.

"Yeah," he said, resolutely. "And then we should climb Denali when we are older."

"I think when you're around eighteen, Denali might be a good thing to try. I really want to take you, your brother, and your mom to the glacier. You can fly out on a little plane and land right on the glacier. It's incredibly beautiful. And I guess the three of us could climb it, if we want."

"That sounds good," Kade said, grinning and dashing out of the room.

Did they really want to do this, or was this like wanting to be a fireman and then a computer hacker and then a spy and then an engineer who invented a real Ironman suit?

Connor chose the painting of Macchapuchhare, a sacred peak—not allowed to be climbed, as it's held to be the home of Lord Shiva—as viewed from the south, and we hung it next to his bedroom door. Kade, meanwhile, chose an impression of Macchapuchhare as seen from the north. Our basecamp on Gangapurna West sat just northeast of that grand peak, and we'd approached it from the south.

"We're going to climb Island Peak in Nepal in 2026," Kade or Connor would tell anyone who would listen—grandparents, teachers, their coaches, pretty much anyone. "Yeah," the other brother would chime in, "and then we're going to climb Denali later."

Turnabout being fair play, I took Connor out for a "date" in mid-December, just after Kade and I had gone on our dry-tooling outing together.

When I asked Connor what he wanted to do, he said, "Scrambling. Well, uh, maybe something that we could do a nice hike to and then get to do some scrambling over some rocks. And then maybe there is a climb we can do at the end."

"That's a lot for one route, especially in winter. Let me see what the weather looks like later this week, and we can decide."

I finally chose Bear Peak, a local peak in the foothills above Boulder that I often used as training. A moderate approach from just east of the Flatirons would take us into a shaded gully called Fern Canyon that ascends steeply to a saddle. From there, we'd catch beautiful views of the snow-capped Indian Peaks Wilderness as we turned south up the summit ridge for another 1,000 vertical feet of short, steep switchbacks leading to a quick scramble up moderate boulders and slabs of red rock. At the summit, we could turn west to see the bigger Colorado mountains or east toward Boulder, and the charismatic, red-tiled Italianate roofs of the University of Colorado campus. The ascent allowed for some good exertion because it gained nearly 3,000 feet in less than three miles, with most of the gain happening over the last mile. Throw on a heavy pack for training weight, and it was a reasonable proxy for the steep flanks of larger peaks. Plus, yes, it had that short scramble at the end.

Come that Sunday, Connor and I woke up with the sun. I wandered into his room, blackout curtains keeping the room dark, and laid out a set of clothing: synthetic underwear with blue and gray stripes; white, thin under-socks and wool, over-the-calf socks in a similar blue-and-gray-striped knit; a black-wool base layer top and matching bottom; a hooded sweat jacket with swirls of emerald-green dancing over a midnight blue; and a navy-blue, hooded, softshell jacket. I patted him on the leg. Then I went back to the door to switch on the light.

"How're you doing this morning? Did you sleep well?"

"Yeah, Dad."

"Ready to go on our hike?"

"A hike with a scramble, right?"

"Yeah, like we talked about: a hike with a scramble. It's that peak I used to help train for Denali and for Gangapurna West. It's a hike to near the top and then a scramble for the final little bit."

"And we aren't going to need ropes, right?"

"Right. No ropes for this. Roped climbing is fun but also takes a while. We don't want to get too cold or take too long with the sun going down so early these days."

"I'm happy we're going to get to do some scrambling. I like scrambling!"

"Well, we have to get up to the scrambling part, first," I warned. "Let's get ready."

In the kitchen, I boiled some water and then poured Connor a liter bottle full of his preferred chai tea: a non-caffeinated rooibos version. I added the hot water to an Arnold Palmer mix in my own bottle, and then added the precious hot drinks and some food to our backpacks.

I turned my attention to bagels and cream cheese for breakfast as Connor trampled down the stairs and onto the hardwood of the main floor. "I'm ready, Dad!" he announced.

At the National Center for Atmospheric Research trailhead, we stepped out of the car, our feet crunching across the frozen clay smeared across the asphalt. A mild breeze carried a winter chill, and the sky was already turning from purple to blue, with only a few wisps of high clouds. The trailhead's namesake research complex, a series of rectangles painted a pinkish-red hue to match the Flatirons, clustered together, reaching up toward our summit objective.

"Are you going to want your navy jacket?" I asked Connor.

"Yeah. Well, no. Maybe not."

"We can always put it on later. It's better to start cold than work up a sweat, right?"

"Right . . ." Connor perked up. "Because if you sweat and it's cold, then all that sweat freezes and makes you *really* cold! Right, Dad?"

"That's right, Connor. So, just put it in your pack, for now. Make sure you have your gloves on, though."

About thirty minutes into the hike, Connor said, "I'm hungry, Dad. Can we take a break?" I had learned over innumerable outings that taking the early break seemed to make the rest of the day relatively complaint free, so we stopped immediately.

"Sure. Let's get our Microspikes on, too," I said. Adding traction to our feet would help as we strode across the compacted snow we were now encountering near the mouth of Fern Canyon.

"Good idea, Dad. We don't want to slip, right?"

"Yeah."

"If we slip on the snow, we could fall and get hurt. That would end our climb really quickly, wouldn't it, Dad?"

"So, let's not slip. Let's get that traction on our feet."

Connor stretched the green silicone around his heel and over the toe of his boot, just as his brother had. Clawing at the rubbery material, he eventually pulled it up to his forefoot, where it naturally snapped into place, holding the small steel spikes firmly against the sole of his boot.

As I pulled at my own red-silicone Microspikes, Connor gazed at the sky. "That cloud looks like a dragon," he said.

I looked up at the wisps in the sky: "Yeah, I guess it does. There's the head . . ."

"Yeah, there's the head, and then you can see one wing and the other. And look, a tail!" he interrupted.

"That's pretty cool."

"You know that Kade and I like dragons, don't you, Dad?"

"Wait, you guys like dragons? I don't know any kids who like dragons."

"Funny, Dad. You know your kids are crazy about dragons—right?"

"Yeah, I guess you both do like dragons an awful lot."

After a couple miles of walking over mildly ascending, snow-crusted clay, we reached the canyon and began a winding, steep hike over snow-covered rock. The temperature dropped considerably as the sun hid itself behind the evergreen trees, traveling in its low, winter arc. Our Microspikes squeaked on the compacted snow. For about an hour, as we gained 800 vertical feet, we raised one foot in front and then rested for the briefest of moments on a straight back leg (also known as the rest step), repeating the process with the trailing foot.

"I like spending time with you," Connor told me.

"I like spending time with you too, kiddo."

At the saddle atop the canyon, we stood looking out at the western expanses and larger mountains beyond—white triangles launching up into the crystalline sky. Out left, on the higher of the two peaks that book-ended the saddle, the trees were swaying to the rhythms of the clearly audible wind. Up on the ridgeback, with no western wall to stop it, the wind had swept some of the snow clean. Our trail became a mix of gray stone, white snow, and red clay.

"Can we have another break? This is a good spot for a break, right?" said Connor. "It's nice and flat right here. And look—there's a great rock we can use for a seat!"

"Sure, let's stop here. Maybe you can drink some more tea? Do you want your peanut butter and jelly?"

"Yeah, I'd like to eat lunch. We always have peanut butter and jelly, don't we, Dad?"

"Well, I wouldn't say 'always,' but I know you like it."

Connor put down his pack and pulled out his navy jacket, putting it on.

"How are you?" I asked. "Are you cold?"

"I'm good. It's better to stay warm than get warm, right?"

Connor brushed snow off of a knee-high rock and took a seat. I found a stance on the windward side of him, deflecting the breeze from his perch.

"Have you climbed any of those mountains, Dad?" Connor asked, pointing to the peaks on the Continental Divide.

"Yeah, a decent number of them. And your mom has, too. And that one there . . ." I said, gesturing out into the distance, ". . . that one with the square top is Longs Peak. Your mom and I climbed that one with your grandpa."

"Your dad?"

"Yeah, my dad."

"That's the one we see from our new house, right?"

"Yep."

"I think I'd like to climb that mountain. And maybe some of the others."

"We can do that. We need to get a little stronger and be able to hike for longer, but days like today will help."

"Yeah. How much are we going up, today? I don't remember."

"Nearly 3,000 feet. In the snow, though, which makes it more difficult."

After finishing his sandwich, Connor pulled on his pack, ran one hand through the leash of his trekking pole, and then started up the summit ridgeline. His face was steady behind his sunglasses despite his heading straight into the wind.

The snow got deeper and the terrain got steeper until we reached an outcropping of red, tumbling, sofa-sized boulders frosted with snow.

Placing one hand on a boulder and wielding his one trekking pole with the other, Connor danced and twisted his way up a slight fissure in the piled stones. He placed his feet firmly; as he reached the pinnacle of this particular formation, and as I poked my head up behind him, I saw about one hundred feet of pyramidal ridge between us and the summit.

Sometimes scooting, sometimes bounding, sometimes taking shuffled steps, Connor made his way across the pointed ridge. The wind whipped at him, tossing his backpack straps into the air. He paused at a knife-edged section of ridge and grasped the edge with two hands; he then swung his feet lower onto the left face, placed his left foot on a hold, and then expertly crossed his right foot through to another foothold. Crystals of snow dust flung up from his feet and burst into a rainbow of colors as we headed into the sun.

Connor reached the summit boulder in a crouch and then stood in a triumphant pose, both arms raised above his head and one trekking pole pointed toward the sky.

"Woo-hoo!" he hollered

He climbed down to the bottom of the rock, this time on the leeward side, allowing me my turn on the summit. As I stood on top, looking out over the white peaks of adventures both past and pending, Connor slung off his pack, dug out an even thicker, puffy blue jacket, threw his arms into its sleeves, and zipped himself up. Then he removed his bottle from its insulated sleeve and sipped his chai.

"Better to stay warm than get warm," he said.

When I was just old enough to notice music on the radio, I was mildly obsessed with two songs. One was "I Love Rock N' Roll" by Joan Jett and the Blackhearts. I never wanted that song to stop. The other was my own tune, a kind of action-hero symphony that I played to myself in my head—an unceasing crescendo like you might hear over a chase scene in a bad 1950s detective movie. From where I got that kind of tune, I don't know; it was 1981.

I only have a few strong memories from my earliest childhood. I remember a snapshot of being (willingly) tied loosely to a tree so that, as part of some soldier game, my brother could rescue me in the middle of a family camping trip. I remember bits and pieces of the day my brother "went missing" as a five-year-old, and we scrambled all over the neighborhood trying to find him only to discover him under the backyard porch swing, sleeping and unmoved despite our frantic calls.

I also remember a day, when I was four, rounding the corner of our home in Albuquerque, dashing past the clubhouse in the backyard, and heading up the side yard and out onto the front driveway. The clubhouse was the dominant feature in the yard—two stories with slot walls. A rope hung on one end, extended from the roof on an overhang, so we could climb to the second story. Inside was a stair-ladder to a hatch that also opened up to the roof. The slots were a minor stroke of parental genius, sold to my brother and I as a way to keep a breeze flowing through the structure, but which also allowed our parents to see whatever was going on in there.

The clubhouse sat in the middle of a sandbox, adding another safety measure, in addition to the roof railing, while simultaneously fostering endless Tonka Truck excavations.

My dad had built the structure. When I was young, he did a lot of work with his hands. I remember that same Albuquerque home being landscaped with the occasional help of colleagues from his work. A rented Bobcat frontend loader, the digging of seemingly endless postholes, and railroad ties being hammered together by way of large spikes make upanother set of vivid, but asynchronous, B-roll in my head.

Ever the engineer, my dad would hand-draw schematics, showing us the plans only after he and Mom had come to agreement. Every angle and every length were documented and measured before any cuts were made.

I remember the crunch of the backyard sand under my feet. Some of it, rather inevitably, spilled out onto the concrete slab of the back patio.

This day, I was wearing a shirt with horiztonal blue-and-red-stripes with white piping between the stripes, sand most certainly clinging to my shoes. As I made my way around the house at a little kid's sprint, my personal anthem played on a loop in my head.

It was a strangely cloudy dusk in arid Albuquerque. A low light was on the western horizon, casting yellow as it dipped beneath the clouds that hung above the cinderblock property wall. I ran down the length of the yard, toward the fading light, and then made my left turn onto the driveway.

My brother, Bryan; his friend and our next-door neighbor, Eric; and I were deep into a spy or soldier or superhero game. The clubhouse stood as our perfect headquarters from where we launched our intrepid missions. Bryan and Eric were already somewhere at the front of the house, readying to execute their part of the plan to save the world, yet again.

I was on my own, carrying out my part of the mission. The urgency and tension of the situation—whatever that was—made the symphonic crescendo in my head feel ever so appropriate. The stakes, clearly, were high; my team was counting on me.

That corner of the house, which I rounded at a sprint, was the same corner where Eric had brought over his boom box one bright, sunny afternoon. That's where "I Love Rock 'N Roll" was introduced to me, pouring from the silver mesh at either end of the black radio and tape deck. And so, both songs from my preschool-boyhood were sprung from this same location.

I don't recall the mission. I don't remember the world-threatening scenario. But I can recall the same few seconds of pure action and replay them over and over and over again: arms pumping high over my head; body leaned a bit too far forward; hands clenched into fists; a stern expression befitting the severity of our concocted purpose.

Moving at speed, I felt a small breeze that blew a bit cool, taking a bite out of the desert heat. The rich cream of our house's stucco flashed by on my left, the gray pallor of the cinderblock walls whipping by on my right. The two barriers converged at a gate in front of me, through which I burst onto the driveway.

Bryan and Eric were next door, on Eric's driveway to my right, kneeling down against the garage and whispering about the next heroic actions to be taken.

I turned left and away from the two of them then awkwardly hopped and danced around and over the low juniper shrubs in our yard. Each foot placement was in earnest, displacing mulch and small river rocks. Reaching the driveway, I resumed my sprint, my feet smacking off the concrete, the sound echoing off our garage door back at me.

Then I was off to the sidewalk and heading up the street, past the home where our friends Clint and his twin brother, Tom, lived. Where I was going, I don't recall. The narrative of all of this is lost, drowned out by that music in my head. But that's okay. It's better than okay. The anthem sticks. I've carried it with me for over forty years now, and it reminds me of a time when the adventure was all still in front of me. I am reminded of a time when I only had to play at making big and weighty decisions to be followed up with decisive and consequential actions.

Summer 2021 faded into fall, and we did end up holding the kids at home a bit longer. A kids' vaccine was enroute to emergency approval from the Food and Drug Administration. The kids would be getting their doses soon. We could hold out that long.

We had just relocated closer to the mountains, moving into our new house in Longmont that September. We already were getting out into the local foothills and were looking forward to being able to access bigger mountains in the winter with less driving, making the shorter days less problematic.

A new home in a new county meant a new school district and a new school. Our new county, district, and school had embraced COVID public-health policies, on the whole, and that gave us an added level of comfort. However, just like everywhere, reactions to the fatiguing, extending COVID reality were all over the map.

The first adult vaccine boosters came out the same month we moved. The political discourse around the vaccines had gotten increasingly toxic. The number of people likely to get the booster was projected to be dramatically smaller than the number who'd gotten the initial doses. The idea of herd immunity surrounding and protecting the immunocompromised population was looking increasingly unlikely.

We embraced the "Swiss-cheese" analogy: layering on different, imperfect forms of protection. Each one has a hole, but the weaknesses are not the same; that is, the holes don't line up to go all the way through the block of cheese. This was just one neologism that was becoming more common around the house, along with N95, social distancing, rapid testing, ventilation, contact duration, and on and on. It was the combination of all these tools that helped us build a modicum of safety for me.

Just over a month after we moved in, the reputable, peer-reviewed journal *Nature* published an article which tabulated that over 38 percent of chronic lymphocytic leukemia patients in the study who were hospitalized with COVID died. The mortality rate for the entire CLL population cohort in the study (hospitalized or not) was over 27 percent, as compared to 17 percent for the population without CLL.

There was talk of the COVID vaccine becoming an annual shot, like the flu vaccine, meaning COVID was not going away. In scientific terms, we were moving from the epidemic to the endemic phase, with certain global regions seeing occasional spikes in the virus before it subsided for a period.

The boys, now fast approaching seven years old, were not long past the age when they had just finished getting the final doses of the various, standard childhood vaccines. I still carried minor emotional scars from holding down their legs at the pediatrician's as they screamed and cried and attempted to avoid the needles that conveyed their tetanus shot or measles shot or pneumonia shot.

When the day came for their COVID vaccines, the boys protested, although only mildly. Kristina and I had been alerting them to the pending day, trying to split the difference between reminding them too much, leading to dread, and reminding them too little, leading to an unpleasant surprise. Judging by the lack of screaming, crying, or running away, maybe we'd managed to find the right balance.

"It keeps us safe, and it keeps Dad safe," Kade said. But his head was tilted down and his shoulders were slumped when he said it, as we gathered in the entryway of our new home. Sunlight from the sidelight window next to the door kept him backlit.

My wife took the boys to the local pharmacy while I stayed home, still avoiding crowded, indoor places when possible.

When I heard the garage door open from my office, I walked downstairs to meet the family at the door. Connor walked into the house with purpose, eyes up, shoulders back. His feet pounded the hardwood floor of our kitchen as he strode past the breakfast island and the sliding glass door to the backyard. He met me at the base of the stairs, which spun down to our front entryway.

Daylight cut behind him from the same sidelight window. It cast his face in darkness until he got nearer to me. His smile stretched from ear-to-ear.

"I did really well getting my shot!"

"Really?! I'm so proud of you!"

I knelt down on my right knee, the scar tissue pressing against the hardwood, and winced at the quick, sharp pain.

Connor wrapped his arms around me, and I wrapped mine around him. He showed me the bandage on his arm: "Yeah, I did good!"

"That's really good, kiddo. Sounds like you did a great job!"

"Yeah, it wasn't too bad. I really wasn't looking forward to it, but sometimes you just have to do things you don't really like, you know?"

"I think that sounds right, Connor."

"I did great, too!" Kade said, filing in as his brother turned to leave.

"You did?!"

"Well, they still kind of hid in the corner of the office, but they did a great job," Kristina said, coming in the door behind them. "It certainly wasn't like their other shots."

"I'm glad to hear it was easier on them—and you," I said with a smile.

"Yeah, it was fine," she replied.

Connor and Kade returned to the kitchen and opened the refrigerator, while I headed back upstairs into our bedroom, closing the door quietly behind me.

A painting of the Annapurna Massif hovered over my shoulder, and I took a beat to follow the ridgeline with my eyes before taking a seat on the bed, sinking deeply into our pillow-top mattress. I stared across the bedroom at the opposite wall, where the south-facing windows threw a wedge of yellow autumn light. The textures of the drywall finish cast tiny shadows, reminding me of the shady relief in so many images I had seen of mountain ranges.

With two or three convulsions, I sobbed, trying desperately to hold in any sound. I looked back up at the wall, now warped and refracted behind tear-soaked eyes, before dragging my forearm across my face.

I gave one full exhale and lay down on the bed, folding my hands across my chest. Numb and unmoving, I waited for a few minutes. The pitter-patter of small feet on the hardwood entryway blended with Kristina's steps. I could hear pots and pans clang and chime as someone took them from the cabinets. The boys were chattering at each other again: something about dragons. My mind finally fell quiet.

Rising, I moved back to the door, opened it, and padded down the stairs with soft feet.

The boys were talking excitedly as I moved across the kitchen to our adjoining living room. Connor's voice was rising and falling in pitch as he and Kade searched for a movie to put on the TV. From over the back of our couch, I glimpsed their dusty hair bouncing up and down and from side to side.

Slipping up behind them, I placed a gentle hand on each of their heads.

The boys returned to public school just before Thanksgiving. That December, the new Omicron variants became dominant and reduced the efficacy of the vaccines. The COVID treatment options for immunocompromised people were nearly nonexistent, and we were still being told to "get vaccinated, but act unvaccinated."

We kept the boys in school.

*Looking back at the entrance to "Hell's Gates" on Gangapurna West (7140m).*

CHAPTER SIXTEEN

# Everything that Rises

It was going to be an expedition. Sure, a kid-sized one, but the mechanics and logistics and itinerary would all be there, if only in less extreme versions. The boys and I would have four days and three nights in the wild, this February of 2022. We would explore and climb and venture into, what was for us, unknown.

We were supposed to spend the first evening traipsing a couple of hours down a frozen, pine-lined forest-service road toward a shadowy gully at the base of an equally-frozen Long Scraggy Peak, in the South Platte region southwest of Denver. Long Scraggy isn't tall, just under 9,000 feet, and trees climb its flanks almost to its summit. But it is defined by a series of rock ribs that march across its spine, from north to south, like the boney plates of a stegosaurus.

After reaching Long Scraggy, we were supposed to have enough time to set up camp, cook and eat dinner, and ready ourselves for bed. I was planning on having an important conversation with the boys on this first night, too; so, I wanted some time for that as well. But the trip began with a significant misstep: I got us to the nondescript Colorado Trail Segment 3 trailhead a bit too late.

As I parked the car, the last streaks of crimson were already hanging low in the sky behind the rocky ridges of the surrounding mountains. To the east, Long Scraggy had turned deep purple, the snow on its flanks bathed in a soft lilac underlying the evergreens that climbed the peak. Like swords, wisps of cloud jutted through the red sky in tones of copper and bronze.

I checked my phone one last time before turning it off. I had just received a new email as we were ending our drive. It was from my climbing mentor, John.

The news hit hard: John's wife, Deb, was entering hospice. Her metastasized cancer was causing liver failure. Things would move quickly now.

I was stunned, and I came to a dead stop, standing there beside the car. My kids were already shouldering their respective blue and red packs. Connor asked me, "Can we start walking now?"

Tilted forward under the weight of a heavy pack, I plodded down the forest road behind the boys. The tightly packed snow squeaked and squealed under our boots with each step. The boys were a bundle of excitement and energy, racing ahead, excited to finally move after our long car ride. The red sky, meanwhile, had given way to steely and navy blues.

The cold bit at my nose. I tucked my head low into my jacket collar, more out of sorrow, though, than for warmth.

As the light drained from the horizon, I spotted a small knoll to our right, rising above our path towards the gully. The knoll was strangely bare on its gently rounded top and looked to be a good campsite. To the north, a tree-covered bluff would block the wind. Wisps of native grass protruded through the snow.

We were still far from our planned camp, but it was also getting dark. I shrugged off my pack and its load of supplies for three people: the tent and bedrolls and sleeping bags and stove. I caught one shoulder strap at the elbow, bent my knees, and tried to lower the pack next to a fallen tree that would make a good bench. The pack still hit with a thud.

Twenty feet away, I set up my phone on a small, plastic tripod and plugged in a portable battery pack.

"Are you going to film us setting up camp, Dad?" Connor asked.

"Yeah, I think people watching our YouTube channel would like to know where our first camp is, don't you? It's kind of an important part of the trip."

A little over a year before, Connor had asked if we could have a YouTube channel about our adventures in the outdoors. I had resisted until Kade was recruited into the lobbying effort. I read up on the basics of cinematography, sound, and editing, and had acquired fairly minimal equipment and software.

As I pulled out our camping gear, Kade asked if he could help set up the stove. I handed him our camp pot. The silver base glinted, reflecting the light from my headlamp; the electric-blue silicone on the pot's upper rim fluttered from dark to vibrant as the light passed over it.

Connor and I fussed with the tent poles, connecting them together over our snow-white tent, which blended into the ground around us. Each of us manning one end of the tent-pole sleeves on the structure's nylon exterior, we slid through one pole and then the next until the dome snapped taut, shaping a portable cave out of nothingness.

"Dad, the stove and fuel are ready. Can you help me connect them?" Kade asked.

"Connor, can you start laying out the sleeping bags? I'll help with the inflatable mattresses in a minute." Then, raising my volume a bit: "Sure, Kade. Be right there!"

I fitted the fuel pump into the aluminum fuel canister and twisted it shut. Taking the hose from the burner, I worked the brass couplings together as best I could while wearing heavy gloves. Eventually, I had to take the gloves off, and my hands stung at the cold touch of metal.

It was a quiet dinner.

Crawling into the tent, I couldn't bring myself to talk to my boys about cancer, as I'd planned. Instead, I powered my phone to life. My thumbs moved awkwardly across my cell phone's virtual keys, and I stamped out a reply to John's heartbreaking email:

> *I am sitting in a tent with my two sons, as I write this. They wanted to do a "mini-expedition." So, we'll be out a few days and will hopefully make a winter summit.*
>
> *I can do this because of the two of you. The love and support you have given me is living on—right now, on this trip—and helping me love and share with my sons in a way that means so much. That love will continue to live on.*
>
> *I am so sorry. I love you both. I always will. Jason*

I shut off my phone. Memories of Deb's quiet tutelage, helping me to be a better instructor, came flooding back. "Show one; have them assist one; then have them do one," was her oft-repeated sentiment. And I remembered our conversations about risk and parenting: "We sat the kids down before we even began planning the Himalayan trip and told them about the risks involved and why, as they were adults now, we felt it was a good choice for us," she'd told me. And I remembered the climbing, holding each other's lives in our hands as we demonstrated ice-climbing skills to the students.

Then my thoughts turned to John, who was losing his best friend. "We are *so* lucky to live in Colorado!" he would always say. I managed a half smile.

I closed my eyes and tried to sleep.

In the morning, the sun rose just off of the shoulder of Long Scraggy, still miles in the distance. As brilliant a gold as I have ever seen hurtled at us through the open vents at the top of our tent, painting the tent walls in a kaleidoscope of warming yellows and reds.

The boys and I zipped up our down jackets and donned our mittens. Sliding cold boots over our feet, we stepped out, raised our arms in a stretch, and greeted the sun.

I repeated my ritual with the stove and fuel, blowing in my hands and voicing the occasional groan as I manipulated the stove's smaller components. The flame eventually lit, and I held my hands over the heat for a few moments.

"Guys, I think maybe we shouldn't climb this mountain. We're still too far away. We didn't get far enough, yesterday, because I made us so late."

"But I want to have an expedition!" Kade replied.

"Yeah, I want an expedition!" piled on Connor.

"I know. I think we can still have one. Do you know what's over there?" I asked, pointing west. The boys shook their heads. Opposite the rising sun was Buffalo Creek Recreation Area and the beginning of Segment 3 of the Colorado Trail. The gently rising slopes contained a seemingly never-ending maze of pink and red granite boulders, rounded towers, and jumbled rock formations anywhere from head height to maybe 300 feet high.

"About a mile or so back that way is where we had our first winter camping trip, which actually is pretty close to where our first ever wilderness camp was located. Do you remember all the boulders and rock towers? I'm sure we can find something to climb."

"Yeah! Okay, Dad!" Connor exclaimed.

"Sounds like fun!" Kade said, beaming.

"Okay, we'll head over there, to the west, rather than east."

Backtracking a bit on the forest road before breaking off onto a forest-canopied trail, the boys scurried and I waddled. The exertion and rising sun warmed my hands, which were slowly recovering from lighting the stove. Our exhaled breath shimmered like crystals when the light caught it.

As some of the scenery became familiar, the boys began telling stories of "remember when we," their excitement quickening their pace.

But as we passed by the familiar into the unfamiliar, the boys slowed and their shoulders sank. Connor began asking if each snow-free spot would make a good campsite; Kade demanded that we go back.

"Guys, I think we can find something pretty cool if we head a little farther up the trail. Look at those rock formations through the trees—do you see them?" I said, spurring them on.

We came to a sharp double back in the trail. The terrain wasn't steep, but a few hundred feet off the bend was a mass of boulders. The biggest was the size of a single-story duplex. The boys once again bubbled into a fervor. One of them yelled, "Look at that fort!" and they both leaned their packs against a tree and dashed forward to scramble up the shoulder of the massive, rounded block.

I dropped my pack (again, awkwardly) and moved briskly to catch up. Connor was already near the top of the right-most portion of rock when I got there. I stopped and looked behind the formation. There was a platform on the other side, a balcony the size of a tennis court, half covered in snow but bare where it was sheltered by the trees.

"This is our camp spot," Connor said. I couldn't disagree.

We returned with our packs to the campsite, where the boys found a particularly friendly-looking tree and declared it the "storage area." Packs were hung from the nubs of broken branches. Trekking poles were leaned with care.

"We want to explore!" Kade yelled as they ran off.

"Okay, but stay close."

I re-pitched the tent under the midday sun, its white sides shining true in the high light. The scent of pine came heavy with each burst of breeze.

After setting up and organizing camp, I found the boys on a low, flat boulder not much smaller than our balcony. It was facing north and was shaded. Kade was kneeling, excavating, working hard with the shovel to scoop up crusty cakes of snow.

"Look, Dad, we're making a snow fort," Connor told me.

"Pretty cool, guys. Do you know, if you use your ice axes, you can carve blocks out of the snow, and they may fit together better? Can I show you?" Kade handed me his axe; I took the pick and dragged it across the crisp snow, making two lines at something close to a right angle.

"Can you do the rest?" I asked, handing Kade back his axe. He completed the square and then wedged his mittened hands under the block.

"Is this good, Dad?"

"Yeah, that's a pretty good block."

"I want to try!" Connor grabbed his axe and plopped down beside us.

"Okay, you guys keep working. I'm going to go check out that rock formation over there," I said, pointing behind us, back across the trail, to a 200-foot-tall jumble of rock towers and boulders. "I think that may be a good thing to climb tomorrow, but I want to take a look. I'll be right back."

"Sure, Dad."

Crossing the trail, I found a low-angled ramp of forest floor, ascending onto the shoulder of a small ridge that rose from left to right, meeting the rocks at mid-height. *Maybe.*

"I think we can try it," I said upon my return.

"Okay, Dad," Kade replied. He was focused on the foundation of their snow structure.

"I'm going to go make dinner. You guys hungry?"

"Yep," from Kade.

"Starving!" Connor emphasized.

When I came back to tell them that dinner was ready, the boys had made something the size of a large doghouse. It even had a roof. Connor crawled in to demonstrate its integrity and their confidence in their work. We then clamored up to our balcony and dug into fried potatoes and cheese.

As we ate, the sky was painted, once again, in sunset reds and coppers. We finished dinner with roasted marshmallows; the kids' faces and fingers were spattered with sticky, stringy sugar.

We boiled water to add to the bottles we would use to keep our feet warm that night. Kade put away the stove and pot under the storage tree, while I folded the foil lining I'd used for the potatoes and placed it in the food bag. Taking a walk to a somewhat distant corner of our surroundings, downwind from us, I threw a tethered cord over a tree limb and hoisted the food bag. Connor scraped their drying socks from day one off of a nearby rock wall and tucked a pair each into the bottom of his and his brother's sleeping bags.

As we climbed into our tent, I placed my phone and portable battery pack above us by wedging them into the cross-section of poles at the tent peak.

"Are you filming our sleeping stuff, Dad?"

"No, Connor. I want to have a talk with you guys."

"For our YouTube channel?"

"No, I don't think this one will go on YouTube."

As I eased back into my sleeping bag, the boys rubbed their eyes, the day's adventure having taken its toll. The white tent walls were doing a good job of catching the remaining light and keeping the inside of the tent bright, illuminating our familiar, and somehow comforting, multicolored tumble of clothing and sleeping bags and camp pillows. As we talked, the rustling of nylon made a constant backdrop of sound.

"So, I need to have a real conversation with you guys."

"Yes, Dad."

"Is that okay?"

"Yes, Dad."

"So, you know when we get back to school on Tuesday, because Monday is a holiday, that masks are optional. But we're still going to wear masks, right?"

"Yeah. You wouldn't let us not wear them, and we wouldn't want to either," Connor said.

"Why wouldn't you want to?"

"We do! Because we want to stay as safe as possible!"

"You guys know that I'll still be wearing a mask, too, when I go places—right?"

"Yes."

"Because I have, umm, what does Mom call them? 'Deadbeat cells,' right?"

"Yeah, 'deadbeat white blood cells,'" Connor answered.

"So, there's two kinds of white blood cells. Well, actually, there are lots of different kinds, but there are B-cells and T-cells. And the B-cells are like the commanders. They tell the T-cells what to go attack . . . My deadbeat cells are some of my B-cells . . . That's part of why our family takes COVID so seriously."

"Yeah, to keep you safe!" Connor said with a smile.

I told them about the need for regular blood tests to make sure I was still healthy enough. I told them that one day I would need treatment, probably a pill to knock back the number of deadbeat cells. I told them that the treatment would weaken my immune system. I told them that, therefore, we'd probably never be done trying to be careful about COVID or other diseases. I told them that I was thankful that they were doing things to help.

We talked about the advances in treatment and that some people using some of the newest treatments are having no measurable disease for so long it feels almost like a cure, or so we think (the treatments were so new that we didn't have enough post-treatment history to know for sure). Kade, in particular, had all sorts of questions about the new treatments, like CAR T-Cell therapy, a process of reprogramming T-cells to attack cancer cells.

We talked about side effects. We talked about what types of

symptoms might cause me to need treatment in the first place. We talked about not knowing how or why I'd gotten these deadbeat cells. We talked about how I'd found all this out during a routine physical.

According to the video, we talked for roughly twenty-five minutes.

"So . . . the three things that I really want you to take away from this are: One, your dad's got this weird thing, and eventually I'm going to have to do something to make it, you know, better. Two, but it's not that bad."

The boys lay there, staring up at the tent ceiling.

"We're still getting out and doing all this stuff. I'm pretty healthy, otherwise."

They still stared straight up.

"And three, we have to manage it. But we have to manage it seriously, and right now managing that seriously means wearing our masks and washing our hands. Even when other people say you don't have to anymore, you're allowed to say, 'Nope. This is what I'm doing.'"

Connor said, "Yes. To keep members of my family safe. Members who have deadbeat white blood cells!" And then he slid his head under his sleeping bag.

"I had to do the same thing when I was a kid. Because, you know I have those food allergies, right?" I said.

"Yeah."

"Well, I once had a teacher . . . we were doing a unit on Native Americans . . . and this teacher was saying that I could smash these nuts. I was like, 'No, I can't because I'm allergic to nuts and I can't inhale the dust.' . . . so, they called my mom . . . and my mom came in and got really mad at that teacher!"

We talked about food allergies a bit longer. I fielded questions about what it feels like and what I do to help myself if I eat the wrong thing by accident. The conversation was clearly winding down.

"Any other questions, guys?"

"No," in unison.

"You guys okay?"

"Yeah."

"You worried about anything?"

"No."

"Okay, I love you both."

"Love you, too," said Connor.

"Yeah, love you, too," said Kade.

I paused, and the kids settled into their sleeping bags. As I rolled over and closed my eyes, I heard Connor mutter, "Sometimes scary stuff gives me nightmares."

Up with the next morning's sun, we took our time with breakfast before filling our packs with a few essentials: first-aid kit, water, clothing, and a few snacks. Grabbing our ice axes, we made our way toward the nearby trail, crossed it, and headed up the ramp to the rocks I had spied the day before.

Progress was easy, at first. The ramp was mostly dry, with just the occasional drifts of snow that were easily avoided. It was unusually warm for a winter day, and we wore just two layers. My shoulders and back radiated heat from underneath my pack. Grasses and decaying branches, almost crumbling after many seasons on the ground, split our strides into uneven steps as we meandered up toward the ridgeline. The rustling of the grass against our boots was penetrated by the occasional crack of a snapping twig.

I pointed to the summit of the rock formation, looming off to our right, its red granite visible through the green pine needles that surrounded us. The boys' voices were loud with excitement.

"Is that what we're going to climb?" Connor asked.

"Well, that's what we are going to *try* to climb. I don't know for sure that there is a way up there, but we can try to find one. That's kind of what happens on expeditions—we have an idea of what we want to try to do, but the plan doesn't always work out."

"Yeah," Connor replied.

"I mean we aren't even on the mountain we were originally going to attempt. But then we found this cool campsite, and now we're going to see if there's a way to the top of this new mountain," I continued.

"So, this is like a real expedition, isn't it, Dad?" Kade called out.

"Yeah, it really is. We had a basecamp, then moved up to the base of this mountain and set a new camp, and now we are going to try to climb it."

"Cool," Kade said, grinning.

At the ridgeline, we turned right into the shadow of the mountain's rocky summit block. The ground was now covered in snow. I took my first step into the pristine white and immediately sunk to mid-shin. The snow was fine and sugary, the unconsolidated stuff that comes when it is very cold as the snow falls. But there wasn't a lot of it, yet. So far, the winter had been unusually dry.

"Okay, boys. Just follow my footprints. Use exactly the same steps I use, so you don't sink too deep."

My focus shifted to taking uncomfortably small strides so that the boys could follow. Each time I pulled a foot out of the hole it had created, I had to consciously set its heel just at the toe line of my standing leg. The boys would be stepping more vertically than me; the same hole that went up to my shin would likely reach their knee or higher. Long strides wouldn't be an option for them as they high-stepped through the snow.

My lower legs started to feel the slow creep of the cold, not uncomfortably but in sharp contrast to my sweaty shoulders and back.

Connor was right on my heels, matching step for step, the navy hood of his jacket bobbing each time I turned around to check on the kids.

Kade was falling behind and starting to grumble. "I hate this!" he barked.

"It's not too bad. We are still going well," I said. "Besides, I can see what's coming up in front of us, and I think it's going to be pretty fun. There's an awful lot of rocks you are going to be able to scramble on!"

"Yeah, Kade," Connor added, "you are going to love this out of your mind!"

The snow ridge steepened as it dissolved into the summit tower of red and pink boulders, our feet now landing on the occasional desk-sized stone under the snow.

Connor and I made our way under the limbs of an aspen tree, and we found ourselves bathed in sun on a football-field-sized plateau. The trees were sparse, the sun was bright, and the ground was dry.

Piles of car-sized, oblong rocks made a labyrinth of short climbs, a story or two from top to bottom. Straight in front of us stood a cliff face, angling gently back, inviting. I scanned the scene: the top of the cliff was the high point.

"I think we want to scramble this face, guys."

Kade's orange hood bobbed up and down beside his brother's navy hood. "It looks like fun!" he said, more positive now that the summit was in sight.

The small cliff was divided into sections by three deep-set, snowy cracks, each about the width of a boot and crossed by a rightward and upward trending ledge that looked wide enough for two feet.

The boys joined me as I slung my pack off of my shoulders, tethered my trekking pole to it, and undid the straps holding my ice axe.

Kade went first. He made his way up the leftmost fissure, driving the pick of his axe into the snow above him, setting it, and then looking down at his feet. He carefully placed one foot above the other. I hovered below him with arms raised in a spotting position. After about ten feet, the cliff face eased back, and Kade accelerated, moving quickly toward the top. He turned and started to make his way from left to right toward the high point of the cliff face. Then he was out of my view.

Connor started within the same crack, but then took the angling ledge up and right across the face. His boots sank up to his ankles at each step, securing his feet, a sight that comforted me. In his right and leading hand, he held his axe near the head, finding small edges on the rock face on which to hook the pick for balance as he twisted his torso to face the rock. His left hand lagged behind, stretched fully away, finding side clings to grasp and release as he made progress.

Again, with arms outstretched overhead, I shuffled along underneath Connor, spotting his ascent.

As Connor was making the final move, swinging his axe up and over the cliff top to wide and flat ground, Kade appeared from behind the rocks. His orange jacket blocked the sun directly behind him, and he cast a striking shadow as he raised his axe overhead in triumph. Connor crawled over the lip, stood up, and joined his brother.

Back at home a few days later, I was sitting in my upstairs office. Deb had died the day following the boys' and my summit, around the time the three of us were hiking back to our car. I found out when I turned on my phone and the flood of replies to an email thread from John made ignorance impossible. Now at home, my computer screen flashed a video of the broad and gently sloping summit at the top of the small cliff the boys and I had climbed. For this shot, the sun was behind me as I filmed, such that Connor's and Kade's packs and jackets exploded in vibrant color as they shrugged them off, pulled snacks from their pockets, and unscrewed their water bottles.

I sank into my chair as I paused the frame. I was facing my library wall. To my left were classics of mountain literature, books like *The White Spider, K2: The Savage Mountain,* and *Buried in the Sky* detailing great climbs in the great ranges, stories of adventures where things never went as expected. To my right were rows of guidebooks, describing routes and inviting forethought and strategies and plans. The reds and blues and yellows of the book spines were ordered neatly by region on the deep-toned, espresso shelves, their popping colors complementing the luminescent images on my computer screen.

And there I sat, at my desk, in the middle.

Scrolling back to the start of the video, I stopped at a sequence of a boy in a green-blue, and quite dirty, down jacket preparing to depart our white-walled tent as the golden sun poured in. As I clicked open the text function, preparing to type out a title block over the image, I felt an arm wrap around my shoulder.

"Making something for our YouTube channel?" Connor asked.

"Yeah. You want to look at the footage with me?" I said.

It was nice to relive these adventures. The pictures weren't tucked away, only to be brought out on rare occasions. The cadence of outings and then storytelling came at a fast clip: every week, we had a chance to see what we had done; every week brought a second round of connection born from our shared experiences.

"That was a good expedition, huh, Dad?" Connor said. I swiveled my chair toward him, our eyes level. His eyes were smiling, and I felt the corners of my own eyes lift in return.

"Yeah, it really was."

"What are we going to do next?"

"I was thinking about teaching you and your brother how to ice climb. What do you think?"

His hazel eyes jumped, and his mouth exploded as he voiced a broad, toothy laugh. "I think that sounds amazing!" he said with a giggle.

"Okay, I'll see what I can figure out. I have an idea where we'll go," I said.

I turned back to my computer, Connor's gaze joining mine at the screen while his arm still lay draped over my shoulder. As the pipe cursor blinked in the title block, I typed in the text: "And Soon, Spring."

***Shortly after the "mini expedition," Connor is at the base of his first ice climb.***

# ACKNOWLEDGEMENTS

Thank you to my wife, Kristina, who not only supported me as I spent long hours typing away only to create a work that undoubtedly holds our lives up to scrutiny, but who also has been my forever-partner in this life. To my kids, Connor and Kade, you are my endless source of inspiration and the motivation that drives me to meet the challenge of each new day. Thanks as well to my mom, Marianne, dad, Alan, and brother, Bryan, who have helped shape me into a halfway-decent human being. Thanks to friends old and new, too numerous for an accounting, that held me up every time I needed holding. And thanks to my editor, Matt Samet, for asking me the hard questions that made this a better book.

## ABOUT THE AUTHOR

Jason Kolaczkowski is a father, husband, son, and brother. He is a lifelong health care analytics professional, used to confronting risk through the lens of numbers and probabilities. He is also a dedicated, amateur climber and is, currently, a cancer survivor—by definition, a transient state. He shares his passion of enabling families to get outdoors through a blog and YouTube channel called Short Guys Beta Works (www.shortguysbetaworks.com) as he, his wife, Kristina, and his twin sons, Connor and Kade, tramp amongst the peaks near their home in Colorado.

ABOUT THE PUBLISHER

Di Angelo Publications was founded in 2008 by Sequoia Schmidt—at the age of seventeen. The modernized publishing firm's creative headquarters is in Los Angeles, California, with its distribution center located in Twin Falls, Idaho. In 2020, Di Angelo Publications made a conscious decision to move all printing and production for domestic distribution of its books to the United States. The firm is comprised of eleven imprints, and the featured imprint, Catharsis, was inspired by Schmidt's love of extreme sports, travel, and adventure stories.

DAP BOOKS

DI ANGELO PUBLICATIONS

www.ingramcontent.com/pod-product-compliance
Lightning Source LLC
LaVergne TN
LVHW050928080826
845145LV00001B/254

* 9 7 8 1 9 6 2 6 0 3 4 5 4 *